DK DORLING KINDERSLEY
—HANDBOOKS—

CATS

DORLING KINDERSLEY
—HANDBOOKS—

CATS

DAVID ALDERTON

Photography by
MARC HENRIE

A Dorling Kindersley Book

Dorling Kindersley

LONDON, NEW YORK, AUCKLAND, DELHI, JOHANNESBURG,
MUNICH, PARIS and SYDNEY

DK www.dk.com

Important Notice
The publisher has made every effort to ensure that the colour of the
cats' fur has been reproduced precisely but, because of the technical difficulties
inherent in colour reproduction, this may not have been achieved in every case.

Editor Irene Lyford
Art Editor Colin Walton
Production Controller Caroline Webber

First published in Great Britain in 1992
Reprinted with corrections in 2000
by Dorling Kindersley Limited,
9 Henrietta Street, London WC2E 8PS

A CIP catalogue record for this book is available
from the British Library

ISBN 0-7513-2776-X

Computer page make-up by
Colin Walton Graphic Design, Great Britain

Text film output by
The Right Type, Great Britain

Reproduced by
Colourscan, Singapore

Printed and bound by
Kyodo Printing Co., Singapore

CONTENTS

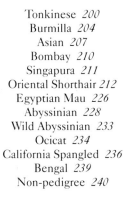

— 🐈 —

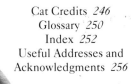

INTRODUCTION

It is now probably 9,000 years since the domestication of the cat began in the Middle East. Down the intervening centuries, domestic cats have had a mixed relationship with people: although worshipped in ancient Egypt, they were widely condemned and persecuted as agents of the Devil during the Middle Ages in Europe. Later, cats were gradually welcomed back into public esteem, not least for their skill in controlling vermin, both in domestic surroundings and on board ships.

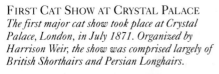

BASTET
The focus of cat worship in Egypt was Bubastis, site of the temple of the goddess Bastet, shown here in the form of a woman with a cat's head.

B Y THE EARLY 19th century, the cat had become a popular companion, but it was not until the latter part of the Victorian era that the breeding of cats for show purposes began in earnest. "Fancying" – the term used to describe the selective breeding of plants and livestock – appealed to the Victorians, and cat shows became popular social events, attracting the nobility and even the occasional presence of Queen Victoria. Inspired by the idea of breeding cats for showing, Harrison Weir became the founding father of the pedigree cat world, and organized the first major cat show, which was held in London on 13th July 1871.

Interest in showing cats was spreading into Europe and further afield, and in 1895 the first American all-breed show took place in New York.

HARRISON WEIR
First president of the National Cat Club, organizer of the first cat show, and notable cat illustrator.

FIRST CAT SHOW AT CRYSTAL PALACE
The first major cat show took place at Crystal Palace, London, in July 1871. Organized by Harrison Weir, the show was comprised largely of British Shorthairs and Persian Longhairs.

The fortunes of individual breeds have changed since these early days, with fashion playing its part. Today, there is an ever-increasing number of breeds and colour varieties already established, with more still in the early stages of development. There are now signs that some breeders are prepared to see quite radical changes in the domestic cat. The Munchkin, a breed developed during the 1990's in the United States, has extremely shortened legs, which restrict its ability to jump up, although it can climb normally. It is in this area that the cat associations must remain vigilant, in order to ensure that the selective breeding of cats does not compromise their health.

THE MUNCHKIN

An example of a breed developed from a chance mutation, in the quest for the unusual. This cat was first shown in the USA in 1991.

THE ROLE OF CAT ASSOCIATIONS

Cat associations are responsible for the recognition of breeds for exhibition purposes and for laying down judging standards for such events. The breed standard is an attempt to set out in words how the "ideal" cat should appear, in terms of type, coloration, and patterning. Breed recognition varies from association to association and from one country to another. New breeds are added as they become more popular and are accepted and recognized.

THE AIM OF THIS BOOK

This book is intended, primarily, to be an identification guide to cats, rather than a show guide. Nevertheless, we have been lucky enough to have the co-operation of many top breeders, and we have aimed to include good examples of type as far as possible. With so many feline registration bodies and different breed standards, however, some discrepancies are inevitable. We have given primary consideration to the standards set by The Governing Council of the Cat Fancy (GCCF), and by the Cat Association (CA) of Britain, as well as to registration bodies in North America and elsewhere in the world.

PEDIGREE CATS

The major distinction between pedigree and non-pedigree cats is that while the pure-bred individuals are typically very similar to each other, much more variability in terms of overall appearance is usually apparent in non-pedigree cats, or moggies, which are of no fixed origins.

THE DEVELOPMENT OF NEW BREEDS

Some of today's breeds have been produced by selective matings that have started with the crossing of two established breeds. The majority, however, are refined variants of cats that have arisen naturally in various parts of

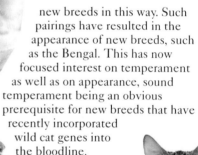

NEW COLOURS
The Oriental group is growing rapidly in terms of colours and patterns, such as this individual. Development is progressing on a long-haired form.

new breeds in this way. Such pairings have resulted in the appearance of new breeds, such as the Bengal. This has now focused interest on temperament as well as on appearance, sound temperament being an obvious prerequisite for new breeds that have recently incorporated wild cat genes into the bloodline.

the world, their particular characteristics then being developed to form the distinctive features of the breed. Out-crossings to other breeds have then been used to increase and diversify the range of coat colours and patterns.

Another trend has been the use of small wild cats in order to introduce their markings into domestic cat bloodlines, a process known as hybridization. Although interest in this area dates from the early days of the cat fancy, it is only recently that serious attempts have been made to develop

BENGAL
The Bengal is the result of hybridization – mating a wild Asiatic leopard cat with a domestic cat.

HOW THIS BOOK WORKS

FOLLOWING the Introduction and the Identification Key, the main breed section of the book is divided into two parts: Long-haired Cats on *pp.40–117* and Short-haired Cats on *pp.118–245*. As conventional classifications of pedigree cat breeds presuppose a fairly extensive knowledge of the subject, this straightforward division is intended to simplify the subject for newcomers, as well as to enhance the book's usefulness as a recognition guide. The annotated example below shows how a typical breed entry is organized.

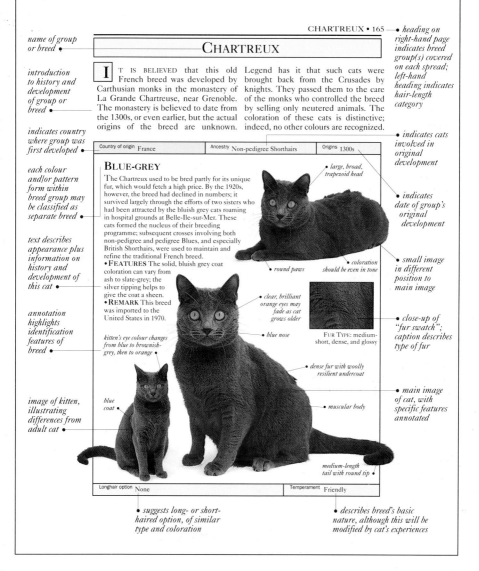

name of group or breed •

introduction to history and development of group or breed •

indicates country where group was first developed •

each colour and/or pattern form within breed group may be classified as separate breed •

text describes appearance plus information on history and development of this cat •

annotation highlights identification features of breed •

image of kitten, illustrating differences from adult cat •

CHARTREUX • 165 — • *heading on right-hand page indicates breed group(s) covered on each spread; left-hand heading indicates hair-length category*

CHARTREUX

I T IS BELIEVED that this old French breed was developed by Carthusian monks in the monastery of La Grande Chartreuse, near Grenoble. The monastery is believed to date from the 1300s, or even earlier, but the actual origins of the breed are unknown.

Legend has it that such cats were brought back from the Crusades by knights. They passed them to the care of the monks who controlled the breed by selling only neutered animals. The coloration of these cats is distinctive; indeed, no other colours are recognized.

| Country of origin | France | Ancestry | Non-pedigree Shorthairs | Origins | 1300s |

BLUE-GREY
The Chartreux used to be bred partly for its unique fur, which would fetch a high price. By the 1920s, however, the breed had declined in numbers; it survived largely through the efforts of two sisters who had been attracted by the bluish grey cats roaming in hospital grounds at Belle-Ile-sur-Mer. These cats formed the nucleus of their breeding programme; subsequent crosses involving both non-pedigree and pedigree Blues, and especially British Shorthairs, were used to maintain and refine the traditional French breed.
• **FEATURES** The solid, bluish grey coat coloration can vary from ash to slate-grey; the silver tipping helps to give the coat a sheen.
• **REMARK** This breed was imported to the United States in 1970.

kitten's eye colour changes from blue to brownish-grey, then to orange

blue coat •

• *indicates cats involved in original development*

• *indicates date of group's original development*

• *small image in different position to main image*

• *large, broad, trapezoid head*

• *round paws*

coloration should be even in tone

clear, brilliant orange eyes may fade as cat grows older

blue nose •

FUR TYPE: medium-short, dense, and glossy

• *close-up of "fur swatch"; caption describes type of fur*

dense fur with woolly resilient undercoat

muscular body •

• *main image of cat, with specific features annotated*

medium-length tail with round tip •

| Longhair option | None | | Temperament | Friendly |

• *suggests long- or short-haired option, of similar type and coloration*

• *describes breed's basic nature, although this will be modified by cat's experiences*

THE CAT FAMILY

WILD CATS are widely distributed around the world, in all inhabited continents except Australia. They tend to live on their own (with the exception of the lion, which lives in groups called prides) and are predatory by nature, hunting a wide variety of prey. Several species have been adversely affected by fur-hunters, but international resolve to regulate this illegal trade has increased

UNDETERMINED TAXONOMY

SUBFAMILY PANTHERINAE

CHEETAHS

Cheetahs are the fastest land mammals in the world. They are capable of achieving speeds of up to 90 km/h (56 mph). They live in open areas, where there is very little cover, so pace is vital.

PANTHERA LINEAGE

Recent work, involving the use of DNA testing, compared the genetic similarities between different species in the cat family. The results suggest that there are actually three main lineages which cut across existing classificatory divisions. These are the Ocelots from South America; the Wild Cats, including the ancestor of the domestic cat; and the Panthera group, which is made up of the remaining members of the sub-families Pantherinae and Felinae.

PANTHERA GROUP
Lion
Tiger
Leopard
Jaguar
Snow Leopard
Clouded Leopard
Marbled Cat
Caracal
Bobcat
North American Lynx
Eurasian Lynx
Spanish Lynx
Serval
African Golden Cat
Asian Golden Cat
Leopard Cat
Fishing Cat
Flat-headed Cat
Rusty Spotted Cat
Bay Cat
Iriomote Cat
Jaguarundi
Puma
Onza

TIGER
Instantly recognizable by its striped patterning, the tiger is the biggest of all wild cats, with Siberian Tigers weighing up to 320 kg (705 lb).

during recent years, and the future of these cats now seems to be more secure.

Most species are well camouflaged by their colouring and the patterning of spots or bars on their coats and this, along with their slow, quiet movements, enables them to get close to prey for a successful kill. The coloration of their coats can be directly influenced by local factors. For example, leopards in Asia, which inhabit forested areas to a greater extent than their African cousins, show an increased tendency towards melanism; this means that their coats become black and this helps to conceal their presence there more effectively.

FELIDAE

SUBFAMILY FELINAE

NEW CATS

Scientists had always been reluctant to accept rumours of a puma-like cat that was said to exist in Mexico – although the cat was known to the Aztecs and to the early Spanish explorers. On 1st January 1986, however, one of these cats was shot; they are now known by the traditional name, the Onza.

OCELOTS

These small cats, some almost unknown due to their shy natures and remote territories, are to be found in a wide range of New World habitats.

OCELOT FAMILY
Ocelot
Geoffroy's Cat
Pampas Cat
Andean Mountain Cat
Margay
Kod Kod
Oncilla

WILD CATS

This Old World group consists of cats living in parts of Europe, Africa, and Asia. The largest member is the Jungle Cat, which can weigh up to 16 kg (35 lb). Most hunt small mammals.

Pallas's Cat
Jungle Cat
Black-footed Cat
Sand Cat
Chinese Desert Cat
Wild Cat
Domestic Cat

OCELOT
In the United States these cats are now found in only a restricted area, but range as far south as Argentina.

WILD CAT
The most widely distributed member of the group, the Wild Cat varies throughout its range in appearance.

DOMESTIC CAT
The domestic cat is thought to be descended from the African Wild Cat. The tabby markings seen on Wild Cats also occur frequently in the domestic form.

WHAT IS A CAT?

DOMESTIC BREEDS of cat show very little variation in appearance, all being of relatively similar size. Precise features, such as the head shape and coat length, may well differ, however, particularly in the case of pedigree cats that have been modified by selective breeding over generations in order to conform to the standards laid down by cat assocations. In many ways, though, domestic cats are still very similar to their wild ancestors, possessing the same athleticism and hunting skills. These features are vividly demonstrated by feral cats – cats that have reverted back to nature, living wild wherever they can find suitable cover.

• *upright carriage*

medium length tail •

• LONGHAIR
The short, bushy tails should be in proportion to the body length; they are often carried low.

• MANX
This breed shows a variable loss of tail. In the Rumpy, the tail is entirely missing.

TAILS
Tails, in a variety of shapes and sizes, play a vital part in the cat's balance and in the "righting reflex" that allows it to land on its feet after falling from a height.

• TAIL
helps the cat's balance as it climbs and walks; held upright here

BODY •
cats are not generally prone to obesity

RIBCAGE •
protects the body organs, such as the heart and lungs, and moves as the cat breathes

• THIGHS
thigh muscles provide the thrust that enables the cat to jump effectively

• REAR PAWS
usually four toes on each of the hind feet

BODY SHAPES

PERSIAN LONGHAIR

BRITISH SHORTHAIR

BURMESE

SIAMESE

The outline of a cat's body usually gives a clear indication of the group to which it belongs. Longhairs, and their relatives, and the British, American, and European Shorthairs, have cobby bodies, set low on the legs. Burmese and Asian cats are of medium size with slender legs, whereas Orientals and Siamese have a slender, svelte body shape.

broad skull • • small ears

broad skull • • round eyes

large ears • triangular head •

flat skull • • large ears

round face • • round eyes

round face • • short nose

long face • slanting eyes •

wedge-shaped head • • oval eyes

LONGHAIR

BRITISH SHORTHAIR

SIAMESE

DEVON REX

EARS •
usually erect, but may be folded or curled in some breeds

• FURNISHINGS
the hair in the ears is more profuse in some cases than in others

HEAD
The shape of the cat's head is an important identification feature; some, such as the British Shorthair, are rounded, whereas others, such as the Oriental, are of a triangular shape when viewed from the front.

EYES •
shape and coloration vary, but all cats are well-equipped to see in the dark

• EYELIDS
serve to protect the eyes from injury, with the colour sometimes contrasting with that of the eyes

• NOSE LEATHER
the hairless area, incorporating the two nostrils

• WHISKERS
an important part of the cat's sensory system, enabling it to assess width

• NECK
the neck contributes to the overall impression of the body shape

• ruff may be less distinctive in the summer

• CHEST
size varies according to breed; in this case it is of medium, semi-cobby type

RUFF •
Some breeds have longer fur around the neck and chest, described as a ruff

carpal pad (front paws only)
helps to prevent cat from sliding on slippery surface when jumping •

FEET
Cats' paws are important, both for climbing and for catching prey in the wild. Many breeds of domestic cat, such as the Longhairs, have large, rounded paws, but in Orientals the paws are much smaller and oval in shape.

sharp claws •

toe pads •

FRONT PAWS •
normally five toes, with the dew claw not in contact with the ground

metacarpal pads •

• dew claw

SENSES AND INSTINCTS

CAT NAPPING
Cats may sleep for up to three quarters of the day, especially when they are young.

Although the domestic cat retains many of the behavioural traits associated with its wild relatives, adaptations to domestic living have occurred, most noticeably in territorial matters. Cats in urban areas inevitably have to share space, rather than maintain large territories, but as they are fed by their owners and do not have to fend for themselves, this does not cause great problems.

WEANING
Kittens may start feeding on their own when they are about three weeks old, but will not be fully weaned from the mother until they are at least two months of age.

ESCAPING
Most female cats are very diligent mothers, and keep a close watch on their kittens; any that stray too far (left) are likely to be carried back, held in the mother's mouth, as shown above.

FIRST MEETING
Cats tend to be cautious when they first meet (left), males being most likely to show aggression.

MAKING FRIENDS
Kittens reared together become close companions, spending most of their time together (right).

HUNTING
Although cats are born with a natural hunting instinct, they have to learn the specific skills required. They do this in early kittenhood by observing their mother and other cats. The skills then have to be practised repeatedly in order to perfect them.

CATCHING
The games that kittens love to play enable them to practise specific hunting skills, such as stalking and catching, as seen here.

BALANCING
Balance is maintained by the semi-circular canals in the ears. If the cat starts to fall, its body will swing round so that it will land on its feet.

CLIMBING
Cats are extremely agile climbers, using both their legs and claws to anchor themselves firmly on a branch. Kittens have to learn these skills by trial and error.

CLEANING
Cats spend time grooming themselves every day. The rough surface of their tongues helps to remove loose hairs as they lick their fur, but, if swallowed, these may form a mat or furball in the stomach.

SCENT MARKING
Male cats who have not been neutered tend to spray their pungent urine both inside and outside the home as a means of staking out their territory. Scratching and rubbing against objects, as well as against people, also serves to mark out territory by scent.

SEEING IN THE DARK
As night hunters, cats rely on a special layer of cells (tapetum lucidum) behind the retina, at the back of their eyes, which reflects light back, increasing its intensity and causing the cat's eyes to glow in the dark.

CATS AND KITTENS

THE APPEARANCE of kittens is often different from that of adult cats; it can take several years for a kitten to develop its full coat and colouring, and this makes it difficult to assess the show potential of a litter of kittens at the stage (from twelve weeks of age) when they are ready to go to new homes. In the case of pedigree kittens, however, it is very important to ensure that they are correctly registered with the appropriate associations at this early stage.

COAT LENGTH
The Cinnamon Angora and her four kittens on the right are of similar colouring, but the silky coats of the kittens are somewhat shorter than that of their mother.

MALE CATS
The Lilac and Chocolate British Shorthairs (left) both show the well-developed jowls of entire, adult males; these are missing from the male kittens (below), as well as in neutered adult males.

PATTERNS AND MARKINGS
These young British Shorthairs show signs of tabby markings. While their coloration may well darken over successive moults, their coloured pattern will not change; the white areas will also remain constant in both their size and shape.

CHANGING COLORATION

The adult cat (left) is much darker than the kitten. Tabby markings in young Blue-creams should disappear as they mature, but the actual pattern of the colours will not alter later.

POINTED COLOURS

The points become visible gradually in kittens, more rapidly in some cases than in others. They appear first on the tips of the ears and on the tail. Siamese kittens lack the "tracings" that connect the mask to the ears in adults.

SPOTTED PATTERNING

The difference in the depth of coloration between kitten and adult is clear here, although the kitten is now showing signs of its adult eye coloration. Its blue spotted patterning will not change, but it should become more distinctive.

TABBY LONGHAIRS

The tabby patterning can become blurred in later life as the coat grows.

It is believed that the kittens showing the darkest markings are likely to develop the best adult coats.

BREED DEVELOPMENT

THE SELECTIVE breeding of cats has been taking place for just over a century; prior to this, no attempt had been made to lay down standards by which entries to cat shows could be judged. Although the standard today is open to interpretation, and may differ from one association to another, two aspects are traditionally included: the first is an attempt to describe what should be the ideal appearance (or "type") of the breed; the second gives guidance on coloration and patterning, depending on the breed concerned. Only recently, in some associations, has temperament come in for scrutiny.

SIAMESE DEVELOPMENT

Since the first Siamese cats were imported to Britain in the 1880s, the type of this breed has altered greatly. Below is a prize-winning Siamese of the early 1900s, with its modern counterpart on the right.

as well as the original Seal Point coloration, shown here, many new colour forms are now available

difference most noticeable on head; now distinctly triangular in shape

body shape now longer and more lithe

selective breeding has eliminated kinks in tail

today's cat has longer legs

PERSIAN DEVELOPMENT

The typical Persian features shown in the cat below, dating from the early 1900s, can also be seen in the contemporary cat on the right, but these have become more exaggerated over the years.

ears smaller; more hair inside

larger, more compact head; shorter nose

body larger; more cobby shape

coat more profuse, and in wider range of colours

well-tufted paws

profuse fur on tail

COLOUR DEVELOPMENT

FELINE GENETICS are now more clearly understood than in the early days of the cat fancy, and this has enabled breeders to develop programmes that are specifically aimed at producing new colours or patterned forms. Because of the random way in which chromosomes carrying the genes combine, however, there is no guarantee of the colour of kittens resulting from a given mating.

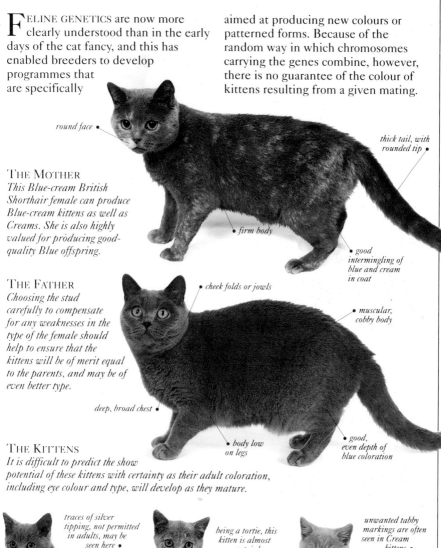

round face •

thick tail, with
rounded tip •

THE MOTHER
This Blue-cream British Shorthair female can produce Blue-cream kittens as well as Creams. She is also highly valued for producing good-quality Blue offspring.

• firm body

• good
intermingling of
blue and cream
in coat

THE FATHER
Choosing the stud carefully to compensate for any weaknesses in the type of the female should help to ensure that the kittens will be of merit equal to the parents, and may be of even better type.

• cheek folds or jowls

• muscular,
cobby body

deep, broad chest •

• body low
on legs

• good,
even depth of
blue coloration

THE KITTENS
It is difficult to predict the show potential of these kittens with certainty as their adult coloration, including eye colour and type, will develop as they mature.

traces of silver
tipping, not permitted
in adults, may be
seen here •

being a tortie, this
kitten is almost
certainly
female •

unwanted tabby
markings are often
seen in Cream
kittens •

BLUE KITTEN

BLUE-CREAM KITTEN

CREAM KITTEN

CHOOSING A CAT

Having decided that you want to acquire a cat, the next question is whether you should choose a non-pedigree or a pure-bred specimen. Non-pedigrees are often easier to find – you could try looking through advertisements in local newspapers, in pet shops, or contact an animal rescue organization.

If you are seeking a pure-bred cat, it may be more difficult to obtain the kitten of your choice, especially one of the rarer breeds. Bear in mind, also, the differences between the various breeds: Longhairs are much more placid than Orientals, and long-haired cats always require more grooming than their short-coated relatives. There are no serious breed weaknesses in cats, however, and both pedigree and non-pedigree animals have a similar lifespan, which can be as much as fifteen years or more.

NON-PEDIGREE CAT
The result of a random mating, such cats show great variation in appearance; like all cats, they are also highly individual in temperament.

If you are hoping to exhibit in the future, it is important to select a kitten that has show potential. Breeders are usually able to assess this by the time that kittens are ready to go to a new home (three months of age). These are likely to be more expensive than kittens with faults, such as obviously poor type or patterning, that would impair their show chances. Such faults, however, will be of little concern if you are simply looking for a healthy and appealing pet.

WHERE TO BUY

If you decide to get a pedigree cat, the advertisement columns of the various cat magazines may help you to find a breeder with kittens available; alternatively, contact one of the cat associations or a specialist breed society. Visiting shows is another way to make contacts if you are searching for a particular breed; you may have to go on a waiting list, as demand for some breeds can outstrip supply.

PEDIGREE (PURE-BRED) CAT
The result of careful selective breeding, this cat has been bred to conform as closely as possible to the recognized "type" specified in the breed standard.

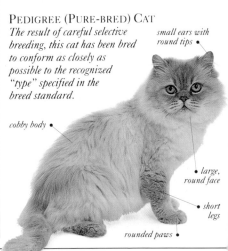

small ears with round tips •

cobby body •

• large, round face

• short legs

rounded paws •

TAKE YOUR PICK

Choosing a kitten is never easy as all young cats are so appealing. Decide in advance whether you want a male or a female. In many breeds, males are slightly larger when mature and should always be neutered, unless required for breeding purposes. This will prevent them from straying from home, and lessen the risk of injuries from fighting. Females will also need to be neutered, around six months of age, if you wish to avoid unwanted pregnancies.

1 OBSERVE THE KITTENS
Spend a few minutes simply observing the kittens: look for an alert, playful, inquisitive individual who does not appear reluctant to be handled.

watchful mother •

• ready to play

interested •

• mischievous

2 CHECK THE COAT
Part the fur and look for any dark specks that are likely to indicate the presence of fleas: these can act as intermediate hosts for tapeworms.

3 CHECK EARS AND EYES
Ears should be clean and free of wax. The third eyelid, or nictitating membrane, should not extend across the eye, nor should there be any discharge from here.

4 CHECK THE MOUTH
Look inside the mouth after prizing the jaws apart. This is vital with older cats, which may have broken teeth, gum disease, or show signs of dental decay.

clean ears •

alert demeanour •

• round, firm chest

5 CHECK THE ANAL AREA
Lift the tail and check that the kitten is not suffering from diarrhoea; there should be no signs of staining here. At the same time check the gender of the kitten: in a female (right), the two openings are close together; in a male they are further apart.

6 MAKING YOUR CHOICE
It is advisable to arrange a veterinary check on your kitten either before or soon after purchase. You should also obtain certified proof from the owner or breeder that the kitten has been vaccinated, as well as a copy of its pedigree.

GROOMING FOR SHOWING

ALL CATS require grooming. Under normal circumstances, they lick their coat, removing dead hairs with the rough surface of the tongue; but the hairs may form a furball in the stomach, which can affect the cat's appetite and its health. Although this is most likely to occur during the moulting period, regular grooming is useful at all times for revealing the presence of parasites such as fleas, ticks, and lice, which will cause the cat to scratch excessively.

On these pages we show just a small selection from the huge range of cat-grooming equipment that is available. A slicker brush is handy for removing dead hair from longhairs, but must be used with caution to avoid pulling out other hairs. Bristle brushes are useful for shorthairs, and some owners like to give their cats a final polish with a chamois leather or with a piece of silk or velvet before a show. You will need a supply of cotton wool for cleaning around the eyes, ears, and nose, as well as talcum or grooming powder, and shampoo.

GROOMING LONGHAIRS
Long-haired cats need daily grooming in order to prevent their coats from becoming matted and tangled.

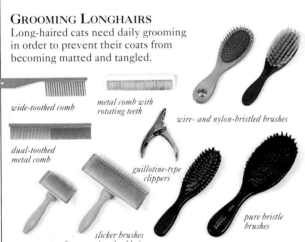

wide-toothed comb

metal comb with rotating teeth

dual-toothed metal comb

wire- and nylon-bristled brushes

guillotine-type clippers

slicker brushes for removing dead hair

pure bristle brushes

1 APPLYING POWDER
Apply non-toxic baby powder or proprietary grooming powder to the coat, section by section. Work the powder well into the coat by hand, ensuring that it is evenly powdered all over.

2 REMOVING POWDER
Using a bristle brush, brush out the coat carefully and thoroughly. The powder adds body to the coat, but no traces must remain on the day of the show.

3 BRUSHING OUT
Brush or comb coat until it stands up all over the body.

4 GROOMING FACE
With a toothbrush, brush the hair on the face, being careful not to get too close to the eyes. Brush or comb the fur around the neck until it forms a ruff.

Bran Bath

For short-haired cats, a bran bath is a very effective means of removing excessive grease and dirt from the coat without having to resort to water and shampoo, which many cats dislike intensely. First, you will need to warm approximately 0.5 – 1 kg bran (available from pet shops) in the oven, set to 150°C, for about 20 minutes. Assemble everything you need before you start: a selection of combs and brushes, an old towel, and a polishing cloth.

1 Rubbing in bran
Stand the cat on newspaper. Massage bran into the coat, avoiding eyes and nose. Some owners wrap the cat in a towel before brushing out the bran.

2 Brushing out bran
Brush out the bran thoroughly and systematically. This method is not suitable for longhairs as any particles left in the coat could cause matting.

Grooming Shorthairs

Shorthairs should generally be combed or brushed in the direction of the fur, from head to tail. Use a fine-toothed comb to smooth the coat and help spot fleas.

rubber brushes

nail clippers

bristle brush for general grooming

metal comb, useful for detecting fleas

chamois / velvet polishing glove

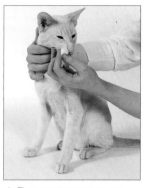

1 Cleaning the face
With a cotton-wool swab and weak salt solution, gently clean around the nose, eyes, and ears.

2 Clipping the claws
If in doubt, ask your vet to show you how to do this without causing injury. Use veterinary clippers that are designed to prevent splitting of the claws.

3 Using a rubber brush
This is useful for shorthairs, but must be used gently to avoid removing too much of the under-coat. It is particularly good for rexes as it won't scratch the skin.

4 Polishing the coat
For a finishing touch to grooming, polish the coat with a polishing mitt that has velvet on one side and chamois leather on the other, or with a piece of silk.

SHOWING

IT IS OFTEN THOUGHT that only pedigree cats can be shown but, in fact, there are also classes for non-pedigrees or "household pets" at most shows. Cat shows are usually advertised in the specialist magazines or you may hear about an event from a fellow enthusiast. In either case you will need to obtain a schedule, listing all the classes, and an entry form. Some cat associations also produce a calendar of shows for the entire year, and there you will find the addresses of the show secretaries. When requesting information about a show, always enclose a self-addressed, stamped envelope of reasonable size, or else you may not receive a reply. Send for details as soon as possible, so that you will have adequate time to enter your cat.

WHEN YOU GET TO THE SHOW

- All cats are vetted-in on arrival, to ensure that only healthy individuals are allowed to compete in the show.
- Give your cat time to settle in its pen before judging takes place. Put a litter tray with clean litter, a water bowl with fresh water, and a clean white blanket in the pen, which will display the same number as the cat's identification tally.

- Give your cat a final grooming, and check eyes, ears, and tail for dirt.
- The cat will be taken to the judging table and assessed against the standard of points for its breed. The judge's comments will be written up and the placings displayed on the award board.

APPLYING FOR ENTRY

Always be sure to read the schedule carefully, so that you can complete the entry form correctly. If you are in any doubt, the show secretary will usually be very pleased to advise you. The entry form must then be sent back well in advance of the closing date, along with the appropriate entry fee.

It is vital that your cat is properly vaccinated before taking part in a show, so check that its inoculations are up-to-date, especially if you are not a regular exhibitor. Should your cat appear unwell for any reason before a show consult your vet without delay, although you will

TRANSPORTING YOUR CAT
The carrier (left) provides a secure means of transporting your cat. The top-opening carrier (right) is easily cleaned, with removable lining.

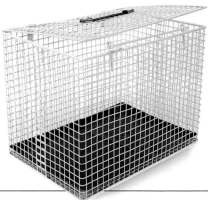

BRITISH SHOW
British cat shows vary in size, from the smaller exemption shows, up to national events.

AMERICAN SHOW
In the United States, owners may enter more shows by registering with several bodies.

probably have to withdraw from the event. This is clearly in the interests of all exhibitors, in order to prevent the possible spread of illness. Similarly, if your cat becomes pregnant, you will not be able to exhibit it.

PREPARING FOR THE SHOW

The regulations concerning equipment vary somewhat, according to the event. If you are in any doubt about this aspect, check beforehand. Careful grooming in the period leading up to the show is essential to ensure that your cat looks its best. Good show cats must also accept handling by strangers, without any resentment; this is why it is so important for kittens to be handled regularly as they grow so they accept it as a matter of routine. You should also get your cat used to travelling from an early age. Check all equipment before leaving, packing the night before if possible. To avoid any last minute panic, be sure you take instructions with you on how to get to the show; leave in plenty of time to get there; and don't let your cat out of the house just before you plan to leave!

SHOW EQUIPMENT
Each cat usually requires a white show blanket, and white food and water containers. You may also require white elastic or ribbon to attach the cat's "tally" around its neck.

A WINNER!
A winning cat can accumulate an impressive collection of rosettes. Once a cat has won three Challenge Certificates, awarded by three separate judges at three different Championship shows, it is recognized as a full Champion.

FUR TYPES

Numerous variations have occurred in the fur types of domestic cats, some having evolved naturally, while others have been produced by selective breeding. Fur type is an individual feature of each breed, independent of colour, and is determined by the specific combination of down, awn, and guard hairs in the fur (*see right*). Close-up photographs of fur are shown throughout this book to help distinguish between the coats of cats of the same colour.

relatively coarse guard hairs

soft, woolly down

thick tips to awn

GUARD
Otherwise known as primary hairs, these constitute the longest and the most visible part of the coat.

DOWN
Short and soft, the down hairs help provide body insulation. Some breeds, however, lack down hairs.

AWN
Slightly longer, bristly hairs that, together with the soft down hairs, constitute the secondary hairs.

LONG-HAIRED CATS

Coat length can be variable, depending on the breed and the season; the density of the coat results largely from the down hair, which also provides the greatest insulation. The Persian Longhair has long guard hairs protruding through the thick down hairs, creating a very dense coat. The hairs of the Angora are finer and less profuse, while the shaggy appearance of the Maine Coon results from the uneven lengths of the individual guard hairs.

FUR TYPE: fine; silky; no woolly undercoat

ANGORA
Sometimes described as semi-longhair, the Angora's coat lies close to the body, especially in summer.

FUR TYPE: long, thick, silky, and fine

PERSIAN LONGHAIR
Persian Longhairs have the longest and densest fur of all domestic cats.

FUR TYPE: thick, silky, and of variable length

MAINE COON
Adapted to living outdoors, these cats have a dense undercoat and a glossy, waterproof top-coat.

SHORT-HAIRED CATS

There is considerable variation in both the appearance and texture of the coats of this group of cats. The Siamese and Orientals have sleek, soft coats with very short, fine-textured hair. In contrast, the Manx has a pronounced double coat – a vital feature of the breed – which serves to emphasize the size of the cat; the undercoat is short and very thick, the guard hairs being just slightly longer. The Russian Blue is another breed that has a very distinctive double coat; this stands up, away from the body, and is soft and silky in texture, as well as being short and thick.

FUR TYPE: short, fine, soft, wavy, and curly

DEVON REX
All three hair types are present, but guard and awn hairs are modified to resemble down hairs, giving a wavy appearance.

FUR TYPE: medium, crimped, and coarse

AMERICAN WIREHAIR
The hairs are crimped into waves, giving the coat a springy, wiry texture.

FUR TYPE: short, dense, and crisp

BRITISH SHORTHAIR
In this case, the coat stands out from the body, giving a rug-like texture, but it must not be too long.

THE "HAIRLESS" SPHYNX

In spite of the name, the Sphynx does have some hair, most conspicuously on the extremities. It also has eyebrows and whiskers, but these are usually shorter than normal. Most of the body has a light covering of down hairs.

FUR TYPE: sparse, very short, and downy

SPHYNX
This highly distinctive breed has not found favour with all cat-lovers.

SEMI-LONGHAIRS

This description is used for cats which have a relatively long top-coat and a greatly reduced undercoat, compared with a Persian or a Colour Pointed Longhair. The group includes breeds that have evolved naturally, such as the Maine Coon, and show a difference in their coat length between winter and summer.

Fur Colours

ALTHOUGH a number of pure colours are now well established within the cat fancy, the basic underlying coloration of the domestic cat is tabby. Actual coloration results from the presence of colour pigments in the hairs, but it is also influenced by light, which may act to dilute the colour of the hairs, so that they appear paler than usual. There are also natural variations of the same colour, so that even litter-mates may differ in the exact depth of their coloration. In particular, some creams may appear much redder than others.

Self Colours

In self-coloured cats, the coloration should be solid from the tips to the roots. Even so, realignment of colour pigment does cause dilution, and this has increased the range of self colours. None of the striping that occurs in tabbies, however, is discernible along the length of the individual hairs of a self-coloured cat. In the case of white selfs, there is no pigment present in the coat, but these are usually not pure albinos.

- solid colour
- standard depth
- no variation in coloration

New Colours

Fawn
This is the dilute form of cinnamon and resembles pale shades of lilac.

Cinnamon
This form of brown is produced by another mutation of the "black" gene.

Dilute Colours

The dilution effect is illustrated here, with dilute colours shown in the upper band above the related dense colour. In the dilute colours, some areas have less pigment than others; thse reflect white light and create a paler impression.

Cream
This is the dilute form of red; it tends to be variable in depth of colour, often with traces of tabby markings.

Lilac
Variations in the precise shade are also common in this colour, some cats being of a lighter shade than others.

Blue
This colour approximates more closely to grey than to pure blue because it is, in fact, a dilute form of black.

White
Caused by a dominant gene, which means that white kittens are likely to occur even if just one of the parents is white.

Red
Sometimes known as Orange but breeders have, in fact, tried to produce a red rather than an orange shade.

Chocolate
This is a dense colour that is now being developed in various breeds, including the Oriental group.

Black
Well known and widely represented in the cat fancy, black should be a pure shade, with no trace of white hairs.

TIPPED

The extent of the tipping on the guard hairs, and also on the awn hairs in some cases, will have a significant effect on

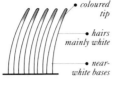

- *coloured tip*
- *hairs mainly white*
- *near-white bases*

the overall appearance of the coat. In the case of the Cream Shell Cameo Persian seen here, the undercoat is almost pure white, while the coloration is confined almost exclusively to the tip of the guard hairs.

CHINCHILLA PERSIAN
The lightest of the silver forms, with the trace of black tipping creating a sparkling effect.

CREAM SHELL CAMEO PERSIAN
The equivalent in the cream series, with white undercoat and cream tipping.

SHADED

In this case, although the undercoat is hardly affected, being largely white, the tipping extends much

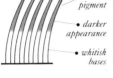

- *more pigment*
- *darker appearance*
- *whitish bases*

further down the length of the guard hairs from their tips, creating a noticeably darker appearance. It is possible to see the paler undercoat when the cat is moving, or simply by parting the fur to reveal the underlying contrasting colour.

CREAM SHADED PERSIAN
Here the cream tipping is more pronounced, leading to a more definite coloration.

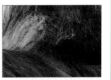

RED SHADED PERSIAN
Identical to the Cream except that, in this case, darker red coloration replaces cream.

SMOKE

This is the darkest form of tipping, most of the guard hair being pigmented. The undercoat still remains lighter,

- *dark coloration*
- *hairs mainly coloured*
- *dense pigmentation*

however, and the contrast is most apparent when the cat walks. The Smoke characteristic is now widely distributed, although the darker forms, in which the distinctive contrast is pronounced, are most popular.

BLUE SMOKE PERSIAN
Pigmentation is most pronounced in the Smokes, so that these cats can resemble selfs.

BLACK SMOKE PERSIAN
Smoke coloration is variable, and some cats will therefore appear lighter than others.

TICKED

Ticking provides a useful means of camouflage for cats. With the coloration broken into bands

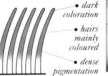

- *tips coloured*
- *variable pigment*
- *lighter banding*

along the length of the individual hairs, the cat's coat becomes less conspicuous. Where the tabby markings are solid, there are hairs with no banding, and this creates further contrast in the coat, sometimes known as disruptive coloration.

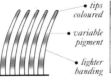

SILVER SORREL SOMALI
Here the white hair is ticked with chocolate, creating an impression of silvery peach.

USUAL ABYSSINIAN
The effect of ticking is to create a distinctive coloration which may be variable in depth over the cat's body.

COAT PATTERNS

MOST CATS have a coat patterning that reflects to some extent the natural tabby markings of their wild ancestors. Breeders have refined these markings, developing them to conform to precise standards. Gradually, by the careful selection of breeding stock, and over successive generations, patterning has been altered in line with the requirements of breeders. An element of luck is required to produce a cat with an ideal coat patterning, but the probability can be greatly increased by following a well-designed breeding programme.

Undesirable features can also be bred out from the cat, as has occurred in the case of the Abyssinian. Its tabby barring has now virtually disappeared, creating the so-called "ticked tabby" pattern.

With few exceptions, a cat's patterning does not change after birth, although the markings may become more distinctive.

PARTI-COLOURS
Many cats have areas of white fur alongside coloured areas. This can vary from the "magpie" appearance of black and white cats, to the tortie and white with its combination of white, black, and red patches.

TORTIE AND WHITE
Clearly defined patches of black, varying shades of red, and white are all visible in this parti-coloured individual •

• BI-COLOURED
It has been possible, by a process of selective breeding, to restrict the proportion of white fur, so that it should cover no more than half of the entire body area

TORTOISESHELL
In the tortoiseshell, the black and red coloration should be evenly intermingled and distributed over the body; a facial blaze of cream or red is considered to be desirable in torties.

TORTOISESHELL •
For genetic reasons, almost all cats showing the tortoiseshell patterning are female

BLUE-CREAM
In these cats, which are otherwise known as Dilute Torties, blue replaces black, and cream replaces red, giving them a distinctive coloration •

POINTED

Cats with pointed markings are instantly recognizable by the darker coloration on the extremities of their bodies, namely the face, ears, legs, feet, and tail. The intensity of colour on the points is affected by body temperature, coat length, and climate.

SIAMESE
The Siamese is the best known of the pointed breeds. The points contrast with the lighter body coloration •

VAN PATTERN
Named after the Turkish Van, but seen also in other breeds; in this case, coloration is mainly restricted to the tail and to part of the head •

TABBY

The different types of tabby patterning seen in domestic cats also occur in wild cats. Such markings provide camouflage, stripes and spots enabling cats to merge easily into their background.

CLASSIC TABBY •
Sometimes known as the blotched tabby, this variety has large, black, oyster-shaped areas on each flank, butterfly-shaped shoulder markings, and numerous rings around the tail

SPOTTED
The tabby stripes are broken up into a pattern of distinct, oval, round, or rosette-shaped spots on the body, which can extend to the tail •

PATCHED TABBY AND WHITE •
This is a tortie tabby, or torbie, which shows both tortoiseshell and tabby characteristics, as well as areas of white fur

MACKEREL TABBY AND WHITE •
This striped patterning is the original form of the tabby variants. Black stripes run vertically down the body, with a narrow, dark, unbroken line along the centre of the spine. The stripes are separated by coloured areas of ticked (agouti) hair

IDENTIFICATION KEY

THIS IDENTIFICATION KEY has been designed to help you to identify both pedigree and non-pedigree cats. The Key is in four stages: in Stage 1, cats are classified according to their coat length; in Stage 2, these categories are broken down further according to face shape; in Stage 3, photographs of one individual from each breed group, with page references, guide you to the appropriate section of the book. Stage 4 covers non-pedigree cats and, as before, photographs of individual cats, with page references, guide you directly to the relevant section.

STAGE 1: LENGTH OF HAIR

A cat's coat is its most striking feature, not just in terms of coloration and pattern, but also in the way that it affects the overall impression of the cat's shape and size. It is for this reason that the classificatory groupings applied to pedigree cats rely in the first instance on coat length. There are, of course, differences also in the texture of the coat. This information is covered fully in in the appropriate breed section entries, in the main part of the book.

LONG-HAIRED CATS
The coat of a long-haired cat is often so profuse that it can double the cat's apparent size, the volume being increased by the undercoat. Some long-haired breeds, such as the Turkish Angora, have a less profuse coat and are sometimes described and classified as semi-longhairs. Like all cats, longhairs may shed a substantial amount of hair during the warmer months, and this can alter their appearance considerably.

SHORT-HAIRED CATS
The coat of a short-haired cat allows you to see more clearly the underlying body shape, which may be sturdy and muscular, or lithe and sleek. The coats of shorthairs can vary in appearance and texture; it may be very short, sleek, and close-lying, or the fur may vary in length on different areas of the body. The texture may be fine or coarse, dense, or plush, and the hairs may be straight, crinkled, curly, or wavy.

"HAIRLESS" CATS
Hairlessness, or relative lack of hair, in pedigree cats is the result of a spontaneous mutation which has subsequently been developed by selective breeding. Although such mutations have been recorded in the past, only one pedigree breed has been developed – the Sphynx – which does, in fact, have a fine covering of down, especially on the face, ears, feet, and tail. For further details of this rather controversial breed, turn to p.178.

STAGE 2: FACE SHAPE

The face shapes of both long-haired and short-haired cats fall into three broad categories, and at this stage you must decide whether the face of the cat you are trying to identify is round, or angular and wedge shaped, or whether it belongs in the middle category of shapes that falls between these two extremes. Face shape can usually be related also to body shape; cats with a round face tend to have cobby bodies, whereas those with wedge-shaped faces typically have a lithe and svelte outline.

It is worth noting that facial characteristics may vary slightly between the sexes, in that unneutered male cats are likely to develop jowls once they mature: jowls are a secondary sexual characteristic, however, and if male cats are neutered before puberty the jowls will not develop. The shape of the face will also vary at different times of the year, according to whether the cat is moulting or in full coat.

LONG-HAIRED CATS

ROUND-FACED
In this case the head is massive and round, with a broad skull and small, round-tipped ears that are set wide apart and low on the head. The face has full, rounded cheeks, and a short, broad nose with a stop.

INTERMEDIATE-FACED
In this group, the head is of medium length. It is well proportioned, with a straight profile, or with a slight break. The ears are usually large, pointed, set well apart, and positioned high on the head.

WEDGE-FACED
This face narrows in straight lines from the widely spaced ears to the muzzle, forming a perfect wedge. The profile is slightly convex, and the nose is long and straight. The ears are large and pointed.

SHORT-HAIRED CATS

ROUND-FACED
The face here is round with full cheeks and good breadth of skull. The broad, short nose is straight, and the profile shows a rounded forehead and a slight break. The small, round-tipped ears are set wide apart.

INTERMEDIATE-FACED
The head here is of medium proportions, slightly broader at the top and tapering to a soft, rounded triangle. The nose can show a shallow indentation, while the ears are medium to large, and broad at the base.

WEDGE-FACED
This is an elegant, elongated face that narrows in perfectly straight lines to the noticeably fine muzzle. The profile is straight, with no break in the long nose. The ears are large, pointed, and wide at the base.

STAGE 3: IDENTIFY YOUR CAT

Having made your decisions about coat length and face shape at Stages 1 and 2, now refer to the appropriate section below where all the pedigree breeds featured in the book can be found. The silhouettes of body shapes that accompany each face are given as an additional identification aid, while the adjacent numbers are page references. Where there are many different colour forms of a breed (such as the Persian Longhairs) we have selected just one representative example for the key; the cat chosen illustrates the typical features of the breed, differing only in colour from the others. It is important to bear in mind that coloration is not necessarily a significant feature in the identification of breeds, and that many breeds can be of similar coloration. However, colour is a guide in the identification of pointed breeds that display darker markings on their body extremities, such as the ears, feet, and tail.

LONG-HAIRED CATS WITH ROUND FACES

Persian Longhair *40*

Persian Tabby *54*

Chinchilla *55*

Colour Pointed Longhair *62*

Birman *68*

Cymric *110*

Scottish Fold *111*

American Curl *112*

LONG-HAIRED CATS WITH INTERMEDIATE-SHAPED FACES

Turkish Angora *74*

Turkish Van *78*

Maine Coon *84*

Norwegian Forest *90*

Siberian Forest *93*

Ragdoll *94*

Somali *96*

Tiffanie *108*

LONG-HAIRED CATS WITH WEDGE-SHAPED FACES

Angora *80*

Javanese *83*

Balinese *102*

SHORT-HAIRED CATS WITH ROUND FACES

British Shorthair *118*

Colour Pointed British Shorthair *132*

Exotic *136*

Manx *140*

Scottish Fold *144*

American Shorthair *148*

American Wirehair *156*

American Curl *158*

European Shorthair *160*

Colour Pointed European Shorthair *164*

Chartreux *165*

Bengal *239*

SHORT-HAIRED CATS WITH INTERMEDIATE-SHAPED FACES

Japanese Bobtail *143*

Russian Shorthair *182*

Korat *183*

Burmese *194*

Burmilla *204*

Asian *207*

Bombay *210*

Singapura *211*

Abyssinian *228*

Wild Abyssinian *233*

Ocicat *234*

California Spangled *236*

SHORT-HAIRED CATS WITH WEDGE-SHAPED FACES

Snowshoe *147*

Cornish Rex *166*

Devon Rex *172*

Sphynx *178*

Selkirk Rex *180*

Siamese *184*

Tonkinese *200*

Oriental Shorthair *212*

Havana *216*

Oriental Tabby *220*

Egyptian Mau *226*

STAGE 4: NON-PEDIGREE CATS

Non-pedigree cats, by their nature, tend not to be of a recognizable type, and there can be wide variation in their appearance, as the examples below illustrate. The range of coat patterns is very variable in non-pedigrees, where there are no restrictions on their breeding. It is not possible to group them meaningfully on the basis of their facial characteristics, either, although there may well be local similarities within a particular area where a degree of in-breeding of related non-pedigree cats has occurred. Selective breeding can then be utilized to reinforce such natural features and a new breed can then evolve, as happened recently with the Singapura. A similar process took place on the Isle of Man where the gene for taillessness arose, breeders then carrying on a development begun by Nature. Many of today's breeds have been developed from such spontaneous mutations.

LONG-HAIRED NON-PEDIGREE CATS

Blue *114*

Cream and White *115*

Silver and White *117*

SHORT-HAIRED NON-PEDIGREE CATS

Black and White *241*

White and Tortie *241*

Blue-cream *242*

Red Tabby and White *243*

Blue Tabby and White *243*

Brown Tabby and White *244*

LONG-HAIRED CATS

PERSIAN LONGHAIR

KNOWN AS LONGHAIRS in the UK and as Persians in North America, these elegant and graceful cats have been popular since Victorian times. They have been bred in an ever-increasing range of colours, but their appearance has changed considerably since the early days. They now have a flatter, more rounded face and the ears are smaller; the coats have also become more profuse and these require daily grooming in order to prevent matting.

Country of origin Great Britain	Ancestry Angoras x Persians	Origins 1880s

ORANGE-EYED WHITE

Some of the earliest Persian Longhairs in Europe and in the United States were white. These cats usually had blue eyes, and this orange-eyed form resulted from subsequent crossings involving Blue, Cream, and Black Longhairs.
• **FEATURES** Pure white, with a long, thick coat, these are quite large cats, with a distinctly cobby profile. On occasion, kittens may show traces of dark markings on the head, but these usually disappear later in life.
• **REMARK** It was only in 1938 that the Blue-eyed and the Orange-eyed White Longhairs were divided into separate categories in Great Britain.

small, round-tipped ears

deep orange or copper eyes

pink nose

short, bushy tail

large, cobby body shape; massive rump

large, round paws, well tufted with fur

dense, pure white coat

FUR TYPE: long, thick, silky, and fine

Shorthair option Orange-eyed White Exotic	Temperament Docile

Country of origin Great Britain	Ancestry Angoras x Persians	Origins 1880s

BLUE-EYED WHITE

Unfortunately, the distinctive blue eye coloration of White Longhairs is frequently linked to deafness, and it has not yet proved possible to eliminate this weakness.
• FEATURES All White Longhairs are born with blue eyes, and this makes it difficult to distinguish, at an early stage, those likely to be handicapped later on.
• REMARK The original White Longhairs appear to have been brought from Turkey to France during the 1500s and were known as Angoras, after the Turkish capital of Ankara.

deep blue shades of eye coloration preferred •

• short, thick neck

• ears set low on head

fine, silky coat •

FUR TYPE: long, thick, silky, and fine

• pure white hair

Shorthair option Blue-eyed White Exotic	Temperament Docile

Country of origin Great Britain	Ancestry Angoras x Persians	Origins 1880s

ODD-EYED WHITE

ears set well apart •

These cats can occur in litters bred from blue-eyed parents or from mixed matings. Deafness, if present, is normally confined to the ear on the same side as the blue eye.
• FEATURES Eyes should be a deep shade of the appropriate colour, with the coat itself being pure white.
• REMARK This breed was recognized in the United States in the 1950s.

• short, broad nose

• ear furnishings

• either eye can be orange or deep copper; the other eye is blue

FUR TYPE: long, thick, silky, and fine

Shorthair option Odd-eyed White Exotic	Temperament Docile

Country of origin Great Britain	Ancestry Angoras x Persians	Origins 1880s

CREAM

The cream coloration resulted from pairings of Tortoiseshells and Red Tabbies, but the offspring produced were almost entirely male.
• **FEATURES** A pale to medium shade of cream is preferred, with no white in the undercoat. Tabby markings in kittens should fade in time.
• **REMARK** The first Cream Longhairs to be produced were of a much darker shade than those seen today, bordering on fawn in some individuals.

• *round forehead*

FUR TYPE: long, thick, silky, and fine

• *deep orange or copper eyes*

• *deep, broad chest*

• *even depth of colour*

Shorthair option Cream Exotic	Temperament Docile

Country of origin Great Britain	Ancestry Angoras x Persians	Origins 1880s

RED

In the early days of the cat fancy it proved difficult to produce these cats, known as "Orange", without traces of darker, tabby markings. This can still cause problems, largely because of fairly widespread crossings with Red Tabbies in the past.
• **FEATURES** A rich, deep red is desirable, with no white hairs evident. Kittens usually have tabby markings, but these disappear in due course.
• **REMARK** A shortage of Red females has been overcome by the pairing of Red males to Tortoiseshell females.

• *broad skull*

FUR TYPE: long, thick, silky, and fine

• *deep orange or copper eyes*

• *full frill*

• *large, round paws*

cobby body shape •

Shorthair option Red Exotic	Temperament Docile

Country of origin Great Britain	Ancestry Angoras x Persians	Origins 1880s

LILAC

The Lilac is a dilute form of the Chocolate Longhair, and the two breeds have been developed along similar lines. Further refinement to the type of these cats is continuing.

• **FEATURES** It has been difficult to create the desired shade of pinkish dove-grey, which must be of an even depth of colour throughout the coat.

• **REMARK** This is one of the newer additions to the Longhair group, dating back only to the 1960s. It is not yet very numerous.

FUR TYPE: long, thick, silky, and fine

massive rump

short, thick neck

pure, even depth of colour

Shorthair option Lilac Exotic	Temperament Docile

Country of origin Great Britain	Ancestry Angoras x Persians	Origins 1880s

BLUE

The earliest Blues were bred from crosses between Black and White Longhairs, and selective breeding eliminated white blemishes from the coat. Queen Victoria kept this breed, thus ensuring its popularity.

• **FEATURES** Kittens often show tabby patterning but, oddly enough, those with the most pronounced markings often develop into the best adults.

• **REMARK** Blue cats originated from Russia, Persia (now Iran), and from neighbouring countries.

FUR TYPE: long, thick, silky, and fine

large orange or copper eyes

ears widely spaced and low on head

broad shoulders

short legs

paws tufted with fur

short, bushy tail

Blue Exotic	Temperament Docile

Country of origin Great Britain	Ancestry Angoras x Persians	Origins 1880s

CHOCOLATE

The Chocolate Longhair originated with the crossing of a Havana and a Blue Longhair. The first example of the breed was exhibited in 1961.
• **FEATURES** The aim has been to produce cats with solid chocolate-brown coloration, and with no other markings of any kind.
• **REMARK** The use of Havana stock tended at first to produce cats with rather elongated faces and large ears. Such flaws have been eliminated by a careful process of selective breeding.

FUR TYPE: long, thick, silky, and fine

• *large, deep orange or copper eyes*

short face •

• *short, sturdy legs*

• *consistent shade of medium to dark chocolate-brown*

Chocolate Exotic		Temperament Docile

Country of origin Great Britain	Ancestry Angoras x Persians	Origins 1880s

BLACK

First on the list of recognized breeds in Great Britain, these cats were exhibited at the first British cat show in 1871. They were equally popular in the United States at this early stage.
• **FEATURES** Good coloration is vital in this breed, with no shading, markings, or white hairs. Kittens may show a grey or rusty hue, but this should fade by about eight months of age.
• **REMARK** The early Black Longhairs had a more foreign type than those seen today.

• *well-spaced, round eyes*

lustrous, raven-black coloration •

• *long, flowing coat of even colour*

short, bushy tail •

FUR TYPE: long, thick, silky, and fine

Shorthair option Black Exotic		Temperament Docile

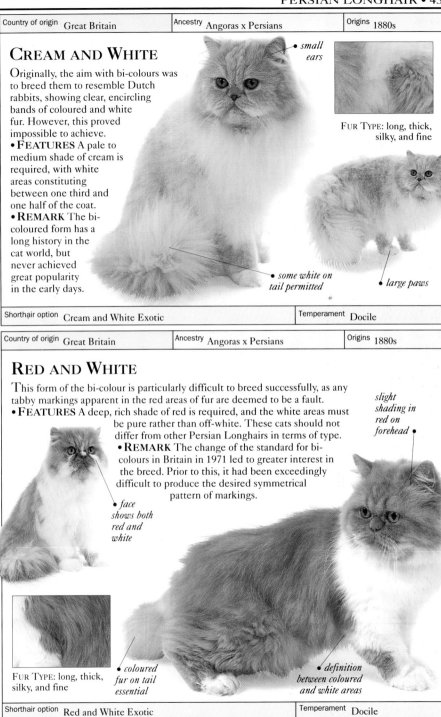

Country of origin Great Britain	Ancestry Angoras x Persians	Origins 1880s

CREAM AND WHITE

Originally, the aim with bi-colours was to breed them to resemble Dutch rabbits, showing clear, encircling bands of coloured and white fur. However, this proved impossible to achieve.
• **FEATURES** A pale to medium shade of cream is required, with white areas constituting between one third and one half of the coat.
• **REMARK** The bi-coloured form has a long history in the cat world, but never achieved great popularity in the early days.

small ears

FUR TYPE: long, thick, silky, and fine

some white on tail permitted

large paws

Shorthair option Cream and White Exotic	Temperament Docile

Country of origin Great Britain	Ancestry Angoras x Persians	Origins 1880s

RED AND WHITE

This form of the bi-colour is particularly difficult to breed successfully, as any tabby markings apparent in the red areas of fur are deemed to be a fault.
• **FEATURES** A deep, rich shade of red is required, and the white areas must be pure rather than off-white. These cats should not differ from other Persian Longhairs in terms of type.
• **REMARK** The change of the standard for bi-colours in Britain in 1971 led to greater interest in the breed. Prior to this, it had been exceedingly difficult to produce the desired symmetrical pattern of markings.

slight shading in red on forehead

face shows both red and white

coloured fur on tail essential

FUR TYPE: long, thick, silky, and fine

definition between coloured and white areas

Shorthair option Red and White Exotic	Temperament Docile

| Country of origin Great Britain | Ancestry Angoras x Persians | Origins 1880s |

LILAC AND WHITE

Initially, only the four traditional colours (black, blue, red, and cream) with white, were permitted as bi-colours. In 1971 this changed and other variants, such as this one, can now be shown.
• **FEATURES** The legs are predominantly white and some white is permitted on the tail.
• **REMARK** It proved quite easy to produce these cats once the Lilac Longhair was established, by simply crossing them with Whites.

even depth of coloration

warm shade of lilac required in coloured areas

broad chest

lilac patch on tail •

FUR TYPE: long, thick, silky, and fine

| Shorthair option Lilac and White Exotic | Temperament Docile |

| Country of origin Great Britain | Ancestry Angoras x Persians | Origins 1880s |

BLUE AND WHITE

Bi-colours are invariably strong and healthy cats, but their coats need careful grooming in order to show the sharp delineation between the white and coloured areas to best effect.
• **FEATURES** Males are likely to develop into massive cats, females being only slightly smaller. There should be no trace of tabby markings in the coat. The profuse hair forms a frill around the shoulders and between the front legs.
• **REMARK** The darker colours, such as this Blue and White, seem to be most popular.

FUR TYPE: long, thick, silky, and fine

powerful jaws

face shows both blue and white •

bushy tail •

clear contrast between blue and white markings

• long fur

| Shorthair option Blue and White Exotic | Temperament Docile |

| Country of origin | Great Britain | Ancestry | Angoras x Persians | Origins | 1880s |

CHOCOLATE AND WHITE

The Chocolate and White variety followed on the development of the Chocolate, the latter being crossed with White Longhairs.
• **FEATURES** The coloured areas should cover between one half and two thirds of the coat.
• **REMARK** The development of this variety was encouraged by the change in the British standard in 1971.

• *round, broad head with good width between ears*

FUR TYPE: long, thick, silky, and fine

• *strong chin*

• *clear delineation between white and chocolate areas essential*

| Shorthair option | Chocolate and White Exotic | Temperament | Docile |

| Country of origin | Great Britain | Ancestry | Angoras x Persians | Origins | 1880s |

BLACK AND WHITE

These bi-colours can be traced back to the early days of the cat fancy when, because of their coloration, they were described as "magpie".
• **FEATURES** As in other bi-colours, a symmetrical pattern of markings is preferred, along with a facial blaze as shown here. The type of these cats should not differ from that of other Persian Longhairs.
• **REMARK** Bi-coloured Longhairs were not recognized for championship status in Britain until 1966, and little progress took place before 1971 when the more realistic standard for markings was introduced.

temporary rusty hue in kitten's coat •

• *lustrous black coloration, with no odd white hairs*

FUR TYPE: long, thick, silky, and fine

• *white collar encircling neck desirable*

| Shorthair option | Black and White Exotic | Temperament | Docile |

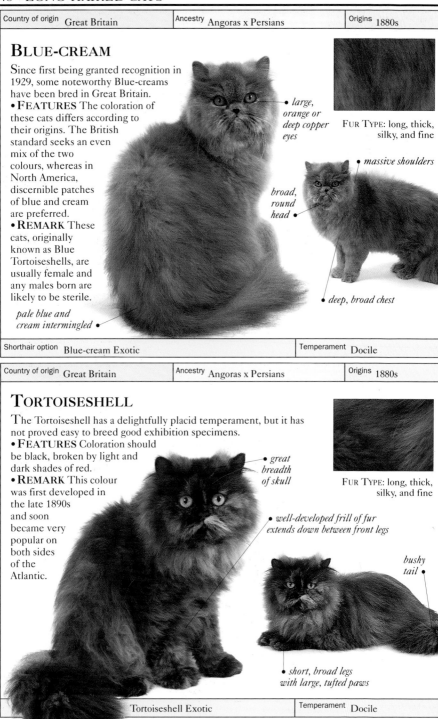

Country of origin Great Britain	Ancestry Angoras x Persians	Origins 1880s

BLUE-CREAM

Since first being granted recognition in 1929, some noteworthy Blue-creams have been bred in Great Britain.
• **FEATURES** The coloration of these cats differs according to their origins. The British standard seeks an even mix of the two colours, whereas in North America, discernible patches of blue and cream are preferred.
• **REMARK** These cats, originally known as Blue Tortoiseshells, are usually female and any males born are likely to be sterile.

large, orange or deep copper eyes

FUR TYPE: long, thick, silky, and fine

massive shoulders

broad, round head

deep, broad chest

pale blue and cream intermingled

Shorthair option Blue-cream Exotic	Temperament Docile

Country of origin Great Britain	Ancestry Angoras x Persians	Origins 1880s

TORTOISESHELL

The Tortoiseshell has a delightfully placid temperament, but it has not proved easy to breed good exhibition specimens.
• **FEATURES** Coloration should be black, broken by light and dark shades of red.
• **REMARK** This colour was first developed in the late 1890s and soon became very popular on both sides of the Atlantic.

great breadth of skull

FUR TYPE: long, thick, silky, and fine

well-developed frill of fur extends down between front legs

bushy tail

short, broad legs with large, tufted paws

Tortoiseshell Exotic	Temperament Docile

Country of origin Great Britain	Ancestry Angoras x Persians	Origins 1880s

BLUE-CREAM AND WHITE

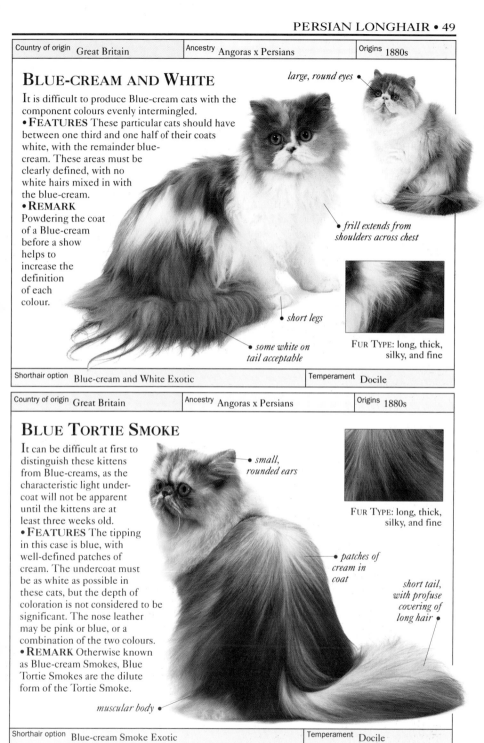

large, round eyes

It is difficult to produce Blue-cream cats with the component colours evenly intermingled.
• **FEATURES** These particular cats should have between one third and one half of their coats white, with the remainder blue-cream. These areas must be clearly defined, with no white hairs mixed in with the blue-cream.
• **REMARK** Powdering the coat of a Blue-cream before a show helps to increase the definition of each colour.

frill extends from shoulders across chest

short legs

some white on tail acceptable

FUR TYPE: long, thick, silky, and fine

Shorthair option Blue-cream and White Exotic	Temperament Docile

Country of origin Great Britain	Ancestry Angoras x Persians	Origins 1880s

BLUE TORTIE SMOKE

It can be difficult at first to distinguish these kittens from Blue-creams, as the characteristic light under-coat will not be apparent until the kittens are at least three weeks old.
• **FEATURES** The tipping in this case is blue, with well-defined patches of cream. The undercoat must be as white as possible in these cats, but the depth of coloration is not considered to be significant. The nose leather may be pink or blue, or a combination of the two colours.
• **REMARK** Otherwise known as Blue-cream Smokes, Blue Tortie Smokes are the dilute form of the Tortie Smoke.

small, rounded ears

FUR TYPE: long, thick, silky, and fine

patches of cream in coat

short tail, with profuse covering of long hair

muscular body

Shorthair option Blue-cream Smoke Exotic	Temperament Docile

Country of origin Great Britain	Ancestry Angoras x Persians	Origins 1880s

TORTIE AND WHITE

Sometimes known by the name of "Calico Longhair", especially in North America, these cats were relatively rare before they were granted recognition in 1950.

• **FEATURES** Between one third and one half of the coat, in this case, should show clearly defined white patches; there must be no white hairs in the coloured areas.

• **REMARK** A slightly different standard for this breed has evolved in North America, where white coloration on the underparts is favoured.

coloured and white areas on the head •

FUR TYPE: long, thick, silky, and fine

• clearly defined patches of colour

• cobby body shape

• large, flattened face

tail must show colour •

Shorthair option Tortie and White Exotic	Temperament Docile

Country of origin Great Britain	Ancestry Angoras x Persians	Origins 1880s

TORTIE AND WHITE VAN

This variant of the Tortie and White Longhair is based on the Turkish Van, being a predominantly white cat with restricted coloured markings on the head, ears, and tail. A range of colours has now been developed.

• **FEATURES** The Tortie and White Van Pattern is a tri-coloured form of the breed, and in this individual the tortie base colour is black and red. Bi-coloured forms of the breed are now becoming more numerous.

• **REMARK** FiFe, the international feline body, granted recognition to this breed in 1986, under the name of "Harlequin".

• colour on head and ears

FUR TYPE: long, thick, silky, and fine

• white body

coloured tail •

up to three small spots of colour permitted on body •

Shorthair option Tortie and White Van Exotic	Temperament Docile

| Country of origin | Great Britain | Ancestry | Angoras x Persians | Origins | 1880s |

CHOCOLATE TORTIE

One of the newer colour combinations to be developed, the Chocolate Tortoiseshell shows to best effect in winter when its coat is most profuse.

• **FEATURES** The basic colour here is chocolate, offset by light and dark red patches. In type, these cats are typical Persian Longhairs, with large heads.

• **REMARK** After the development of the Chocolate Longhair, Chocolate combinations, such as this essentially female-only tortie variety, could be produced.

• *deep orange or copper eyes*

• *clear stop between forehead and nose*

• *fur may be up to 15 cm (6 in) long*

• *short, thick neck*

rounded rump •

• *large, tufted paws*

FUR TYPE: long, thick, silky, and fine

| Shorthair option | Chocolate Tortie Exotic | Temperament | Docile |

| Country of origin | Great Britain | Ancestry | Angoras x Persians | Origins | 1880s |

CHOCOLATE TORTIE TABBY

Most long-haired tabbies show classic patterning, as in this case; the mackerel form is comparatively scarce. Tabby markings tend to be less distinctive in Longhairs.

• **FEATURES** In this case, chocolate tabby markings are combined with the tortoiseshell colours of light and dark red. The basic tabby patterning itself consists of a bronze agouti ground colour, with rich, chocolate-coloured markings. Paw pads can be chocolate, pink, or a combination of both.

• **REMARK** These cats are sometimes known, in the United States, as "patched tabbies" or "torbies".

• *broad, round head with short, wide muzzle*

• *strong chin*

• *pads may be either chocolate or pink, depending on distribution of red*

FUR TYPE: long, thick, silky, and fine

• *short, full tail*

| Shorthair option | Chocolate Tortie Tabby Exotic | Temperament | Docile |

Country of origin Great Britain	Ancestry Angoras x Persians	Origins 1880s

LILAC TABBY

Although bred from Lilac Longhairs, which date back to the 1960s, these tabbies are one of the more recent additions to the Persian Longhair category.
• FEATURES The ground colour should be a beige agouti shade, offset by dense, clearly defined lilac markings. These should be evident both on the sides of the body and running down the back in stripes.
• REMARK Tabby markings, long evident in Longhairs, have been introduced in association with new colours as these have become available.

clear "M"-shaped marking on forehead •

• lilac "necklaces" present on neck and chest

• lilac spotting on underparts

FUR TYPE: long, thick, silky, and fine

Shorthair option Lilac Tabby Exotic	Temperament Docile

Country of origin Great Britain	Ancestry Angoras x Persians	Origins 1880s

BLUE TABBY

The earliest Blue Tabbies occurred in litters of Brown Tabby Longhairs, but they can also be bred by crossing a Blue self with a Brown Tabby.
• FEATURES There is good contrast in these cats, with dark blue markings and a pale blue ground colour.
• REMARK These cats were granted recognition in the United States in 1962, but in the UK they have achieved only preliminary recognition.

• blue nose

FUR TYPE: long, thick, silky, and fine

• tightly grouped dark lines

clearly defined outline of "M" •

cobby body; low on legs •

good fur covering on tail •

• bushy tail

Shorhair option Blue Tabby Exotic	Temperament Docile

| Country of origin | Great Britain | Ancestry | Angoras x Persians | Origins | 1880s |

RED TABBY

Red Tabby Longhairs were being shown during the last century, but suffered a decline in numbers following World War II.

• **FEATURES** The basic coloration of these cats should be a rich shade of red, with a series of darker tabby markings.

• **REMARK** Originally called Orange Tabbies, this variety has always been popular in North America.

• small, well-tufted ears with rounded tips

FUR TYPE: long, thick, silky, and fine

• solid red back, with darker colour running in three stripes here

| Shorthair option | Red Tabby Exotic | Temperament | Docile |

| Country of origin | Great Britain | Ancestry | Angoras x Persians | Origins | 1880s |

SILVER TABBY

Silver Tabby kittens that are mainly black at birth, showing just traces of markings, are likely to develop into the best-marked adult cats.

• **FEATURES** The ground colour is silver with contrasting dense black markings. There must be no trace of white or brown fur in the coat.

• **REMARK** Silver Tabby Longhairs were popular in show circles even in the late 1800s. In terms of their markings, there are few more striking cats.

tabby markings clearly discernible •

FUR TYPE: long, thick, silky, and fine

• short tail with no signs of a kink

• barring, or "bracelets" on legs

| Shorthair option | Silver Tabby | Exotic | Temperament | Docile |

| Country of origin Great Britain | Ancestry Angoras x Persians | Origins 1880s |

BROWN CLASSIC TABBY

Brushing the coat in the direction of the lie of the fur will intensify the contrast between the light coat and dark markings.
• **FEATURES** The basic coat colour should be a rich, tawny shade of sable, with solid black markings. The eye coloration should be orange or copper, with no trace of a green rim. The nose leather must be brick-red. The pads can be either black or brown.
• **REMARK** One of the earliest specialist cat clubs in Britain, The Brown Tabby Persian Cat Society, was founded to promote this breed in Victorian times.

characteristic "M"-shaped marking on forehead •

• black line running back from corner of each eye

FUR TYPE: long, thick, silky, and fine

tail well ringed with black •

barring on legs •

• short neck

| Shorthair option Brown Classic Tabby Exotic | Temperament Docile |

| Country of origin Great Britain | Ancestry Angoras x Persians | Origins 1880s |

TORTIE TABBY

These Longhairs show typical tabby patterning and tortoiseshell markings in shades of red, both of which should be clearly visible.
• **FEATURES** In this case the tabby markings are black, superimposed on the basic coppery-brown agouti fur coloration. Tortoiseshell coloration is also visible. The pads are pink or black.
• **REMARK** Tortie Tabbies, or "Torbies", are likely to be bred only as females.

colours clearly defined •

• tabby markings clearly evident

FUR TYPE: long, thick, silky, and fine

short, bushy tail •

| Shorthair option Tortie Tabby Exotic | Temperament Docile |

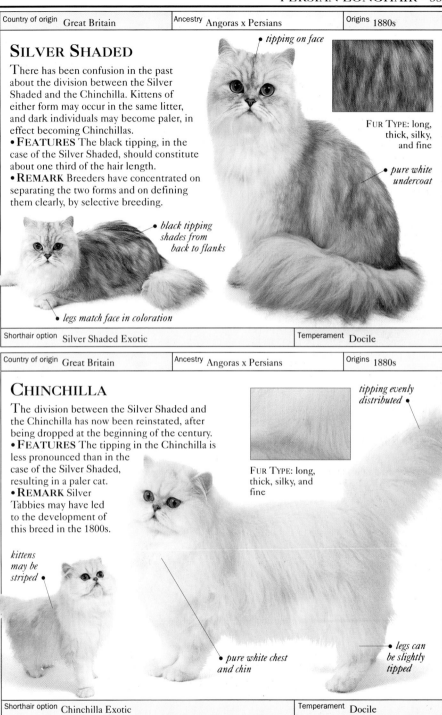

| Country of origin | Great Britain | Ancestry | Angoras x Persians | Origins | 1880s |

SILVER SHADED

There has been confusion in the past about the division between the Silver Shaded and the Chinchilla. Kittens of either form may occur in the same litter, and dark individuals may become paler, in effect becoming Chinchillas.
• FEATURES The black tipping, in the case of the Silver Shaded, should constitute about one third of the hair length.
• REMARK Breeders have concentrated on separating the two forms and on defining them clearly, by selective breeding.

tipping on face

FUR TYPE: long, thick, silky, and fine

pure white undercoat

black tipping shades from back to flanks

legs match face in coloration

| Shorthair option | Silver Shaded Exotic | Temperament | Docile |

| Country of origin | Great Britain | Ancestry | Angoras x Persians | Origins | 1880s |

CHINCHILLA

The division between the Silver Shaded and the Chinchilla has now been reinstated, after being dropped at the beginning of the century.
• FEATURES The tipping in the Chinchilla is less pronounced than in the case of the Silver Shaded, resulting in a paler cat.
• REMARK Silver Tabbies may have led to the development of this breed in the 1800s.

tipping evenly distributed

FUR TYPE: long, thick, silky, and fine

kittens may be striped

pure white chest and chin

legs can be slightly tipped

| Shorthair option | Chinchilla Exotic | Temperament | Docile |

| Country of origin Great Britain | Ancestry Angoras x Persians | Origins 1880s |

CREAM SMOKE

The contrast in this case may not be quite as pronounced as in the darker colours, but it is nevertheless very attractive.

• **FEATURES** The basic body coloration is cream, shading to white on the sides and flanks. The undercoat becomes most evident as the cat walks.

• **REMARK** This variety needs very frequent grooming in order to show the Smoke effect to best advantage. As with all Smokes, kittens need to be at least six months old before they can be shown.

• cream mask with no markings

• cream feet

• white frill extending from shoulders, and creating ruff on chest

FUR TYPE: long, thick, silky, and fine

• short, bushy tail

| Shorthair option Cream Smoke Exotic | Temperament Docile |

| Country of origin Great Britain | Ancestry Angoras x Persians | Origins 1880s |

BLUE SMOKE

All Longhairs need extensive grooming; excessive grease in the coat can be overcome by rubbing cornflour into the coat then brushing it out.

• **FEATURES** The blue coloration shades to silver on the sides of the body; the undercoat should be as white as possible to create an impressive contrast. The head and feet are also a deep shade of blue.

• **REMARK** The number of Blue Smokes has fluctuated as their popularity has risen and declined over the years.

• blue coloration clearly evident along back

• silver frill around neck

FUR TYPE: long, thick, silky, and fine

| Shorthair option Blue Smoke Exotic | Temperament Docile |

Country of origin Great Britain	Ancestry Angoras x Persians	Origins 1880s

BLACK SMOKE

There is some variation in the depth of black coloration in these cats. British breeders prefer the darker individuals. The contrast between the white undercoat and the black tipping on each hair is pronounced in the Black Smoke, frequent grooming being needed to emphasize the effect.

• **FEATURES** These cats resemble other Longhairs in type having a broad, round head, and cobby body. Their eye coloration should be orange or copper.

• **REMARK** Black Smokes date back to the 1860s, and are the traditional colour form.

blackish back •

• silver frill around neck

black body coloration showing white undercoat when parted •

well-furnished tail •

FUR TYPE: long, thick, silky, and fine

Shorthair option Black Smoke Exotic	Temperament Docile

Country of origin Great Britain	Ancestry Angoras x Persians	Origins 1880s

BLUE-CREAM SMOKE

When assessing the potential of young Smoke kittens, choose those whose undercoats are lightest as they are likely to become the best adults in terms of their coloration. Regular grooming is especially important in maintaining the appearance of these cats.

• **FEATURES** In the case of the Blue-cream Smoke, the tipping should be a mixture of blue and cream, mingled together to create an attractive appearance. The contrasting undercoat should be as white as possible.

• **REMARK** Crossings involving Blue-cream Longhairs were used in the past to improve the type of other Smokes.

facial blaze •

• coloration often most intense across head

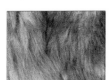

FUR TYPE: long, thick, silky, and fine

tufted paws •

short, powerful legs •

Shorthair option Blue-cream Smoke Exotic	Temperament Docile

Country of origin Great Britain	Ancestry Angoras x Persians	Origins 1880s

TORTIE SMOKE

The tipping here, as for other Smokes, is significantly more extensive than in Shaded Longhairs, making their coloration more clearly defined. A facial blaze of cream or red is a desirable feature of this almost entirely female variety.

• **FEATURES** These cats should resemble Tortoiseshell Longhairs, with their patches of red, cream, and black fur, but when they move the white undercoat becomes visible and creates a distinctive contrast.

• **REMARK** Crossings of Smokes with Tortoiseshell Longhairs created this particular form.

mottled colours

short nose

large, round paws

short, bushy tail

FUR TYPE: long, thick, silky, and fine

Shorthair option Tortie Smoke Exotic	Temperament Docile

Country of origin Great Britain	Ancestry Angoras x Persians	Origins 1880s

PEWTER

While there is a noticeable similarity between the Pewter and Silver Shaded Longhairs, they can be distinguished quite easily on the basis of their eye coloration. In the case of the Pewter Persian, the eyes are orange or copper.

• **FEATURES** The coat is white, with black tipping creating a pewter mantle. The undercoat is also white, with darker shading apparent on the legs. The nose is brick-red, with a black outline.

• **REMARK** Pewter Longhairs derive from Chinchilla stock.

large, round, orange or copper eyes

broad, round head with widely spaced ears

short tail

FUR TYPE: long, thick, silky, and fine

Shorthair option Pewter Exotic	Temperament Docile

| Country of origin | Great Britain | Ancestry | Angoras x Persians | Origins | 1880s |

GOLDEN PERSIAN

The distinctive colouring of these cats results from the shading on the individual hairs.

• **FEATURES** The undercoat varies from apricot to gold, with seal-brown or black tipping on the head, back, flanks, and tail. The legs can be shaded, with a solid coloured area that corresponds to the colour of the tipping, extending from the paw up to the heel. Paw pads may be seal-brown or black.

• **REMARK** Only seal-brown tipping is allowed in North America, which results in a less pronounced effect.

pale apricot ear tufts

blue-green eyes

tabby markings often seen in kittens

pronounced frill present on chest

FUR TYPE: long, thick, silky, and fine

short, thick legs

| Shorthair option | Golden Shaded Exotic | Temperament | Docile |

| Country of origin | Great Britain | Ancestry | Angoras x Persians | Origins | 1880s |

TORTIE CAMEO

Good contrast is an essential feature of the Tortie Cameo, both in terms of the undercoat and the contrasting tipping on the guard hairs, and in the distinct patches of the tortoiseshell coloration itself.

• **FEATURES** The cream, red, and black tortoiseshell coloration should be well broken into patches, especially on the face. There should be no solid coloration evident on either the legs or the feet, but the tipping can be of any shade.

• **REMARK** Daily grooming is essential, not only to show the markings to best effect, but also to prevent the coat from becoming matted.

FUR TYPE: long, thick, silky, and fine

colours well broken into patches over face

bright copper eyes

short, broad, snub nose

short, bushy tail

pure white undercoat

| Shorthair option | Tortie Cameo Exotic | Temperament | Docile |

Country of origin Great Britain	Ancestry Angoras x Persians	Origins 1880s

CREAM SHADED CAMEO

The stunning appearance of these cats results from the contrast between the white undercoat and the cream shading.

• **FEATURES** The most pronounced cream areas occur on the mask and along the back to the tip of the tail. The legs and feet are well shaded; the ear tufts, flanks, frill, and underparts are pale.

• **REMARK** Cameos were developed in the United States, during the 1950s.

copper eyes, surrounded by deep cream mask •

• flowing tail   FUR TYPE: long, thick, silky, and fine

prominent neck ruff •

• even cream shading creates impression of cream mantle

Shorthair option Cream Shaded Exotic		Temperament Docile

Country of origin Great Britain	Ancestry Angoras x Persians	Origins 1880s

CREAM SHELL CAMEO

Shell Cameos are lighter in the depth of their coloration than Shaded Cameos or darker Smokes; this difference is the result of shorter tipping on the individuals hairs.

• **FEATURES** The sparkling appearance of these cats results from the combination of predominantly white fur and slight cream tipping, giving a somewhat misty effect. The pads and the nose leather should be pink.

• **REMARK** Cameos were established in Australia, New Zealand, and North America in the 1960s. The first European Cameo was bred in Holland in 1962, two years after recognition in North America.

copper eyes •

FUR TYPE: long, thick, silky, and fine

• short, bushy tail with no kink

Shorthair option Cream Shell Cameo Exotic		Temperament Docile

Country of origin Great Britain	Ancestry Angoras x Persians	Origins 1880s

RED SHADED CAMEO

Although odd Cameos had been known for many years, it was not until the 1950s that a determined attempt was made, by a breeder called Dr Rachel Salisbury, to develop them. The American Cat Fanciers' Association accepted these cats in 1960, and they have since become widely known. The description "cameo" is used for red equivalents of tipped colours such as the chinchilla, shaded, and smoke. The difference between these three forms is in the extent of the tipping, which in turn influences the coloration. The tipping on the Red Shaded is of an intermediate shade.

deepest coloration apparent along cat's back

• **FEATURES** The white undercoat has red tips, creating contrast over the coat. The red coloration is most pronounced on the upper body, extending from the mask along the back to the tip of the tail. The underparts are pale, apart from the shaded legs and feet.
• **REMARK** There should be no tabby markings on the coat.

bushy tail

small ears

massive rump

tufted paws

broad, compact nose with clear stop

relatively large body carried on short legs

short tail

large, round paws

coppery eyes

pink nose

muscular body

frill of longer hair begins over shoulders, extending between front legs

upper surface of tail redder than underside

paler coloration on flanks

FUR TYPE: long, thick, silky, and fine

Shorthair option Red Shaded Cameo Exotic	Temperament Docile

COLOUR POINTED LONGHAIR

T HESE CATS ARE known in North America as Himalayans. The dark coloration on the points is seen in other Himalayan animals, such as rabbits, and results from the Himalayan gene. Long-haired cats with distinctive patterning such as this were originally developed in the 1920s by a Swedish geneticist, Dr Tjebbes, for scientific study. Only when a later investigation into feline genetics attracted publicity was the potential for a new breed appreciated.

Country of origin USA	Ancestry Longhairs x Siamese	Origins 1920s

CREAM POINT

The quest to establish this breed began in 1935, using the results obtained from the original American breeding programme. The crossing of a Black Longhair with a Siamese had produced three black, short-haired kittens. Two of these were then mated and a long-haired kitten resulted. When this cat, called *Debutante*, was paired with her father, a pointed Longhair kitten was born. This showed that the normal self coloration and short-haired characteristics were dominant, but that the kittens carried both the pointed and the long-haired genes.
• FEATURES The body coloration is creamy white, with the points a darker shade of cream. In type, these cats resemble typical Longhairs, with large, round heads and cobby bodies.
• REMARK The mask tends to be more extensive in males of the breed.

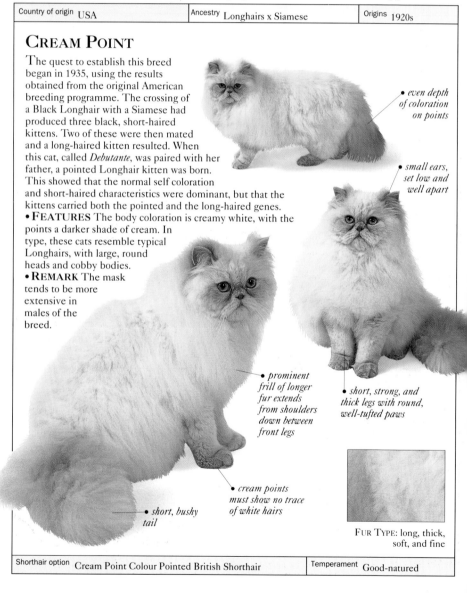

• even depth of coloration on points

• small ears, set low and well apart

• prominent frill of longer fur extends from shoulders down between front legs

• short, strong, and thick legs with round, well-tufted paws

• cream points must show no trace of white hairs

• short, bushy tail

FUR TYPE: long, thick, soft, and fine

Shorthair option Cream Point Colour Pointed British Shorthair	Temperament Good-natured

Country of origin USA	Ancestry Longhairs x Siamese	Origins 1920s

LILAC POINT

The early Colour Pointed Longhairs were much closer in type to Siamese than those seen today. The solid point colours were the first to be developed and, once the desired colour had been introduced, improving the type became a priority.

• **FEATURES** The warm-toned, lilac colour of the points contrasts with the magnolia-white body coloration. The eyes must be a pure shade of blue.

• **REMARK** Few cats have more placid natures. Colourpoint Longhairs resemble Persian Longhairs in temperament and need a similar amount of grooming.

traces of body shading on shoulders as well as flanks

• *short, bushy tail, in proportion to length of body*

• *body carried low on legs*

well-tufted paws •

FUR TYPE: long, thick, soft, and fine

Shorthair option Lilac Point Colour Pointed British Shorthair	Temperament Good-natured

Country of origin USA	Ancestry Longhairs x Siamese	Origins 1920s

CHOCOLATE POINT

One of the major problems faced by the early breeders of Colour Pointed Longhairs was how to establish the desired blue eye coloration. Initially it was thought that crossings involving Longhairs with pale eyes would be necessary but, in fact, those with deep copper-coloured eyes proved most valuable.

• **FEATURES** The points in this case should be of a warm chocolate shade, and the body should be ivory-white. The depth of coloration on the points should be even.

• **REMARK** Kittens are fairly slow to develop their pointed markings to their full extent.

• *clear contrast between points and body coloration*

FUR TYPE: long, thick, soft, and fine

• *cobby body*

thick, powerful legs •

• *large, round paws*

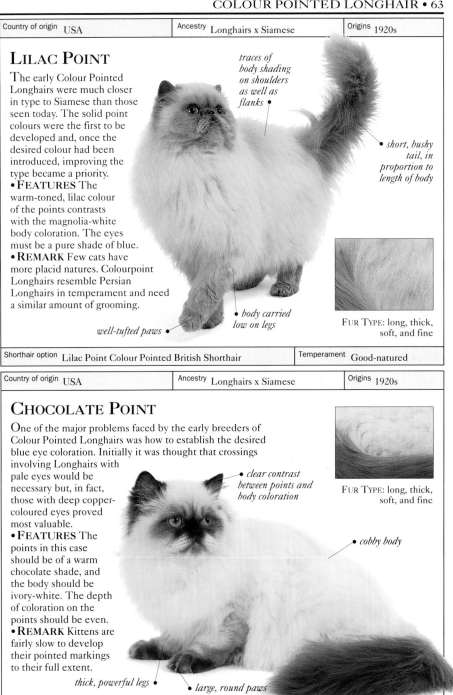

Shorthair option Chocolate Point Colour Pointed British Shorthair	Temperament Good-natured

| Country of origin | USA | Ancestry | Longhairs x Siamese | Origins | 1920s |

BLUE POINT

All Colour Pointed Longhair kittens are born with a short, fluffy, pure white coat. The points start to appear when the kittens are several days old, and it can take 18 months for these to develop to their full potential.
• **FEATURES** The blue coloration of the points contrasts with the glacial white fur covering the body. The rims of the eyes, nose, and pads should also be blue in colour.
• **REMARK** Colourpoints mature earlier than other Longhairs, reflecting their Siamese ancestry.

massive, round head •

• clear delineation between coloration of points and body

• bushy tail

• cobby body

• paws should be well tufted, and round in shape

FUR TYPE: long, thick, soft, and fine

| Shorthair option | Blue Point Colour Pointed British Shorthair | Temperament | Good-natured |

| Country of origin | USA | Ancestry | Longhairs x Siamese | Origins | 1920s |

SEAL POINT

While dark coloration on the points is desirable, this can never be as deep as in the Seal Point Siamese, because the longer hair provides insulation from the temperature extremes that affect colouring.
• **FEATURES** The creamy white body contrasts with the dark seal-brown coloration of the points. The colour of the eyes, as in all Colour Pointed Longhairs, should be a clear, deep blue hue.
• **REMARK** Slightly darker shading may develop on adult cats. This must match the points and should be confined to the shoulders and flanks.

FUR TYPE: long, thick, soft, and fine

• coat length may be up to 13 cm (5 in)

good contrast between points and body coloration essential •

• deep seal-brown points

| Shorthair option | Seal Point Colour Pointed British Shorthair | Temperament | Good-natured |

Country of origin USA	Ancestry Longhairs x Siamese	Origins 1920s

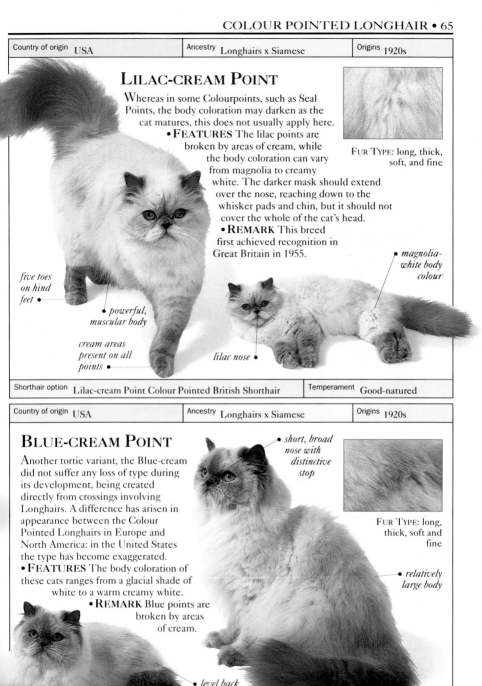

LILAC-CREAM POINT

Whereas in some Colourpoints, such as Seal Points, the body coloration may darken as the cat matures, this does not usually apply here.
• **FEATURES** The lilac points are broken by areas of cream, while the body coloration can vary from magnolia to creamy white. The darker mask should extend over the nose, reaching down to the whisker pads and chin, but it should not cover the whole of the cat's head.
• **REMARK** This breed first achieved recognition in Great Britain in 1955.

FUR TYPE: long, thick, soft, and fine

magnolia-white body colour

five toes on hind feet •

• powerful, muscular body

cream areas present on all points •

lilac nose •

Shorthair option Lilac-cream Point Colour Pointed British Shorthair	Temperament Good-natured

Country of origin USA	Ancestry Longhairs x Siamese	Origins 1920s

BLUE-CREAM POINT

Another tortie variant, the Blue-cream did not suffer any loss of type during its development, being created directly from crossings involving Longhairs. A difference has arisen in appearance between the Colour Pointed Longhairs in Europe and North America: in the United States the type has become exaggerated.
• **FEATURES** The body coloration of these cats ranges from a glacial shade of white to a warm creamy white.
• **REMARK** Blue points are broken by areas of cream.

• short, broad nose with distinctive stop

FUR TYPE: long, thick, soft and fine

• relatively large body

• level back and massive rump

Shorthair option Blue-cream Point Colour Pointed British Shorthair	Temperament Good-natured

Country of origin	USA	Ancestry	Longhairs x Siamese	Origins	1920s

RED TABBY POINT

Here both red coloration and tabby markings are combined with Himalayan patterning. This relatively recent development reflects the scope that exists for future breeding programmes.
• **FEATURES** Tabby characteristics are apparent on the head, with an "M"-shaped scarab marking on the forehead and "spectacle" traces around the eyes.
• **REMARK** Whisker pads should be spotted.

small ears with round tips •

FUR TYPE: long, thick, soft, and fine

lighter coloured hair within ears, creating pale rim •

broken tabby rings on legs •

• apricot-white body colour, with rich red markings on light apricot agouti points

• tabby markings on tail

Shorthair option	Red Tabby Point Colour Pointed British Shorthair	Temperament	Good-natured

Country of origin	USA	Ancestry	Longhairs x Siamese	Origins	1920s

LILAC TABBY POINT

The various lilac forms of the Colour Pointed Longhair evolved originally from chocolate stock, and they have since become very popular. They must show the typically round, massive head, with no suggestion of a Pekinese face. The eyes are rounded in shape and relatively large.
• **FEATURES** The magnolia-white body coloration is offset by the lilac tabby markings.
• **REMARK** Tabby Points are often described in the United States as "Lynx Points".

• widely spaced ears emphasize rounded face shape

• clear, brilliant blue eyes

• short, thick neck leads to broad, deep chest

solid point colour on back of hind legs •

• tabby markings on hind legs

FUR TYPE: long, thick, soft, and fine

Shorthair option	Lilac Tabby Point Colour Pointed British Shorthair	Temperament	Good-natured

Country of origin USA	Ancestry Longhairs x Siamese	Origins 1920s

BLUE-CREAM TABBY POINT

The introduction of new features meant that the type of these cats initially showed a deterioration. Breeders then relied upon matings with Longhairs to bring the type back to that of the Colourpoint.

• **FEATURES** The body coloration can vary from a glacial to a creamy shade of white, with the points a combination of blue and cream; this is variable in depth of coloration, depending on the individual cat.

• **REMARK** The "M"-shaped scarab marking, characteristic of all tabbies, should be well defined.

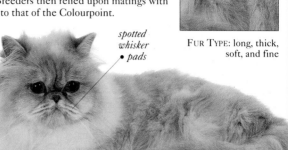

spotted whisker pads

FUR TYPE: long, thick, soft, and fine

broken rings, confirming tabby patterning, extend up front legs from the toes

Shorthair option Blue-cream Tabby Pt Colour Pointed British Shorthair	Temperament Good-natured

Country of origin USA	Ancestry Longhairs x Siamese	Origins 1920s

CHOCOLATE TABBY POINT

It is the darker forms of Tabby Point, such as the Chocolate, that show the clearest patterning. Kittens are much paler than adult cats.

• **FEATURES** The chocolate markings are displayed against a light bronze agouti background, offset by the ivory-white body coloration. It is acceptable for the fur above the nose to be bronze, with the nose itself corresponding in colour to the points. The head markings include "spectacles".

• **REMARK** The "thumb-marks" on the ears are usually quite distinct in the darker forms.

FUR TYPE: long, thick, soft, and fine

lighter hair in ears

massive rump

adult cat showing darker points

five-and-a-half-month-old kitten with pale points

Shorthair option Chocolate Tabby Point Colour Pointed British Shorthair	Temperament Good-natured

BIRMAN

L EGEND HAS IT that a white temple cat called *Sinh* came up to the head priest, Mun-Ha, as he lay dying. Whereas the cat's paws remained white where they had touched the priest, his yellow eyes were changed to blue. His head, tail, and legs took on an earthy brown hue, and the fur along his back became golden. The appearance of the other temple cats was then transformed to golden brown so that they resembled *Sinh*, the ancestor of the Birman breed.

Country of origin Burma (Myanmar)	Ancestry Non-pedigree cats	Origins Unknown

CREAM POINT

Although the traditional form of the Birman is the Seal Point, this is one of the newer, more recently developed forms. Contrast is not as marked in this case as in varieties with darker points but the characteristic white areas on the paws, extending partly up the hind legs, must be apparent.
• **FEATURES** The body coloration of the Cream Point is off-white with traces of a golden hue. The points are cream. In mature Birman cats, the colour of the mask extends over the whole of the face, including the pads of the whiskers.
• **REMARK** There is no link between the Birman and the short-haired Burmese breed.

pink nose •

• *slightly curled fur on stomach*

FUR TYPE: long and silky in texture

• *deep blue eyes, almost round in shape*

widely spaced ears with rounded tips •

• *broad, rounded head*

strong hind-quarters •

• *medium nose with slight indentation*

• *round paws*

• *bushy, medium-length tail*

Shorthair option None	Temperament Intelligent; gentle

Country of origin Burma (Myanmar)	Ancestry Non-pedigree cats	Origins Unknown

RED POINT

Another recent addition to the Birman group, the Red Point shows an identical pattern of markings. On the front paws, the white gloves extend across the paw in a straight line and must be symmetrical; on the hind legs the white "gauntlets" cover both paws completely.

• **FEATURES** Cream body hue, often with a hint of gold, is offset against a warm shade of orange-red on the nose, ears, and legs.

• **REMARK** Slight freckling, especially on the nose and ears, is not judged too serious a flaw.

FUR TYPE: long and silky in texture

• *medium ears*

• *medium-length, thick-set legs*

• *all points must be of even shade*

good contrast between points and body coloration •

Shorthair option None	Temperament Intelligent; gentle

Country of origin Burma (Myanmar)	Ancestry Non-pedigree cats	Origins Unknown

LILAC POINT

Although the Birman's coat is less susceptible to matting than that of Longhairs daily grooming is essential, particularly during the moulting period. Regular grooming will prevent loose hair collecting in the cat's stomach and forming a fur-ball, which can cause an obstruction.

• **FEATURES** The off-white magnolia body coloration contrasts with the soft, pink-grey colour of the points.

• **REMARK** The Birman often proves to be a playful breed.

FUR TYPE: long and silky in texture

• *distinctive ruff of longer hair around neck*

pure white gloves •

• *pinkish grey mask connected to ears by matching trace lines in mature cats*

Shorthair option None	Temperament Intelligent; gentle

Country of origin Burma (Myanmar)	Ancestry Non-pedigree cats	Origins Unknown

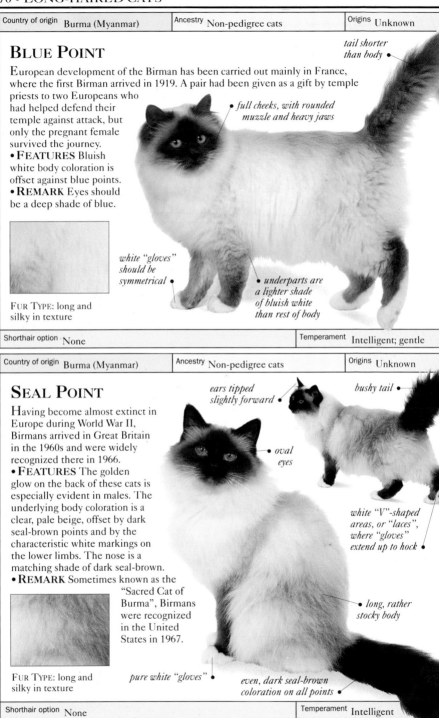

BLUE POINT

tail shorter than body •

European development of the Birman has been carried out mainly in France, where the first Birman arrived in 1919. A pair had been given as a gift by temple priests to two Europeans who had helped defend their temple against attack, but only the pregnant female survived the journey.

• full cheeks, with rounded muzzle and heavy jaws

• **FEATURES** Bluish white body coloration is offset against blue points.
• **REMARK** Eyes should be a deep shade of blue.

white "gloves" should be symmetrical •

• underparts are a lighter shade of bluish white than rest of body

FUR TYPE: long and silky in texture

Shorthair option None	Temperament Intelligent; gentle

Country of origin Burma (Myanmar)	Ancestry Non-pedigree cats	Origins Unknown

SEAL POINT

ears tipped slightly forward •

bushy tail •

Having become almost extinct in Europe during World War II, Birmans arrived in Great Britain in the 1960s and were widely recognized there in 1966.

• oval eyes

• **FEATURES** The golden glow on the back of these cats is especially evident in males. The underlying body coloration is a clear, pale beige, offset by dark seal-brown points and by the characteristic white markings on the lower limbs. The nose is a matching shade of dark seal-brown.

white "V"-shaped areas, or "laces", where "gloves" extend up to hock •

• **REMARK** Sometimes known as the "Sacred Cat of Burma", Birmans were recognized in the United States in 1967.

• long, rather stocky body

FUR TYPE: long and silky in texture

pure white "gloves" •

even, dark seal-brown coloration on all points •

Shorthair option None	Temperament Intelligent

Country of origin Burma (Myanmar)	Ancestry Non-pedigree cats	Origins Unknown

CHOCOLATE POINT

As one of the darker-coloured Birmans, the Chocolate may show some body shading, especially when adult, but this must match with the coloration of the points, and clear contrast must still be quite apparent.

• **FEATURES** The points in this case are of milk-chocolate coloration, offset against an ivory body coloration. In terms of type, these cats do not differ from other Birmans, having a relatively flat forehead and a dip in profile along the nose. The eyes should be as deep a shade of blue as possible; the nose leather should be chocolate-coloured.

• **REMARK** Although the coat of these cats is quite long, it does not mat and grooming is therefore straightforward.

• well-spaced ears

• full frill around neck; some curling of fur on stomach

bushy tail •

FUR TYPE: long and silky in texture

white "gauntlets" cover hind paws •

long fur on back •

• mask covers entire face, including whisker pads; dark tracings connect this area to matching ears

broad, rounded skull •

• round feet

• medium-length tail, in proportion to body size

• symmetrical white "gloves" on front paws

Shorthair option None	Temperament Intelligent; gentle

Country of origin Burma (Myanmar)	Ancestry Non-pedigree cats	Origins Unknown

SEAL TORTIE POINT

It is always difficult to produce quality Birmans that excel in type, coloration, and in gloved patterning, but once tortie patterning is introduced the task becomes even harder.

red and seal-brown fur evident on tail •

• *facial blaze in mottled colours*

• **FEATURES** The body coloration is a light fawn, shading to warm brown or red colour on the back and sides.
• **REMARK** This is a female-only breed.

intermingling of colours essential at each point •

FUR TYPE: long and silky in texture

• *white paws and hocks*

Shorthair option None	Temperament Intelligent; gentle

Country of origin Burma (Myanmar)	Ancestry Non-pedigree cats	Origins Unknown

SEAL TORTIE TABBY POINT

An additional element, in the form of tabby markings, is apparent in this cat. The typical tabby patterning should therefore be visible on the coat alongside the tortie coloration. The distribution of the markings is not significant.

• *tabby markings on head*

FUR TYPE: long and silky in texture

• **FEATURES** The fawn body coloration is transformed unevenly into a more evident shade of brown, often merged with red, on the back and flanks. The points are seal-brown.
• **REMARK** The nose colour in this case is a combination of mottled pink and darker markings.

• *actual coloration of Birmans can be variable in depth*

• *ruff of fur around neck*

bushy, well-coloured tail •

Shorthair option None	Temperament Intelligent

Country of origin	Ancestry	Origins
Burma (Myanmar)	Non-pedigree cats	Unknown

BLUE TABBY POINT

Tabby markings are apparent on these cats although the "gloves" are unaffected. Good contrast, always an important feature in Birmans, tends to become more marked in the darker tabby forms, as seen here.
• **FEATURES** The blue points are offset against a light beige, agouti ground colour with the body itself bluish white. A tail showing lighter and darker rings is preferred but such markings may occur only on the underside.
• **REMARK** It has not yet proved easy to develop good tail markings in Tabby Point Birmans.

colour on coat is more evident as cat grows older

"spectacle" marking at corner of eye

FUR TYPE: long and silky in texture

coloured legs

darker tabby barring on legs

Shorthair option	Temperament
None	Intelligent; gentle

Country of origin	Ancestry	Origins
Burma (Myanmar)	Non-pedigree cats	Unknown

SEAL TABBY POINT

Because Birmans shed much of their longer coat during the summer months, their appearance is likely to vary through the year.
• **FEATURES** Tabby Point Birmans must show solid markings above the "gauntlets" on the hind legs. The pale beige body with its golden hue is contrasted here against seal-brown markings over the points.
• **REMARK** All Birmans are born with a short, whitish coat.

"M"-shaped tabby markings clearly defined on forehead

seal-brown area above "gauntlet"

clear delineation of white "gloves"

brown tail slightly barred

FUR TYPE: long and silky in texture

Shorthair option	Temperament
None	Intelligent; gentle

TURKISH ANGORA

A S THE ANGORA became scarce, both in its native Turkey and elsewhere, the Turkish government set up a breeding programme at Ankara Zoo during the 1960s with the aim of reviving the breed's fortunes. Surplus cats from the programme were obtained by other breeders, particularly in the United States. The first overseas litter was born in 1963, but such cats did not reach Britain until the late 1970s. Turkish Angoras are one of the oldest surviving breeds and bloodlines must be kept pure for breeding purposes.

Country of origin Turkey	Ancestry Non-pedigree Longhairs	Origins 1400s

WHITE

White is the traditional colour of this breed, which was originally known as the Angora. This name, however, was subsequently chosen for the recent re-creation of the breed, using Oriental cats, which led to some confusion. The native form is now known as the Turkish Angora.

• **FEATURES** The Turkish Angora has a rounder and shorter head than the Angora, being less Oriental in its overall type. Its ears are less prominent too. Eye coloration in the white is variable, and deafness is likely to occur in blue-eyed forms.

• **REMARK** Traditionally, it is the odd-eyed variety, known as *Ankara kedi*, that is accepted as the original form, but the breed also occurs in other colours and patterned forms.

FUR TYPE: fine, silky; no undercoat

• *almond-shaped eyes; one eye blue and one orange in this case*

• *graceful body*

wide base to ears •

long, slender legs •

longer ruff of hair around neck •

• *full plume of long hair on tail*

• *traces of colour in white kittens permitted up to age of two*

Shorthair option None	Temperament Playful and friendly

Country of origin Turkey	Ancestry Non-pedigree Longhairs	Origins 1400s

BLACK

This ancient breed has yet to achieve worldwide recognition, despite the fact that many of the breeds to which it has probably contributed, such as the Longhairs, are well established in the cat fancy.
• **FEATURES** The coloration of these cats should be a pure shade of dense black, with no hint of rusty brown in the coats. Scattered white hairs are considered to be a serious flaw.
• **REMARK** Crosses with other breeds are not permitted, and Turkish Angora bloodlines must be kept pure.

well-plumed tail •

• *widely spaced, pointed ears*

• *rounded eyes*

• *medium-length nose*

• *slim, elegant neck*

• *coat becomes shorter during summer months*

FUR TYPE: fine, silky; no undercoat

Shorthair option None	Temperament Playful and friendly

Country of origin Turkey	Ancestry Non-pedigree Longhairs	Origins 1400s

BLUE-CREAM

For many years, the white form was the only recognized colour of Turkish Angora, but tabby, tortoiseshell, and Smoke forms are now being bred alongside the solid colours. The Blue-cream is essentially a female-only variety, as in other breeds.
• **FEATURES** The blue color-ation may vary in shade from light to medium, as can the depth of the cream in the coat.
• **REMARK** The coats of these cats are softer and lighter than those of Longhairs. The distinctive tail is often carried lower than the body, although when they are moving fast it is more likely to be curled forward, almost reaching to the head.

• *tufted ears*

• *relatively small head, compared with body size*

• *amber eyes*

• *longish legs contribute to fine-boned appearance*

FUR TYPE: fine, silky; no undercoat

long, tapering tail •

Shorthair option None	Temperament Playful and friendly

Country of origin Turkey	Ancestry Non-pedigree Longhairs	Origins 1400s

CREAM CLASSIC TABBY

The graceful shape of these cats is emphasized by their long, lithe body shape. Mature males are typically larger than females and may have jowls, but they should still appear lean and muscular in build.

- **FEATURES** The lighter shades of cream, and amber eyes, are preferred. The head is fairly small and wedge shaped. The fur on the underparts is slightly wavy.
- **REMARK** The overall appearance of these cats is fine boned, in contrast to the larger, cobby type of the Persian Longhair to which they have contributed.

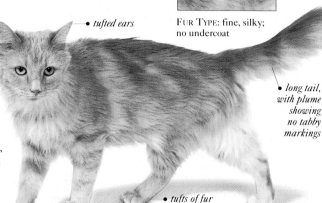

• *tufted ears*

FUR TYPE: fine, silky; no undercoat

• *long tail, with plume showing no tabby markings*

• *tufts of fur between toes*

Shorthair option None	Temperament Playful and friendly

Country of origin Turkey	Ancestry Non-pedigree Longhairs	Origins 1400s

CREAM CLASSIC TABBY AND WHITE

darker blotch signifies classic tabby patterning •

Like other Angoras, these cats tend to shed much of their longer fur in summer, so that they resemble shorthairs, although still retaining the distinctive plume of hair on the tail.

- **FEATURES** Both the cream and white areas in the coat should be prominent and clearly defined; the dark cream markings contrast with paler cream body coloration.
- **REMARK** The highly distinctive silky fur of the Angora shows little tendency to become matted, and the sleek appearance is emphasized by the complete absence of an undercoat. Regular daily grooming is still needed, however.

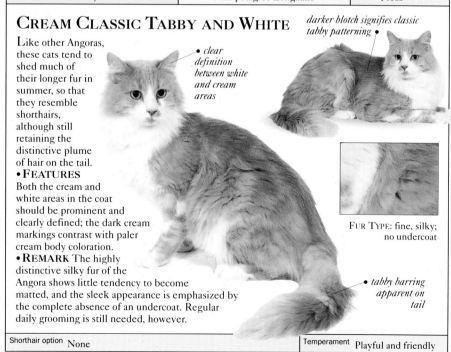

• *clear definition between white and cream areas*

FUR TYPE: fine, silky; no undercoat

• *tabby barring apparent on tail*

Shorthair option None	Temperament Playful and friendly

| Country of origin | Turkey | Ancestry | Non-pedigree Longhairs | Origins | 1400s |

BLUE MACKEREL TABBY

Blue Turkish Angoras have the same delightful temperament as other Turkish Angoras, being lively, playful, and affectionate, but they are not suited to apartment-living as their naturally curious natures encourage them to explore outdoors.
• **FEATURES** A light bluish shade which contrasts well with the darker blue tabby markings is preferred. The main characteristic is the narrow lines running down the sides of the body from the spine.
• **REMARK** Amber eye colour predominates in the case of the Turkish Angora.

typical tabby "M"-shaped marking

FUR TYPE: fine, silky; no undercoat

flat skull

unbroken darker "necklaces" on neck and upper chest

evenly spaced rings on tail

| None | | Temperament | Playful and friendly |

| Country of origin | Turkey | Ancestry | Non-pedigree Longhairs | Origins | 1400s |

BLACK TORTIE SMOKE

Another variety of the Turkish Angora, first documented in Britain in the late 1800s, the Smoke has been combined with Tortoiseshell in this case.
• **FEATURES** Only the typical tortoiseshell patterning of cream, red, and black is visible until the cat begins to move. The Smoke appearance is derived entirely from the silver-grey coloration at the base of the individual hairs.
• **REMARK** Several Victorian naturalists, including Charles Darwin, suggested that the Turkish Angora had evolved from Pallas's cat, not the African wild cat, but this is now thought unlikely.

medium in overall size

amber eyes

tail curls forward to shoulders, tapering along its length

FUR TYPE: fine, silky; no undercoat

angular chest

clearly defined areas of colour, with paws correspondingly marked

| Shorthair option | None | Temperament | Playful and friendly |

TURKISH VAN

THESE CATS all have a distinctively coloured chalky white coat, which should display no hint of yellow. Their restricted markings should ideally be confined to the head and tail, although some cats may have localized "thumb-prints" of colour on their bodies. Auburn and cream, the two most widely recognized colours, each exist in three different forms, distinguished on the basis of their eye coloration. The eyes can be either amber or blue, or an odd-eyed combination of both of these colours, with pink rims in all cases. Deafness is associated with blue-eyed Turkish Vans, and odd-eyed cats may well be afflicted with deafness on the side corresponding to the blue eye.

Country of origin Turkey	Ancestry Non-pedigree local cats	Origins 1600s

CREAM

Although their coats are relatively long, the grooming of Turkish Van cats is straightforward because they lack a thick woolly undercoat. A daily combing is still to be recommended, particularly in early summer when these cats are moulting.
• **FEATURES** Cream markings contrast with the chalky white colour of the coat. A vertical white blaze, extending over the nose, separates the coloured areas of fur on the head. These are localized to the area above the eyes, not extending beyond the base of the rear of the ears. The ears themselves are white, with shell-pink interiors. The tail should be a solid shade of cream, which can extend slightly onto the back.
• **REMARK** Darker rings may be present on the tail; these are most likely to be apparent in kittens.

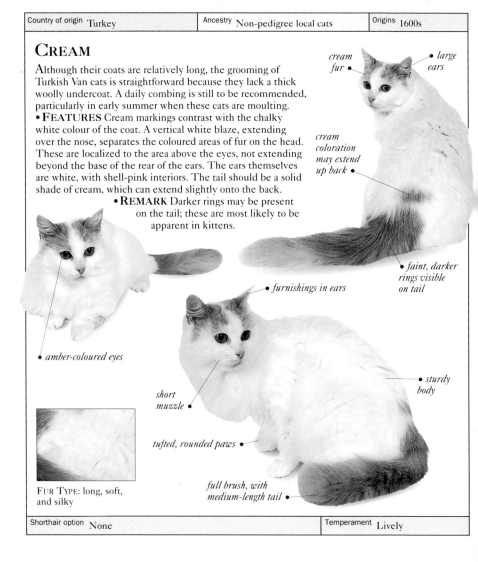

cream fur •

• large ears

cream coloration may extend up back •

• faint, darker rings visible on tail

• furnishings in ears

• amber-coloured eyes

short muzzle •

tufted, rounded paws •

• sturdy body

full brush, with medium-length tail •

FUR TYPE: long, soft, and silky

Shorthair option None	Temperament Lively

Country of origin Turkey	Ancestry Non-pedigree local cats	Origins 1600s

AUBURN

These cats originate from the vicinity of Lake Van, in south-east Turkey. Their coat length varies throughout the year, being noticeably shorter in summer; in the winter it is much thicker, providing protection against the freezing winters of their homeland. The development of this breed in Britain began in 1955, when a pair of kittens was brought back by two photographers who had become entranced by the cats.

• **FEATURES** The pattern of markings is significant in this case, with the auburn areas on the head confined to the area above the eyes and not extending behind the ears. The nose is white, and a clear white vertical blaze separates the auburn areas on the head. The tail is auburn.

• **REMARK** These cats are unusual in several respects, including their apparent affinity with water – they swim quite readily. Turkish Vans are also agile climbers, and have a surprisingly melodious voice.

chalky white coloration with no hint of yellow

large ears, set high

long, sturdy body

amber-coloured eyes with pink rims

short, wedge-shaped head

medium-length legs

fur long and silky to roots

medium-length tail with full brush

FUR TYPE: long, soft, and silky

Shorthair option None		Temperament Lively

ANGORA

THESE CATS ORIGINATED in Turkey, being named after the capital city Angora (or Ankara), and have been known in Europe since the 1600s. They were well known in Victorian times, contributing to the development of the Longhair, but they then declined and later vanished. The breed known by this name in Britain today is an artificial re-creation, from a breeding programme based on Oriental Shorthairs which carried the long-haired gene.

Country of origin Great Britain	Ancestry Oriental Shorthair crosses	Origins 1960s

BLUE-EYED WHITE

The prolific nature of the Oriental bloodlines helped to ensure that these cats increased quite rapidly in numbers. Although they have evolved to resemble the original Turkish Angora, they have retained the more vocal natures of their Oriental ancestors. Breeders have placed particular emphasis on coat quality, and have developed these cats in a much wider range of colours than formerly. In appearance, however, they can still be distinguished from the traditional Turkish form by their longer, more angular heads and larger ears.

• FEATURES White has traditionally been the most significant fur colour in cats originating from Turkey. Although there is a clear link between blue-eyed white cats and deafness, such individuals have remained popular. In the case of Odd-eyed Whites, deafness may affect the ear on the side of the blue eye.

• REMARK Turkish legends suggest that the famous ruler Atatürk would be reincarnated as a deaf, white cat.

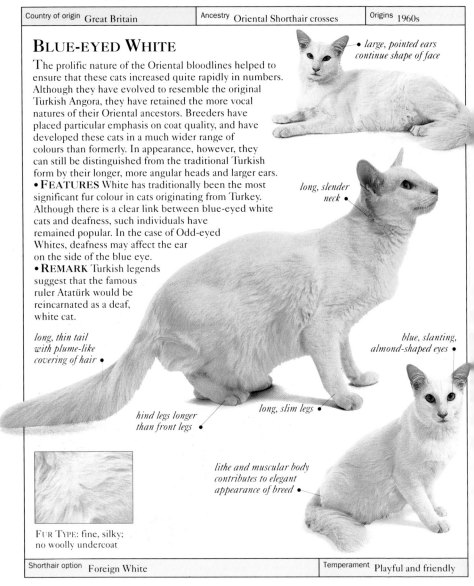

large, pointed ears continue shape of face

long, slender neck •

blue, slanting, almond-shaped eyes •

long, thin tail with plume-like covering of hair •

hind legs longer than front legs •

long, slim legs •

lithe and muscular body contributes to elegant appearance of breed •

FUR TYPE: fine, silky; no woolly undercoat

Shorthair option Foreign White	Temperament Playful and friendly

Country of origin Great Britain	Ancestry Oriental Shorthair crosses	Origins 1960s

GREEN-EYED WHITE

The unusual combination of bright green eyes with a pure white coat stems from the use of Oriental blood when the Angora breed was re-created. In fact, green eyes are not a typical feature of the traditional Turkish Angora, but they do create an attractive contrast.
• FEATURES The graceful shape of these cats is emphasized by their wedge-shaped heads, slender necks, lithe bodies, and gently tapering tails.
• REMARK These cats are not affected by deafness.

eyes slant in direction of nose, with no squint •

• pure green eyes

• small, dainty paws with tufts of hair developing on toes

• all kittens are born with blue eyes

FUR TYPE: fine, silky; no woolly undercoat

Shorthair option Foreign White	Temperament Playful and friendly

Country of origin Great Britain	Ancestry Oriental Shorthair crosses	Origins 1960s

LILAC

This is one of the newer colours. The coat lies relatively flat against the body and is a little shorter than that of most long-hairs, especially during the summer when Angoras tend to moult heavily. They can then be confused with shorthairs, although the plume of longer hair on the tail is a consistent feature.
• FEATURES The body coloration should be frosty grey, with an overall pinkish hue. The eyes are green.
• REMARK These slender cats have an almost tubular body outline.

tapering tail •

fine muzzle •

• wide bases to ears; typically large and tufted

• tubular body

• dainty, tufted paws

FUR TYPE: fine, silky; no woolly undercoat

Shorthair option Foreign Lilac	Temperament Playful and friendly

Country of origin Great Britain	Ancestry Oriental Shorthair crosses	Origins 1960s

CINNAMON

The long wedge of the head is an important feature of this breed, forming straight lines that extend from the base of the nose up to the tips of the ears, and creating a triangle within this area. The only acceptable variance is in the case of mature males, whose jowl development distorts their facial contours, creating a more rounded appearance.
• **FEATURES** Coloration should be a warm shade of cinnamon-brown throughout the coat, with no white hairs apparent. The pads can vary in colour from pink to cinnamon-brown.
• **REMARK** Litters comprising fewer than three kittens are rare.

• *green eyes*

• *ruff of fur*

FUR TYPE: fine, silky; no woolly undercoat

• *tail tapers to point*

Shorthair option Foreign Cinnamon	Temperament Playful and friendly

Country of origin Great Britain	Ancestry Oriental Shorthair crosses	Origins 1960s

CHOCOLATE

The Angora has large, broad-based ears set on a flat skull. Another characteristic is that there is no stop in the nasal area, the face effectively extending in a straight line from the skull to the nostrils. The tip of the chin is also roughly in line with the end of the nose in this variety.
• **FEATURES** It can take up to two years for this rich shade of chestnut-brown colour to develop; the nose and paws must be similarly coloured. These cats are sometimes known as Chestnut, notably in North America.
• **REMARK** This chocolate colour has not yet been recognized in the Turkish Angora.

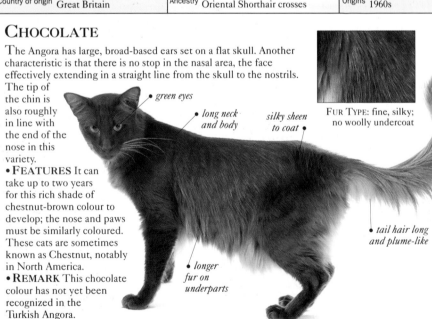

• *green eyes*

• *long neck and body*

silky sheen to coat •

FUR TYPE: fine, silky; no woolly undercoat

• *tail hair long and plume-like*

• *longer fur on underparts*

Shorthair option Havana	Temperament Playful and friendly

JAVANESE

C ONFUSION STILL ARISES over cats known by this name. In North America, the name is often applied to forms of the Balinese that do not correspond to the four traditional Siamese point colours, while in New Zealand it is the self and spotted forms of the Balinese that are so called. In Great Britain, however, the name Javanese is given to the cats that emerged from a breeding programme aimed at re-creating the Angora.

Country of origin Great Britain	Ancestry Abyssinian / Siamese hybrids	Origins 1973

CINNAMON

Cuckoo, one of the kittens from the original breeding programme, was noted to be very similar in appearance to the old Turkish Angora. He was distinguished by a whitish undercoat, which contrasted with his longer chocolate-brown hair. All of these Javanese cats resulted from a breeding programme that attempted to re-create the traditional Angora. The breed was granted championship status in 1984. In October 1989 the breed's name was changed from Angora to Javanese, to accord more with its Oriental appearance.

• **FEATURES** The Javanese shows the typical features of an Oriental cat, being graceful and lithe, with a wedge-shaped head. It has now been developed in a range of colours and patterns.

• **REMARK** The Javanese has more recently been introduced in the United States, where there is already one Supreme Grand Champion.

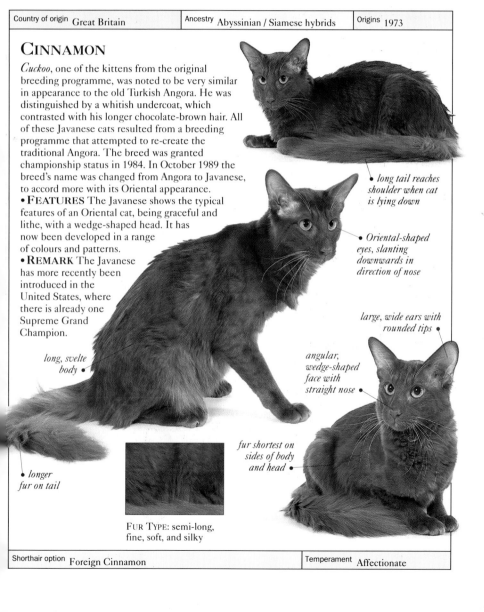

• long tail reaches shoulder when cat is lying down

• Oriental-shaped eyes, slanting downwards in direction of nose

large, wide ears with rounded tips •

long, svelte body •

angular, wedge-shaped face with straight nose •

fur shortest on sides of body and head •

• longer fur on tail

FUR TYPE: semi-long, fine, soft, and silky

Shorthair option Foreign Cinnamon	Temperament Affectionate

MAINE COON

THIS IS THE FIRST long-haired breed to have emerged naturally in North America. As the name suggests, the breed originated on the east coast, in the vicinity of Maine. These are large cats, and the males can weigh up to 8 kg (18 lb); the females are only slightly lighter. They are tough, hardy cats with a dense, rugged coat, which is longer on the back and legs. The undercoat is soft and fine, and the tail fur is long and profuse.

Country of origin USA	Ancestry Non-pedigree Longhairs	Origins 1770s

GOLDEN-EYED WHITE

Maine Coons were probably being taken to sea before rodenticides made their skills at vermin-control redundant, and this may account for their strange habit of sleeping in small nooks around the home in positions that look most uncomfortable.
• **FEATURES** The wedge-shaped head appears small relative to the size of the body. In mature male Maine Coons, the jowls provide extra width. These cats have large, prominent ears, tipped with tufts of hair. They are muscular and broad chested, with powerful legs as befits their working ancestry.
• **REMARK** The Maine Coon's long-haired ancestors may have arrived from Europe and Asia during the 18th century.

golden eye coloration •

fur increases in length down back •

• long, flowing fur on tail

• width of head less than length

long tail, equivalent to length of back •

FUR TYPE: thick, silky, and of variable length

• tufted paws

Shorthair option White American Shorthair	Temperament Independent

Country of origin USA	Ancestry Non-pedigree Longhairs	Origins 1770s

BLACK

Maine Coons are very affectionate, but they do like the freedom to explore out-of-doors, making them most suitable for rural living. The Black is a particularly imposing cat.
• **FEATURES** The coat is pure black, as are the paw pads, nose, and eye rims.
• **REMARK** At the first cat show in New York in 1860 this breed was prevalent, but its numbers had declined by 1900.

FUR TYPE: thick, silky, and of variable length

ruff runs from base of ears around throat

firm chin •

• longer fur towards hindquarters

long tail fur •

Shorthair option Black American Shorthair	Temperament Independent

Country of origin USA	Ancestry Non-pedigree Longhairs	Origins 1770s

BLUE AND WHITE

One remarkable feature of the Maine Coon is the way it grooms its long tail by wrapping it around a front leg and then spiralling around. During hot weather, these cats frequently shed their longer hair and the ruff becomes less distinctive.
• **FEATURES** While having typical Maine Coon proportions, the bi-colour forms should display white fur covering one third of the body, as well as on the face and underparts. Clear delineation of white and coloured areas is also desirable.
• **REMARK** One of the earliest Maine Coons to be exhibited, in 1861, was a Black and White male.

• large, pointed ears

• large, wide-set eyes

• longish neck and back emphasize body length

white paws •

long tail, with wide base tapering towards tip •

FUR TYPE: thick, silky, and of variable length

Shorthair option Blue and White American Shorthair	Temperament Independent

Country of origin USA	Ancestry Non-pedigree Longhairs	Origins 1770s

SILVER TABBY

• "M"-shaped marking

These intelligent cats sometimes use their front paws to pick up food and twigs. They are not averse to water: their dense coat provides protection against the elements, and in the home they often delight in playing with water dripping from a tap.

• **FEATURES** The basic ground colour in this case should be silver, with black tabby markings that are dense and well defined.

• **REMARK** Both classic and mackerel tabby patterning have been long associated with Maine Coons, but this particular colour is relatively scarce.

• *tabby patterning*

• *large, round paws*

FUR TYPE: thick, silky, and of variable length

Shorthair option Silver Tabby American Shorthair	Temperament Independent

Country of origin USA	Ancestry Non-pedigree Longhairs	Origins 1770s

CREAM SILVER TABBY

Maine Coons can be bred in a vast array of colour forms, this being one of the more unusual combinations currently available. These cats do not differ significantly in temperament, and all members of the breed have an unusual, chirping call.

• **FEATURES** The ground colour in this case is silver, offset by rich cream tabby markings. The pads and nose are pink.

• **REMARK** Maine Coons were first seen outside North America, in West Germany, in 1978.

• *wide-based, pointed ears*

FUR TYPE: thick, silky, and of variable length

• *some white markings permitted on chin*

flowing tail •

• *tabby markings on leg*

Shorthair option Cream Silver Tabby American Shorthair	Temperament Independent

| Country of origin USA | Ancestry Non-pedigree Longhairs | Origins 1770s |

BROWN CLASSIC TABBY

The striped tail of this breed may have given rise to the name "Coon", as the tail is similar to that of the raccoon, or coon as these animals are popularly known in North America.

ruff around neck

• **FEATURES** The ground coloration in this case should be a warm shade of copper, with contrasting black tabby markings. In the classic tabby form, the markings should be blotched on the body and solid in colour. The nose leather should be brick red.

broad chest

ears well spaced and high on head

• **REMARK** Brown Classic Tabbies are a common form of the Maine Coon.

FUR TYPE: thick, silky, and of variable length

black tip to tail

| Shorthair option Brown Classic Tabby American Shorthair | Temperament Independent |

| Country of origin USA | Ancestry Non-pedigree Longhairs | Origins 1770s |

BROWN TABBY AND WHITE

This form of Maine Coon has been developed from the more common Brown Tabby ancestry.

"M"-shaped tabby marking on head

• **FEATURES** Brown coloration should predominate in this case, with the tabby markings clearly evident. White fur should be confined essentially to the underparts and the feet.

FUR TYPE: thick, silky, and of variable length

moderately long neck

• **REMARK** Originally known in Europe as American Forest Cats, the Maine Coon first arrived in Britain in 1984.

characteristic mackerel markings

wide base to tail

bushy, flowing tail

| Shorthair option Brown Tabby and White American Shorthair | Temperament Independent |

Country of origin USA	Ancestry Non-pedigree Longhairs	Origins 1770s

TORTIE TABBY AND WHITE

Maine Coons are very easy to train and can be taught to walk with a harness and leash. Although they are not prolific breeders, and often produce just one litter a year, they are good mothers.
• **FEATURES** The ground colour is a warm shade of copper agouti, with darker red areas and black tabby markings. The white fur is somewhat variable in distribution, but should ideally be restricted to the face, chest, and belly, and down the legs to the feet.
• **REMARK** More than 60 different colour and patterning combinations have been recorded to date for the Maine Coon.

wide-set eyes •

• firm chin

• clear division between white and coloured areas

• solid, muscular body

FUR TYPE: thick, silky, and of variable length

tail at least as long as body •

Shorthair option Tortie Tabby and White American Shorthair	Temperament Independent

Country of origin USA	Ancestry Non-pedigree Longhairs	Origins 1770s

SILVER TORTIE TABBY

When viewed from the front, the head of this cat is similar to that of a shorthair, the longer fur being most apparent on the sides of the body.
• **FEATURES** These cats are distinguished from the Silver Tabby by their red and cream patching. The ground colour is silver, offset by clearly defined, darker black tabby markings.
• **REMARK** This variety is better known in its homeland as the "Silver Patched Tabby".

FUR TYPE: thick, silky, and of variable length

• "M"-shaped head marking

• black tabby patterning clearly apparent

• powerful legs with large, round paws

• barring on legs

Silver Tortie Tabby American Shorthair

	Temperament Independent

Country of origin USA	Ancestry Non-ped. Longhair	Origins 1770s

BLUE SILVER TORTIE TABBY

Because of the wide range of colours within this breed, there is
usually great diversity in the coloration of the kittens in any litter.
• **FEATURES** The ground colour is a pale, clear shade of bluish
silver. Tortoiseshell markings, in the form of patches of cream, are
apparent in the coat, as well as the denser, dark blue tabby markings.
• **REMARK** The diversity in coloration and markings in this breed
has resulted partly from its widespread
natural evolution; this may change as the
breed is now restricted
to pedigrees only.

profuse tail fur

*full,
round
eyes*

tortie coloration

tabby markings

FUR TYPE: thick, silky,
and of variable length

Shorthair option Blue Silver Tortie Tabby American Shorthair	Temperament Independent

Country of origin USA	Ancestry Non-pedigree Longhairs	Origins 1770s

BLACK SMOKE AND WHITE

Although there can be considerable variation in the size of these cats, this
factor alone is not sufficient to determine the quality of a cat.
• **FEATURES** The coat markings of this variety are equivalent to other
Smokes; the white undercoat is most clearly visible when the cat walks,
showing through the black tipping on individual outer hairs. The ear tufts
and flanks are lightest in colour; the head, back, and legs are darkest.
• **REMARK** Smoke forms of all the
self colours, and Tortie and White
combinations, are now being bred.

*ears wide
at base*

*rectangular
body shape
desirable*

*prominent ruff
around neck*

*well-tufted
white paws*

FUR TYPE: thick, silky,
and of variable length

plume-like end to long tail

Shorthair option Black Smoke and White American Shorthair	Temperament Independent

NORWEGIAN FOREST

THIS BREED is not dissimilar to the Maine Coon, and may even have contributed to the development of that breed. Known in their Norwegian homeland as *Norsk Skaukatt*, these cats are very well adapted to survival there during the freezing winter months. The long, double-layered coat is water-repellent and is not affected by even heavy rain. Although, in the past, Norwegian Forest Cats have not been well known outside their homeland, they are now being more widely kept. However, this is not a breed that thrives in a totally urban environment; they are best kept where there is space for them to roam, climb, and hunt, as they do in their native Scandinavia.

Country of origin Norway	Ancestry Angoras x Shorthairs	Origins 1520s

BLACK AND WHITE

The origin of these cats is something of a mystery, although it has been suggested that they were developed from Angoras that had been brought by ship to Norway, where they mated with the local shorthairs. Yet despite the fact that the breed has been kept in Norway for centuries, it was only during the 1930s that they attracted any serious interest from breeders.
• **FEATURES** Large and muscular, these cats are solidly built. The head has the shape of an equilateral triangle, with a long, straight profile.
• **REMARK** A breeding programme for these cats was begun in earnest in 1973 and, since then, a number have been sent overseas.

long, bushy tail

• long tufts of hair growing out of ears

• semi-long, water-repellent coat

FUR TYPE: glossy outer coat; woolly undercoat

clearly defined black and white areas •

• long, glossy hair forms knickerbockers

Shorthair option Black and White European Shorthair	Temperament Adventurous

Country of origin Norway	Ancestry Angoras x Shorthairs	Origins 1520s

BLUE TABBY AND WHITE

In spite of its similarity to the Maine Coon, the Norwegian Forest Cat is distinctive in type, having hind legs longer than the forelegs. The eyes of adult cats should be almond shaped and slightly angled, with the inner corner lower than the outer. In young cats, the eyes may be more rounded.
• FEATURES White fur, when present, is confined to the chest and paws. There may be a slight difference in coat type between the different colours, with tabbies tending to have the thickest coats.
• REMARK Colour has never been as important a feature of this breed as its type and coat.

FUR TYPE: glossy outer coat; woolly undercoat

• large, open, obliquely set eyes

• glossy top coat

• long, flowing tail

large, round, tufted paws •

Shorthair option Blue Tabby and White European Shorthair	Temperament Adventurous

Country of origin Norway	Ancestry Angoras x Shorthairs	Origins 1520s

BLUE TORTIE SMOKE AND WHITE

This form of the Norwegian Forest Cat reflects the wide range of colours that are associated with the breed. As a tortie, it is essentially a female-only variety and is therefore smaller than other forms in which males are invariably larger.
• FEATURES Straight noses are preferred, but they may sometimes display a slight curve along the length.
• REMARK Traditionally, torties of this breed have softer, smoother coats than those of tabbies.

tufted ears •

FUR TYPE: glossy outer coat; woolly undercoat

• long tail should reach to neck

Shorthair option Blue Tortie Smoke and White European Shorthair	Temperament Adventurous

Country of origin Norway	Ancestry Angoras x Shorthairs	Origins 1520s

BLACK SMOKE AND WHITE

The distinctive double coat is a feature of this breed and pressing on it ought to leave an indentation in the fur. During the summer months much of the coat is shed but the tufts of hair on the toes, as well as the long, flowing tail, will remain evident, indicating the true, semi-long-haired nature of the breed.

• **FEATURES** The Smoke coloration results from the contrast between the white undercoat and the dark shading on the outer fur.

• **REMARK** All colours, except chocolate, lilac, and Siamese-style points, are permitted for showing.

long, flowing tail with bushy appearance •

FUR TYPE: glossy outer coat; woolly undercoat

white normally present on the chest •

Black Smoke and White European Shorthair	Temperament Adventurous

Country of origin Norway	Ancestry Angoras x Shorthairs	Origins 1520s

BROWN TABBY AND WHITE

An important feature of this breed is the neck ruff, consisting of a full bib, a short back, and, in winter, a final section sometimes called "side mutton-chops".

• **FEATURES** The fur of these cats is affected by their living conditions: those kept indoors, in the warmth, have shorter and softer coats than those living outdoors in Scandinavia.

• **REMARK** The ears of the Norwegian Forest Cat are high and open, and wide at the base, with lynx-like tufts.

triangular head with strong chin •

full ruff •

• *solid bone structure*

FUR TYPE: glossy outer coat; woolly undercoat

• *strong, long legs*

Shorthair option Brown Tabby and White European Shorthair	Temperament Adventurous

SIBERIAN FOREST

I T IS NOW THOUGHT that these cats could be the ancestral form of all long-haired breeds, including the original Persians and Angoras. It is not clear when this coat mutation first appeared, but there is some evidence to suggest that these cats have been in existence for a thousand years or more, and have altered little during that time. Studies in the former USSR have shown that the greatest incidence of the long-haired gene is in the vicinity of St Petersburg (formerly Leningrad), and it seems likely that these cats first emerged in the northern part of the country. The extra thickness of the coat would have been very beneficial in the harsh weather conditions of that area.

Country of origin Russian	Ancestry Non-pedigree longhairs	Origins 1000s

BROWN SPOTTED AND WHITE

There is a relatively high incidence of tabby markings in this breed, possibly due to matings with wild cats, and this is thought to reduce the likelihood of self colours developing in the breed. Although not yet being selectively bred to any extent, there are moves to develop the Siberian on formal lines, as happened with the Norwegian Forest Cat, another "natural" breed from a northern region. The traditional colour of the Siberian Forest is the golden tabby.

• **FEATURES** In this case, the spotted tabby markings are clearly off-set against the white areas of the coat.
• **REMARK** Although known outside their homeland, Siberian Forest Cats are still relatively scarce.

• *broad, round head*

• *long, water-repellent coat, with obvious ruff around neck*

• *coat short at birth, with no guard hairs until three months*

• *visible ear furnishings*

• *long fur-covering on hindquarters and tail*

• *long fur on sides of face*

• *powerful legs*

• *well-muscled, relatively long body*

FUR TYPE: glossy top-coat; dense undercoat

Shorthair option None	Temperament Shrewd and active

RAGDOLL

IN THEIR EARLY DAYS, Ragdolls were reputed to be insensitive to pain, but this is entirely fallacious; the belief arose when the original white Longhair gave birth to her kittens after having been injured in a road accident. These cats do, however, become extraordinarily relaxed, like limp ragdolls, when being stroked by their owners, and they make ideal family pets, as they are usually very tolerant towards children.

Country of origin USA	Ancestry White Longhair x Birman	Origins 1960s

SEAL POINT

There are currently three coat patterns, the Seal Point being an example of the Colour Pointed variety. Blue, Chocolate, and Lilac Points are identical in markings, differing simply in their coloration. Ragdolls are large cats, and take three years or so to reach full adult size and coloration.

- **FEATURES** The head is large and wedge shaped, with a flat-topped skull and rounded muzzle. There is a slight stop on the short nose. Coat length is long on the neck, giving the impression of a bib. The coat grows longer in cold weather, and is then moulted during the summer. Females are smaller and lighter in colour than males.
- **REMARK** The early development of this breed was controlled by the original breeder, by franchise.

• broad hind-quarters

• even, dense shade of seal-brown on tail

beige coloration shading to cream on belly and chest •

• large, heavy body

• heavy-boned legs

• large, rounded, seal-brown paws

FUR TYPE: medium-length, silky, and dense

Shorthair option None		Temperament Docile and quiet

Country of origin USA	Ancestry White Longhair x Birman	Origins 1960s

BLUE MITTED

The Ragdoll was granted recognition in the United States in 1965, and in Great Britain in 1983, two years after its arrival there.
• **FEATURES** Similar to the equivalent Colour Pointed form, the Mitted Ragdoll is distinguished by the white "mittens" on its front paws, which must be evenly matched in size and which should not extend beyond the angle of the paw and the leg. The white "boots" on the hind legs continue up to the hocks; the entire underbody, from chin to tail, is also white.

large, blue eyes

• **REMARK** Ragdoll kittens start to develop their characteristic points at roughly one week of age.

blue-grey mask •

FUR TYPE: medium-length, silky, and dense

• white "boots" extend up to hock

• pure white, matching "mittens"

Shorthair option None	Temperament Docile and quiet

Country of origin USA	Ancestry White Longhair x Birman	Origins 1960s

SEAL BI-COLOUR

In order to preserve their unique patterns and type, Ragdolls are always mated to other Ragdolls. In the Bi-colour, a limited amount of white is allowed on the body.
• **FEATURES** The white fur on the underparts should not extend into the pointed, seal-brown areas. Eye coloration is deep blue. The body is long and muscular, with a broad chest and strong, short, heavy-set neck.
• **REMARK** The "V"-shape on the face is an important feature.

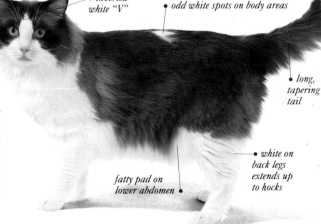

• inverted white "V"

• odd white spots on body areas

• long, tapering tail

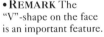

FUR TYPE: medium-length, silky, and dense

fatty pad on lower abdomen •

• white on back legs extends up to hocks

Shorthair option None	Temperament Docile and quiet

SOMALI

T HESE CATS are named after the country of Somalia, which borders Ethiopia (formerly Abyssinia), in Africa, and the name was chosen to reflect the breed's close relationship with the Abyssinian. Long-haired kittens had occurred in Abyssinian litters for a number of years, but it was only in 1967 that the first steps were taken to develop these cats into a new breed. Somalis display ticking along each hair similar to that of the Abyssinian.

Country of origin USA	Ancestry Long-haired Abyssinians	Origins 1967

SORREL SILVER

The Somali is a medium-sized cat of muscular build and harmonious proportions. The head is wedge shaped, with soft contours and a slightly curved profile. A slight nose break is essential. The pricked ears are widely spaced and tufted at the tips.
• FEATURES All silver forms of the Somali should have white hair with appropriate ticking; in this case, the chocolate ticking gives rise to a sparkling, silvery peach impression. The ears and tail should each be tipped with chocolate coloration.
• REMARK Although breeders in many countries welcomed the development of the Somali, it was not until 1983 that the breed was recognized by the Cat Association of Britain, and the breed only received championship status from the GCCF in 1991.

lithe, muscular body

chocolate-brown tufting between toes

dark skin on eyelids, with lighter "spectacles" encircling eyes

almond-shaped hazel-coloured eyes

medium-length coat, shorter over shoulders

long, tapering tail

five toes on front foot

chocolate tip to tail

FUR TYPE: very soft, fine, and dense

Shorthair option Sorrel Silver Abyssinian	Temperament Extrovert

| Country of origin USA | Ancestry Long-haired Abyssinians | Origins 1967 |

SORREL

This breed has a double-layered coat, with at least three bands of ticking along each hair.
• **FEATURES** The warm, copper-coloured fur is ticked with chocolate, and the ears and tail are similarly tipped. The undercoat is deep apricot.
• **REMARK** Two Sorrel Somali kittens, born in a litter with four Sorrel Abyssinians in 1971, caused controversy when they were exhibited in Britain.

FUR TYPE: very soft, fine, and dense

• *rich copper coloration preferred*

• *short hair on head*

• *soft, curved wedge*

fine, long legs •

tail with full brush •

| Shorthair option Sorrel Abyssinian | Temperament Extrovert |

| Country of origin USA | Ancestry Long-haired Abyssinians | Origins 1967 |

USUAL

This form of the Somali, which is better known in some countries as the "Ruddy", was one of the first colours, along with the Sorrel Somali, to be recognized for show purposes in Britain.
• **FEATURES** The coloration should be a rich, golden brown with black ticking most evident on the spine and tail. The underparts are apricot, with no trace of darker markings.
• **REMARK** A ruff around the neck and "breeches" of longer fur on the legs are desirable.

bands of ticking with dark tips •

• *ruff gives full-coated appearance*

black tip to tail with no trace of rings •

• *fur longer on underparts*

"breeches" of longer fur •

FUR TYPE: very soft, fine, and dense

| Shorthair option Usual Abyssinian | Temperament Extrovert |

| Country of origin | USA | Ancestry | Long-haired Abyssinians | Origins | 1967 |

BLUE

The popularity of the Somali is increasing rapidly, and these cats are being produced in an ever-expanding array of colours.
• **FEATURES** The depth of blue coloration varies between individuals, but the ticking should be darker in all cases. The undercoat can be cream or a slightly deeper shade, often described as oatmeal.
• **REMARK** Because the coat of the Somali is not woolly, it shows no tendency to mat.

FUR TYPE: very soft, fine, and dense

• *broad-based ears set wide apart on head*

• *oatmeal-coloured underparts*

mauvish blue pads •

• *tufted toes*

| Shorthair option | Blue Abyssinian | Temperament | Extrovert |

| Country of origin | USA | Ancestry | Long-haired Abyssinians | Origins | 1967 |

CREAM SILVER

pricked ears •

Somali kittens can take up to 18 months to develop their pattern of adult ticking. Although Somalis mated together will produce only Somali kittens, either coat length may result from Somali x Abyssinian pairings.
• **FEATURES** The base hair in this typical Somali is white with cream ticking, so that the resulting impression is of a cat with a sparkling, silvery cream appearance. The ears and tail are cream, and the underparts are whitish.
• **REMARK** In a mixed litter, Somalis tend to be slightly larger than Abyssinians.

• *silvery underparts*

• *medium, wedge-shaped head with rounded chin*

full, plumed tail •

FUR TYPE: very soft, fine, and dense

| Shorthair option | Cream Silver Abyssinian | Temperament | Extrovert |

Country of origin USA	Ancestry Long-haired Abyssinians	Origins 1967

LILAC

As in other Somalis, the Lilac is characterized by the agouti markings on its coat. Darker shading is seen on the back, down the sides of the body, and along the tail.
• **FEATURES** The basic coloration in this case is a warm, pinkish dove-grey, with contrasting tipping of a darker shade. Both the nose and pads should be mauvish pink, with the area between the pads corresponding to that of the body coloration.
• **REMARK** There may be a noticeable difference in type between North American and European Somalis, reflecting the difference in their ancestors.

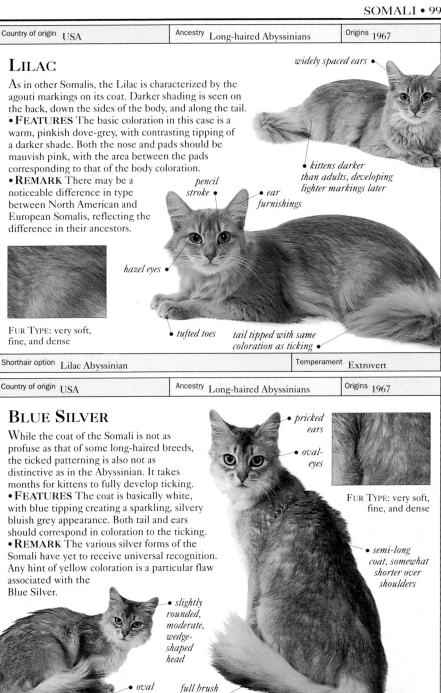

widely spaced ears •

• kittens darker than adults, developing lighter markings later

pencil stroke •

• ear furnishings

hazel eyes •

FUR TYPE: very soft, fine, and dense

• tufted toes

tail tipped with same coloration as ticking •

Shorthair option Lilac Abyssinian		Temperament Extrovert

Country of origin USA	Ancestry Long-haired Abyssinians	Origins 1967

BLUE SILVER

While the coat of the Somali is not as profuse as that of some long-haired breeds, the ticked patterning is also not as distinctive as in the Abyssinian. It takes months for kittens to fully develop ticking.
• **FEATURES** The coat is basically white, with blue tipping creating a sparkling, silvery bluish grey appearance. Both tail and ears should correspond in coloration to the ticking.
• **REMARK** The various silver forms of the Somali have yet to receive universal recognition. Any hint of yellow coloration is a particular flaw associated with the Blue Silver.

• pricked ears

• oval eyes

FUR TYPE: very soft, fine, and dense

• semi-long coat, somewhat shorter over shoulders

• slightly rounded, moderate, wedge-shaped head

• oval feet

full brush to tail •

Shorthair option Blue Silver Abyssinian		Temperament Extrovert

Country of origin USA	Ancestry Long-haired Abyssinians	Origins 1967

SILVER

The Somali is actually a ticked tabby, and the presence of the silver gene in this case results in a glacial white ground colour. There is no hint of gold or reddish hues in the ground colour.

• **FEATURES** The combination of a white undercoat and black ticking creates an impression of silver in the coat. There should be no ticking or any other dark markings on the underparts. The pads can be either brown or black in colour, with the black coloration extending up along the hind legs. This cat has five toes on each of the front feet, and only four on the back.

• **REMARK** The quality of the coat is an important feature, and there should be at least three bands of ticking on each of the hairs. The dark coloration of the eyelids emphasizes the colour of the eyes, which can range from amber, through hazel, to green.

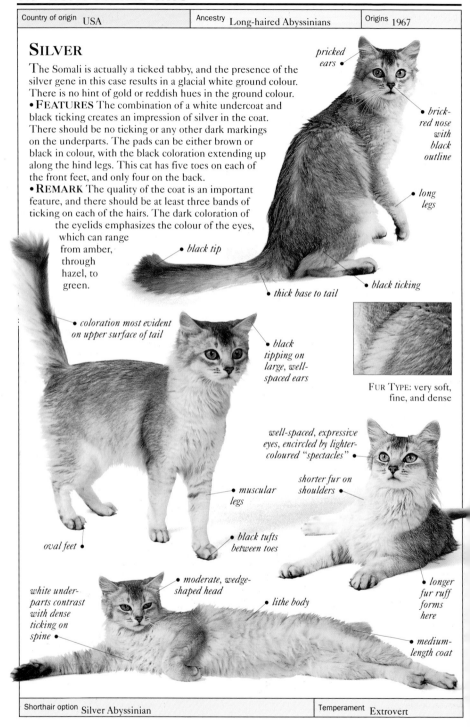

pricked ears •

• brick-red nose with black outline

• long legs

• *black tip*

• *thick base to tail*

• *black ticking*

• *coloration most evident on upper surface of tail*

• *black tipping on large, well-spaced ears*

FUR TYPE: very soft, fine, and dense

well-spaced, expressive eyes, encircled by lighter-coloured "spectacles"

shorter fur on shoulders •

• *muscular legs*

oval feet •

• *black tufts between toes*

• *longer fur ruff forms here*

white under-parts contrast with dense ticking on spine •

• *moderate, wedge-shaped head*

• *lithe body*

• *medium-length coat*

Shorthair option Silver Abyssinian	Temperament Extrovert

Country of origin USA	Ancestry Long-haired Abyssinians	Origins 1967

CHOCOLATE SILVER

The alternate light and dark bands of ticking on the individual hairs create the distinctive patterning of Somalis. There can be up to four distinct light and dark bands along the length of any one hair.

• **FEATURES** Dark ticking on the white base hair gives these cats a sparkling, silvery chocolate appearance.

• **REMARK** Kittens are darker in coloration.

• short, dark "pencil" stroke extends vertically above each eye

• ruff of fur clearly apparent around neck

FUR TYPE: very soft, fine, and dense

dark chocolate toe-tufts •

• "breeches" of longer fur on hind legs

• chocolate-brown pads, with colour extending up hocks

Shorthair option Chocolate Silver Abyssinian	Temperament Extrovert

Country of origin USA	Ancestry Long-haired Abyssinians	Origins 1967

BLUE TORTIE

Somali kittens are born with short hair, which very quickly turns fluffy, but they only gradually acquire their smooth, sleek coat as they mature.

• **FEATURES** The blue-grey coloration is here mixed with a rich shade of cream, the coloration of the belly reflecting that of the underlying base hair. Colouring on the back, hind legs, and the tip of the tail should be darker. The areas of tortie patterning may be even on both sides of the cat's body, or entirely random, with a blaze present in some cases.

• hazel-green, almond-shaped eyes with dark rims and lighter coloured "spectacles"

• medium-length nose

• legs quite long in relation to body size

tail thickest at base •

FUR TYPE: very soft, fine, and dense

Shorthair option Blue Tortie Abyssinian	Temperament Extrovert

BALINESE

BALINESE are the long-haired counterpart of the Siamese and, as such, can be easily distinguished from Colour Pointed Longhairs by their distinctly Siamese type – as compared with the typically cobby shape of the Persian Longhair. It is thought that the long-haired gene was most probably introduced from Angoras, which were occasionally paired with Siamese in Great Britain in the 1920s and later formed the basis of the Balinese breed.

Country of origin USA	Ancestry Siamese x Angoras	Origins 1940s

LILAC POINT

When they first appeared in what were believed to be pure Siamese bloodlines, breeders had little interest in these cats, but gradually the appeal of the Balinese spread, and the breed began to evolve. Since long hair is a recessive characteristic, any two Balinese mated together will inevitably produce Balinese kittens, but out-crossings to preserve Siamese type were also used.
• **FEATURES** Balinese have a long, wedge-shaped head, and a slim, elegant body. Fur may grow to 5 cm (2 in) in length.
• **REMARK** The name of this group of cats stems from the graceful dancers on the island of Bali in Indonesia. The first known breeder was Marion Dorsey, of California, who collaborated on a breeding programme with another cat fancier in New York, during the 1960s.

• *well-plumed, tapering tail*

even depth of colour on points •

• *long, wedge-shaped head*

magnolia body colour •

lavender-pink paw pads •

• *frosty grey points with pinkish tone*

FUR TYPE: medium-length, fine, and silky

Shorthair option Lilac Point Siamese	Temperament Lively

| Country of origin | USA | Ancestry | Siamese x Angoras | Origins | 1940s |

BLUE POINT

Kittens are born with white coats and only later does the characteristic coloration begin to develop. Adult cats, on the other hand, become somewhat darker as they start to age.

• **FEATURES** The colour of the body is a glacial shade of bluish white, which is darker on the back. The points should be slate-blue, with matching pads and nose coloration.

• **REMARK** The first Balinese to reach Europe arrived from the United States in the mid-1970s.

vivid, deep blue eyes

lithe, graceful body

well-balanced appearance

FUR TYPE: medium-length, fine, and silky

| Shorthair option | Blue Point Siamese | Temperament | Lively |

| Country of origin | USA | Ancestry | Siamese x Angoras | Origins | 1940s |

CHOCOLATE POINT

Balinese were recognized as a breed for the first time in the United States in 1963, and a specialist breed club was formed for them five years later.

• **FEATURES** The ivory body colour contrasts with warm, milk-chocolate points. The nose and paw pads are a cinnamon-pink shade.

• **REMARK** Grooming is easy, as the silky hair texture helps to prevent matting.

shading matches points

FUR TYPE: medium-length, fine, and silky

front legs shorter than hind legs

long, thin, well-plumed tail

| Shorthair option | Chocolate Point Siamese | Temperament | Lively |

Country of origin USA	Ancestry Siamese x Angoras	Origins 1940s

SEAL TORTIE POINT

This is one of the more striking Balinese, with its pronounced contrast between body colour and points.
• **FEATURES** The body colour matches that of the Seal Point, being pale fawn on the back, and warm cream over the rest of the body. The points are a deep seal-brown, with patches that can be varying shades of red.
• **REMARK** Breeders in the United States recognize only the four "pure" colours, variants there being known as "Javanese".

wedge-shaped head

shoulders equal in width to hips

plume apparent on tail

small, oval-shaped paws

FUR TYPE: medium-length, fine, and silky

Shorthair option Seal Tortie Point Siamese	Temperament Lively

Country of origin USA	Ancestry Siamese x Angoras	Origins 1940s

SEAL POINT

The Balinese is less assertive than the Siamese and has a quieter voice.
• **FEATURES** The coloration of the points must be a solid, even shade of dark seal-brown, with matching nose and pads. Body coloration is pale fawn on the back, becoming a warm cream colour on the sides of the body, and it is lighter still on the underparts.
• **REMARK** Out-crossings to Siamese have meant that some American strains have been affected by a reduction in coat length. In Europe, the more widespread use of Angoras has tended to prevent this problem from arising.

complete mask with dark lines extending to ears

seal-brown mask

hair forming tail plume up to 5 cm (2 in) long

lighter underparts

good contrast between points and body colour

slim legs

FUR TYPE: medium length, fine, and silky

Seal Point Siamese	Temperament Lively

| Country of origin | USA | Ancestry | Siamese x Angoras | Origins | 1940s |

SEAL TORTIE TABBY POINT

plume-like tail •

The coat obscures the markings in Tortie and Tabby Points, especially on the tail. During judging the tail is held at its tip, shaken, and assessed from behind for a clear view of the patterning.

• **FEATURES** The combination of tortie and tabby markings is reflected by the presence of shades of red superimposed on the basic tabby patterning.

• **REMARK** Cats with these markings are sometimes described as "torbies".

• "M"-shaped tabby marking on head

• broken stripes

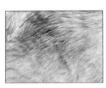

FUR TYPE: medium-length, fine, and silky

• relatively smooth fur with no ruff

| Shorthair option | Seal Tortie Tabby Point Siamese | Temperament | Lively |

| Country of origin | USA | Ancestry | Siamese x Angoras | Origins | 1940s |

CHOCOLATE TORTIE POINT

bright blue eyes •

In the same way that desirable features of the Siamese have been bred into the Balinese, so faults can also arise; the most likely to appear are signs of an obvious squint or the trace of a kink in the tail.

• **FEATURES** In this breed, the coat lies close over the whole body, with no woolly undercoat present. Young cats have shorter coats than those of adults. Tufts are sometimes apparent on the ears, and the absence of a frill is preferred.

• **REMARK** As in the case of other tortie varieties, these cats are usually exclusively female.

• large ears with wide bases

• pale chocolate and apricot shades on back and sides

• ivory underparts more visible when cat is sitting

graceful body shape, with long, slender legs •

milk-chocolate points broken and mixed with red •

• mottled colouring

FUR TYPE: medium-length, fine, and silky

| Shorthair option | Chocolate Tortie Point Siamese | Temperament | Lively |

Country of origin USA	Ancestry Siamese x Angoras	Origins 1940s

RED TABBY POINT

Better known in the United States as the "Red Lynx Point Javanese", these cats are Siamese in type and have a desirable ermine-like coat. They are a playful, intelligent, and naturally friendly breed.

• **FEATURES** Here, the basic body colour is creamy white, with points varying from orange through to red, contrasting with blue eyes. Tabby markings must be clearly evident on the head and on the legs and tail.

• tabby rings apparent on legs

• **REMARK** The Javanese category was introduced in the United States in 1980.

• large, pointed ears

• "M"-shaped tabby marking on head

FUR TYPE: medium-length, fine, and silky

• tapering tail showing tabby markings

contrast between points and body colour •

Shorthair option Red Tabby Point Siamese	Temperament Lively

Country of origin USA	Ancestry Siamese x Angoras	Origins 1940s

BLUE TABBY POINT

Elegance and balance are vital features of the Balinese, with all parts of the cat's body in proportion to each other. The body is lithe with slender legs, and the long, tapering tail emphasizes the body length.

• **FEATURES** The body is pale, glacial white, becoming more blue on the back. Points are light blue, set against darker blue tabby. Definite stripes surround the eyes and nose; tail markings are not as clear.

FUR TYPE: medium-length, fine, and silky

• **REMARK** This breed is known in the United States as the "Blue Lynx Point Javanese".

• almond-shaped blue eyes slant towards nose

• triangular head

well-plumed, long tail •

Shorthair option Blue Tabby Point Siamese	Temperament Lively

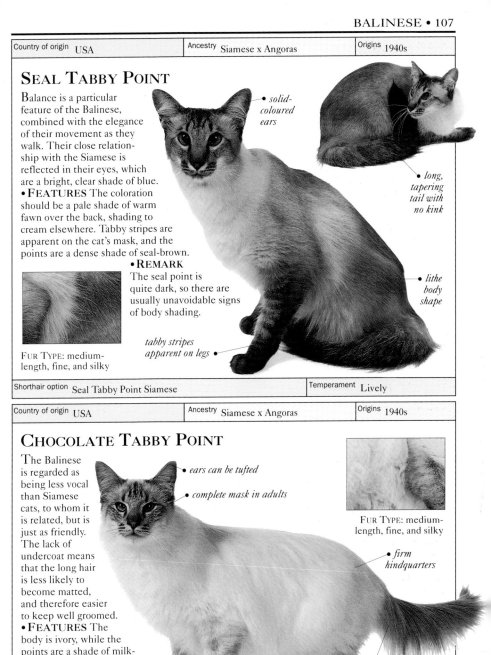

Country of origin USA	Ancestry Siamese x Angoras	Origins 1940s

SEAL TABBY POINT

Balance is a particular feature of the Balinese, combined with the elegance of their movement as they walk. Their close relationship with the Siamese is reflected in their eyes, which are a bright, clear shade of blue.

• **FEATURES** The coloration should be a pale shade of warm fawn over the back, shading to cream elsewhere. Tabby stripes are apparent on the cat's mask, and the points are a dense shade of seal-brown.

• **REMARK** The seal point is quite dark, so there are usually unavoidable signs of body shading.

• solid-coloured ears

• long, tapering tail with no kink

• lithe body shape

tabby stripes apparent on legs •

FUR TYPE: medium-length, fine, and silky

Shorthair option Seal Tabby Point Siamese	Temperament Lively

Country of origin USA	Ancestry Siamese x Angoras	Origins 1940s

CHOCOLATE TABBY POINT

The Balinese is regarded as being less vocal than Siamese cats, to whom it is related, but is just as friendly. The lack of undercoat means that the long hair is less likely to become matted, and therefore easier to keep well groomed.

• **FEATURES** The body is ivory, while the points are a shade of milk-chocolate brown.

• **REMARK** The long tail, spread out like a plume, is a distinctive feature of this breed.

• ears can be tufted

• complete mask in adults

FUR TYPE: medium-length, fine, and silky

• firm hindquarters

• long, tapering tail, with no kink

• long, slim legs

Shorthair option Chocolate Tabby Point Siamese	Temperament Lively

TIFFANIE

O RIGINALLY called Asian Longhairs, these cats are, essentially, the long-haired form of the Burmese. Similar in type to the Burmese, with a medium, wedge-shaped head and a short nose, they have well-spaced ears that are slightly rounded at the tips. The widely spaced eyes are set slightly obliquely, and the Burmese ancestry is reflected in the eye coloration, which can vary in shade from yellow to amber, although a rich golden yellow colour is preferred.

Country of origin UK	Ancestry Burmese crosses	Origins 1980s

RED

It was originally thought that this breed was the same as the Tiffany in the USA, and so its name was changed, but it has since emerged that they are of different origins. The Tiffanie in the UK was created as a result of the development of the Burmilla breed.
• **FEATURES** The coloration matches that of the Red Burmese, but the fur itself is noticeably longer, forming a ruff around the neck, as well as being much longer on the tail.
• **REMARK** The name 'Tiffany' could not be used in the UK because it was already in use as a stud name, so it was decided to adopt the alternative spelling.

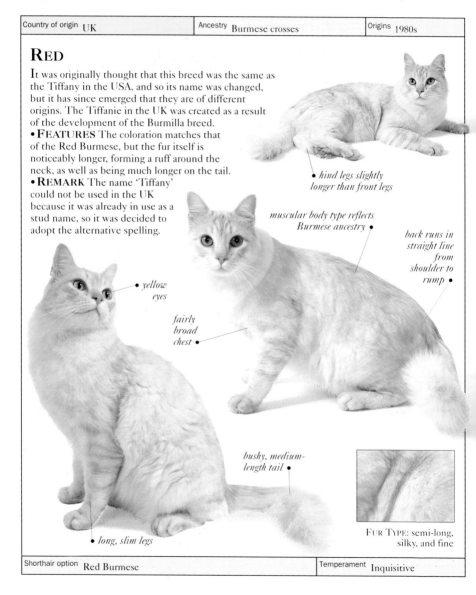

• hind legs slightly longer than front legs

muscular body type reflects Burmese ancestry •

back runs in straight line from shoulder to rump •

• yellow eyes

fairly broad chest •

bushy, medium-length tail •

• long, slim legs

FUR TYPE: semi-long, silky, and fine

Shorthair option Red Burmese	Temperament Inquisitive

| Country of origin | UK | Ancestry | Burmese crosses | Origins | 1980s |

BROWN

Although Tiffanys are now bred in a wide range of colours, this is in effect the traditional variety, being the long-haired version of the Brown Burmese.

• **FEATURES** Kittens' coats are shorter than those of adults, and take several months to grow; they also tend to be paler.

• **REMARK** The Tiffanie now has a more elegant conformation than the Tiffany, which is named after the Tiffany Theatre in Los Angeles, reflecting the breed's exotic appearance.

warm brown colour

tail tapers slightly to rounded tip

fine, silky fur

ruff around neck

FUR TYPE: semi-long, silky, and fine

| Shorthair option | Brown Burmese | Temperament | Inquisitive |

| Country of origin | UK | Ancestry | Burmese crosses | Origins | 1980s |

BLUE TIPPED SILVER

This is one of the more exotic colour forms of the Tiffanie to be developed. Breeders have used good-quality Burmese stock to produce cats that do genuinely approximate to long-coated Burmese in type.

• **FEATURES** Blue tipping of the silver coat creates an attractive colour contrast, just as distinctive as in the Blue Tipped Silver Burmilla.

• **REMARK** The long-haired gene that enabled this breed to develop was introduced by pairing Chinchilla Longhairs with Burmese during the development of the Burmilla.

widely spaced eyes

"M"-shaped marking on head reflects Burmilla ancestry

darker coloration clearly evident along back

FUR TYPE: semi-long, silky, and fine

| Shorthair option | Blue Tipped Silver Burmese | Temperament | Inquisitive |

CYMRIC

T HE CYMRIC is the long-haired form of the Manx and, as such, it is distinguished by a similar absence of tail. There are three different forms: Rumpy Cymrics have no trace of a tail, but just a hollow at the base; Stumpies have some vertebrae present in this area; the Longie has a tail that is only slightly shorter than that of other breeds. In coloration and markings, most forms are recognized by those associations that accept the breed.

Country of origin Canada	Ancestry Long-haired Manx	Origins 1960s

ORANGE-EYED WHITE

Although the Cymric (pronounced KUMRIC, after the traditional name for Wales) is a long-haired breed, its dense coat does not mat easily, and it is quite easy to groom. Because of the lethal gene associated with taillessness, Cymrics are never mated together, and the longer-tailed forms play an important part in breeding programmes.

• **FEATURES** All colours, except for Chocolate, Lilac, and Himalayan forms, are accepted with eye coloration matching the coat. The Cymric is similar to the Manx in terms of its type.

• **REMARK** Evolved directly from Manx, these cats are best known, at present, in North America and the United Kingdom.

neat, rounded paws •

large, wide ears with pointed tips •

body has arched profile from shoulder to rump •

FUR TYPE: thick under-coat; glossy top-coat

• broad, round head

• muscular thighs and deep flanks

• no trace of tail in exhibition Cymrics

short forelegs •

• hind legs longer than front legs

Shorthair option Orange-eyed White Manx	Temperament Intelligent

SCOTTISH FOLD

T HE LONG-HAIRED gene appears to have been present in the original bloodline of these cats. Although the first recorded Scottish Fold was actually short-haired (*see p.144*), both she and her daughter *Snooks* went on to produce long-haired cats with the characteristic folded ears. Later, the use of British Shorthair breeds probably contributed further long-haired genes, via previous Longhair crosses, and long-haired kittens frequently crop up in today's Scottish Fold litters. The short-haired form was the first to be recognized, and it was not until May 1987 that the long-haired Scottish Fold was given championship status for the first time by The International Cat Association (TICA). These cats are gradually making a big impact on the show scene.

Country of origin Scotland	Ancestry Non-pedigree Shorthairs	Origins 1950s

BLUE-CREAM AND WHITE

Scottish Folds make ideal companions, being very amenable and generally tolerant of other pets, dogs included. They should display the same rounded face as their short-haired counterparts, with the medium-sized ears lying rather like a cap on the side of the head. There is a slight stop on the nose, and the large, round eyes emphasize the friendly nature of these cats.

• **FEATURES** The coloured areas of fur should be discrete, and not merge with the white hair. The distinctive medium-length coat stands away from the body.

• **REMARK** It takes about two weeks for the ears of a Scottish Fold kitten to start folding over.

FUR TYPE: medium-length; dense; resilient

bushy tail

medium-sized ears

semi-cobby body

muscular thighs

sturdy legs

tightly folded ears

large, round eyes

strong, muscular neck

short legs

flexible tail

clearly defined patches of coloured and white fur

rounded face

Shorthair option Blue-cream and White Short-haired Scottish Fold	Temperament Placid

AMERICAN CURL

THE HIGHLY UNUSUAL appearance of these cats results from a mutation affecting the ears. Originally seen in long-haired cats, the mutation has now been transferred to short-haired cats; both forms are now popular.

The breed first appeared in 1981, when two kittens were adopted by John and Grace Ruga, of Lakewood, California. The Rugas noticed that the ear cartilage of one of the kittens, named *Shulasmith*, curled backwards. When she had her first litter, *Shulasmith* produced four kittens, two of whom had curled ears. This confirmed that the trait could be passed on from one generation to the next, and provided the potential to develop the breed.

Country of origin USA	Ancestry Non-pedigree Curl	Origins 1981

BLACK

Mercedes, one of the original curly-eared kittens, and her offspring were spotted in California by Nancy Kiester, who obtained both a long- and a short-haired specimen. She and the Rugas then decided to exhibit *Shulasmith* and the two kittens at a show in Palm Springs in October 1983. The cats attracted considerable attention and, as a result, the Rugas and another breeder set out to establish a breed standard and to provide a sound base for the development of these cats.

• **FEATURES** All kittens in a litter of American Curls are born with apparently normal ears; about half then develop curled ears. The changes may become evident from four to seven days of age.

• **REMARK** All colours and coat patterns are accepted in this breed.

• *cartilage at base of ears feels firm to touch*

legs moderately thick, with rounded paws •

• *plumed tail quite wide at base, tapering along length*

curled tip •

silky coat, with little undercoat •

FUR TYPE: semi-long and silky

• *hind legs slightly longer than front legs*

Shorthair option Black Short-haired American Curl	Temperament Gentle

Country of origin USA	Ancestry Non-pedigree Curl	Origins 1981

BLACK AND WHITE

It can take up to six months for the adult shape of the ears to become apparent, although they may continue unfurling for a time after this stage. The American Curl is relatively slow to mature, taking two or three years; it is of medium size, with a weight of 2–4.5 kg (5–10 lb).
• FEATURES The ears curl through at least 90 degrees, and usually through a greater angle. The cat actually swivels its ears so the tips point towards each other.
• REMARK Judges assess both the size and shape of the ears and their positioning, as well as the degree of curl and the ear furnishings.

• tufts on ears considered desirable

muscular body •

FUR TYPE: semi-long and silky

• medium-length coat lies flat

• short, straight legs

Shorthair option Black and White Short-haired American Curl	Temperament Gentle

Country of origin USA	Ancestry Non-pedigree Curl	Origins 1981

BROWN MACKEREL TABBY AND WHITE

The American Curl is a muscular, medium-sized cat with a softly rounded face and a straight nose. The silky, medium-length coat lies flat on the body.
• FEATURES The ears of the American Curl should be angled towards the middle of the back of the skull. The hair in the ears, known as furnishings, needs to be clearly visible. The eyes are quite large and slanted towards the nose and contribute to the friendly and alert appearance of this popular breed.
• REMARK American Curls make intelligent and playful companions and appear to suffer no ill effects from their unusual ear formation.

tips of ears may be soft to touch •

• furnishings clearly apparent within ears

typical mackerel stripes •

FUR TYPE: semi-long and silky

• plumed tail

• long tail, reaching to shoulders when folded forwards

• tight, round paws

Shorthair option Brown Tabby Short-haired American Curl	Temperament Gentle

NON-PEDIGREE

A S WITH WILD CATS, it is likely that the coats of domestic cats evolved in response to their environment. Cats that originated in colder northern areas have longer, thicker fur, while those from south-eastern Asia are often short-haired. The first long-haired cats in Great Britain came from France.

Country of origin Turkey	Ancestry Cross-bred cats	Origins 1500s

BLUE

Since they have not been bred to specific standards, the appearance of non-pedigree longhairs can be quite variable. Their coats can be less profuse than those of pure-bred longhairs, and the depth of coloration may vary between individuals.
• **FEATURES** There are often traces of tabby markings and small white areas that would be penalized in pure-bred Blue Longhairs. The head shape is less rounded than in pedigree Blue Longhairs.
• **REMARK** There was very little interest in establishing strains of pure colours until the advent of cat shows at the end of the last century. The earliest Blue Longhairs of that period were probably rather like the non-pedigree cats of today.

• *narrow head shape*

longish fur on tail •

• *largish, upright ears*

• *straight legs*

• *fur tufts between toes unlikely in non-pedigrees*

• *relatively little frill extending around shoulders and between legs compared to pedigree Longhairs*

FUR TYPE: thick and soft

Shorthair option Blue Non-pedigree Shorthair	Temperament Friendly

Country of origin Turkey	Ancestry Cross-bred cats	Origins 1500s

BLACK

Black coloration may have been one of the first domestic colour mutations, and Persian Longhairs, although scarce, were much in demand in Victorian Britain. Today, these cats are most commonly to be found in urban areas.

• **FEATURES** Non-pedigree cats can be quite diverse in appearance, resulting from random matings. Coloration may include greyish or brownish hues.

• **REMARK** Black cats may have originated in the eastern Mediterranean region, about 2,000 years ago.

FUR TYPE: thick and soft

stocky body shape with variable fur length
shorter hair on large paws
fluffy tail

Shorthair option Black Non-pedigree Shorthair	Temperament Friendly

Country of origin Turkey	Ancestry Cross-bred cats	Origins 1500s

CREAM AND WHITE

Bi-colour non-pedigree cats are very appealing, although they do not show the precise pattern of markings of their pedigree counterparts. Such cats can be found in any of the usual colour combinations.

• **FEATURES** The fur of non-pedigrees is usually quite short compared with that of exhibition Longhairs.

• **REMARK** Most non-pedigree longhairs are the result of entirely random matings.

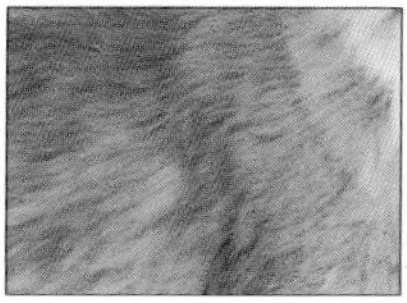

FUR TYPE: thick and soft

cream coloration may show traces of tabby markings
stocky legs
medium-long tail

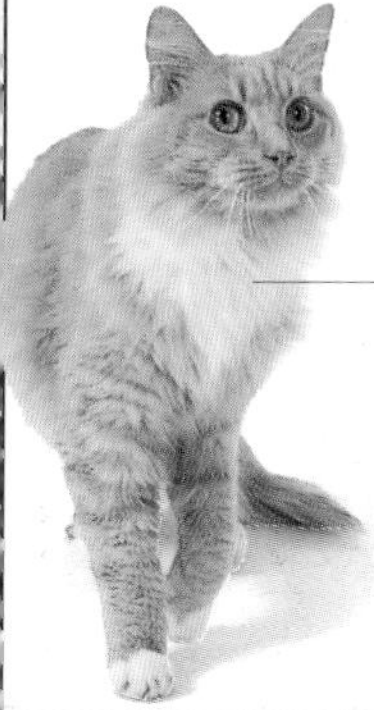
clear delineation between coloured and white areas is common

Shorthair option Cream and White Non-pedigree Shorthair	Temperament Friendly

Country of origin Turkey	Ancestry Cross-bred cats	Origins 1500s

RED SPOTTED

Cats of this colour are better known as "ginger" rather than red. It is believed that the colour may be of Asiatic origin.
• FEATURES The spotted markings are random and the coloration and coat length vary, so some individuals will be more attractive than others.
• REMARK There is often a class for non-pedigrees at cat shows, judging being based on beauty, condition, and temperament.

narrow head

longish tail, less bushy than in pedigree longhairs •

• *rounded cheeks with relatively short fur*

tabby markings •

FUR TYPE: thick and soft

• *tabby markings on legs*

Shorthair option Red Spotted Non-pedigree Shorthair	Temperament Friendly

Country of origin Turkey	Ancestry Cross-bred cats	Origins 1500s

BROWN TABBY

Tabby patterning in cats dates back to the earliest days of their domestication, about 5,000 years ago. However, longer coat length may tend to obscure these markings.
• FEATURES Tabby cats have darker patterning, offset against their basic colour, which in this case is light brown. In non-pedigree tabbies, the tabby markings are less precise. For example, the tip of this cat's tail does not terminate in black fur, as specified by the show standard for a pedigree Brown Tabby Longhair.
• REMARK Cats showing this patterning have been common for centuries.

agouti coat with dense black markings •

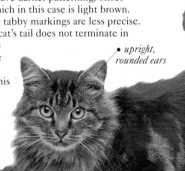

• *upright, rounded ears*

• *strong body*

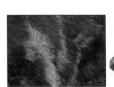

FUR TYPE: thick and soft

slight ruff evident here •

Shorthair option Brown Tabby Non-pedigree Shorthair	Temperament Friendly

Country of origin Turkey	Ancestry Cross-bred cats	Origins 1500s

SILVER AND WHITE

clear white areas •

Today's pure-bred longhairs have been selectively developed from non-pedigree stock over the past 120 years. However, non-pedigree cats are no less attractive than their pure-bred counterparts – they are simply of a different type. Although they are bred in the usual combinations, rarer variants, such as this silver and white, also arise.

• **FEATURES** Cats that are the result of shorthair x longhair pairings often have shorter coats than those bred from long-haired parents.

• **REMARK** In pedigree circles, the Tipped Silver Longhair is better known as the Chinchilla.

• *darker tipping on outer fur, with white undercoat, produces silver effect*

FUR TYPE: thick and soft

fluffy tail •

Shorthair option Silver and White Non-pedigree Shorthair	Temperament Friendly

Country of origin Turkey	Ancestry Cross-bred cats	Origins 1500s

TORTIE AND WHITE

These cats have a reputation for being excellent mothers and mousers; these skills, however, are passed on by example as well as by inheritance. Being torties, they are predominantly female.

• **FEATURES** Variable blotches of black, red, and white fur distinguish these cats, with the patterning largely depending on the individual. No two cats will have identical markings.

• **REMARK** Traditionally associated with farms, Tortie and White cats have evolved into a pure breed since 1956, with a rigorous standardization of type and patterning being imposed.

• *colours clearly defined*

• *cobby body shape*

• *round head*

FUR TYPE: thick and soft

bushy, mottled tail •

Shorthair option Tortie and White Non-pedigree Shorthair	Temperament Friendly

SHORT-HAIRED CATS

BRITISH SHORTHAIR

BRED ORIGINALLY from ordinary domestic cats, and then refined in terms of size, British Shorthairs are now distinguished by their massive, cobby shape and rounded faces. Adult males are considerably larger than females.

Following a period of decline at the turn of the century, interest in these cats revived during the 1930s. The self colours have always been in great demand and new colours, such as the Lilac, are still being developed.

Country of origin Great Britain	Ancestry Non-pedigree Shorthairs	Origins 1880s

ORANGE-EYED WHITE

There are three forms of the White British Shorthair, distinguished by eye coloration. Congenital deafness is not associated with the orange-eyed variety as it is with Blue-eyed Whites. Like other white cats, however, they can be at risk from sunburn.

• **FEATURES** Some white strains show a higher incidence of a condition known as polydactylism, which literally means "many digits". Although this is considered a serious show fault, the condition does not cause any handicap and will not prevent the cat from proving a healthy and delightful companion.

• **REMARK** White cats have always been very popular, in contrast to their black counterparts, which have been regarded as symbols of darkness and evil.

• *eyes may vary from deep gold, through orange, to copper*

• *round, massive head*

deep chest and broad shoulders •

• *cobby body shape*

• *pure white coat with no hint of yellow*

FUR TYPE: short, dense, and crisp

Longhair option Orange-eyed White Persian Longhair	Temperament Placid and friendly

Country of origin Great Britain	Ancestry Non-pedigree Shorthairs	Origins 1880s

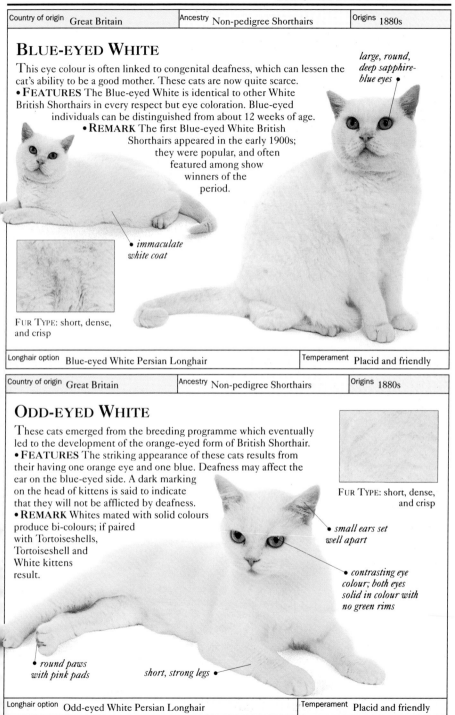

BLUE-EYED WHITE

This eye colour is often linked to congenital deafness, which can lessen the cat's ability to be a good mother. These cats are now quite scarce.
• **FEATURES** The Blue-eyed White is identical to other White British Shorthairs in every respect but eye coloration. Blue-eyed individuals can be distinguished from about 12 weeks of age.
• **REMARK** The first Blue-eyed White British Shorthairs appeared in the early 1900s; they were popular, and often featured among show winners of the period.

large, round, deep sapphire-blue eyes

• *immaculate white coat*

FUR TYPE: short, dense, and crisp

Longhair option Blue-eyed White Persian Longhair	Temperament Placid and friendly

Country of origin Great Britain	Ancestry Non-pedigree Shorthairs	Origins 1880s

ODD-EYED WHITE

These cats emerged from the breeding programme which eventually led to the development of the orange-eyed form of British Shorthair.
• **FEATURES** The striking appearance of these cats results from their having one orange eye and one blue. Deafness may affect the ear on the blue-eyed side. A dark marking on the head of kittens is said to indicate that they will not be afflicted by deafness.
• **REMARK** Whites mated with solid colours produce bi-colours; if paired with Tortoiseshells, Tortoiseshell and White kittens result.

FUR TYPE: short, dense, and crisp

• *small ears set well apart*

• *contrasting eye colour; both eyes solid in colour with no green rims*

• *round paws with pink pads*

short, strong legs •

Longhair option Odd-eyed White Persian Longhair	Temperament Placid and friendly

Country of origin Great Britain	Ancestry Non-pedigree Shorthairs	Origins 1880s

CREAM

This has been a popular colour since the 1950s, but it is one that represents a considerable challenge for the breeder. At first, the genetics of the colour were not fully understood.
• **FEATURES** Many cats show permanent traces of tabby markings, or a more reddish coloration than is considered desirable. The eye coloration can vary in shade from deep gold to copper.
• **REMARK** By a process of selective breeding, the incidence of tabby markings in these cats has been reduced.

short neck •

• *pale cream coat*

FUR TYPE: short, dense, and crisp

Longhair option Cream Persian Longhair	Temperament Placid and friendly

Country of origin Great Britain	Ancestry Non-pedigree Shorthairs	Origins 1880s

LILAC

One of the newest colours in the British Shorthair category, the Lilac has been derived from crossings involving Lilac Longhairs, to create a self-coloured, short-haired breed.
• **FEATURES** In type, the Lilac resembles other British Shorthairs, with a typically cobby body shape. Lilacs should have a pinkish nose and pads. Eye coloration can vary in shade from deep gold, through orange, to copper.
• **REMARK** The Lilac colour form is relatively scarce at present.

• *rounded face shape*

tabby markings disappear as kittens grow up •

• *frosty grey coat with pinkish tone*

• *medium-length, thick tail*

FUR TYPE: short, dense, and crisp

Longhair option Lilac Persian Longhair	Temperament Placid and friendly

Country of origin Great Britain	Ancestry Non-pedigree Shorthairs	Origins 1880s

BLUE

This is probably the most popular of all the self colours.
• **FEATURES** British Blues have a typically rounded face and stocky body shape. Males of the breed may develop prominent jowls as they mature, especially if they have not been neutered early in life.
• **REMARK** This breed nearly became extinct during World War II, due to a shortage of male cats, and did not begin to recover until the 1950s. The quality of the coat had to be maintained by a process of selective breeding.

round-tipped ears •

• *eye colour varies from deep gold to copper*

• *blue pads*

• *even coat coloration with no tabby markings*

FUR TYPE: short, dense, and crisp

Longhair option Blue Persian Longhair	Temperament Placid and friendly

Country of origin Great Britain	Ancestry Non-pedigree Shorthairs	Origins 1880s

CHOCOLATE

The Chocolate is not yet very common, but the attractive coloration should ensure their popularity as they become more readily available.
• **FEATURES** This breed should be of obvious British type, and any tendency towards the Havana in body type is seen as a serious fault.
• **REMARK** This breed originated from the use of Chocolate Longhairs followed by careful breeding to maintain the coat type of the British Shorthair. These cats are not currently recognized by all associations.

FUR TYPE: short, dense, and crisp

• *rich dark brown coloration*

short, straight nose •

• *tabby markings may be present in kittens*

large jowls •

tail slightly rounded at tip •

Longhair option Chocolate Persian Longhair	Temperament Placid and friendly

Country of origin Great Britain	Ancestry Non-pedigree Shorthairs	Origins 1880s

BLACK

Black British Shorthairs were often seen at the early cat shows, but had lost their popularity by the outbreak of World War I, and only started to become a common sight at cat shows again in the 1950s.

• **FEATURES** Cobby in shape, with a short, glossy coat, this is a very striking cat. A potential fault is any hint of green in the eye coloration, thought to be a legacy of out-crosses with Blues early in their development. Eyes should be copper, orange, or deep gold.

• **REMARK** These cats should be discouraged from sun-bathing because this can bleach the coat slightly, and give it a rusty brown hue.

broad chest •

• *short, level back*

• *pure black coat*

• *powerful, muscular body*

• *thick tail*

FUR TYPE: short, dense, and crisp

Longhair option Black Persian Longhair	Temperament Placid and friendly

Country of origin Great Britain	Ancestry Non-pedigree Shorthairs	Origins 1880s

CREAM AND WHITE

Bi-coloured cats have never been as popular in show circles as their self-coloured counterparts, possibly because of the difficulty in breeding well-marked individuals.

• **FEATURES** The white areas should be restricted to no more than one half of the body area and preferably only one third. The markings should be symmetrical, but this is impossible to predict with certainty, even in the case of well-marked parents.

• **REMARK** The Cream and White is the rarest of the four traditional bi-coloured forms, the other variants being black, blue, and red, all combined with white.

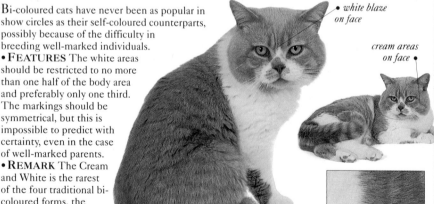

• *white blaze on face*

cream areas on face •

• *no white hairs in coloured areas*

cobby body shape •

FUR TYPE: short, dense, and crisp

Longhair option Cream and White Persian Longhair	Temperament Placid and friendly

Country of origin Great Britain	Ancestry Non-pedigree Shorthair	Origins 1880s

BLUE TORTIE AND WHITE

All forms of the tortoiseshell are highly valued as pets, being gentle and affectionate by nature. This more unusual breed is no exception to the rule.

• **FEATURES** This is the "dilute" version of the Tortoiseshell and White British Shorthair, in which blue replaces black, and cream replaces red. The white areas should constitute between one third and one half of the coat. A blaze is desirable.

• **REMARK** The name "tortie" is simply an abbreviation of "tortoiseshell", and applies to any cat in the group.

medium-length, tapering tail

light to medium blue

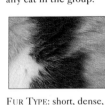

clear coloration

FUR TYPE: short, dense, and crisp

rounded paws

Longhair option Blue Tortie and White Persian Longhair	Temperament Placid and friendly

Country of origin Great Britain	Ancestry Non-pedigree Shorthairs	Origins 1880s

TORTIE AND WHITE

This ancient variety was originally known in Britain as the "Chintz and White"; in the United States it is known as the "Calico".

• **FEATURES** Unlike the Tortoiseshell, this is a patched variant, with each of the three colours being distinctly visible in different areas of the coat. Kittens are invariably duller than adults, and take about nine months to acquire their full colour.

• **REMARK** Although males are rare in this variety, one named *Ballochmyle Batchelor* won at a show in London in 1912. His winning career continued, but he obviously sired no kittens, tortoiseshell males being invariably sterile.

white facial blaze

deep orange eyes

pale red fur

white fur covers one third to one half of body

dense black

FUR TYPE: short, dense, and crisp

Longhair option Tortie and White Persian Longhair	Temperament Placid and friendly

Country of origin Great Britain	Ancestry Non-pedigree Shorthairs	Origins 1880s

BLUE SPOTTED

Cats with spotted markings date back to the days of ancient Egypt. Although they used to be known as spotted tabbies, this name was not strictly correct as tabby markings take the form of stripes rather than spots.

• **FEATURES** Although the spots do not have to be of a consistent size or shape, they must be quite distinctive.

• **REMARK** After having disappeared for the first half of this century, these cats, known affectionately as "Spotties", began to regain their popularity in the 1960s.

FUR TYPE: short, dense, and crisp

• *blue nose*

faint line along spine acceptable •

• *numerous spots on body*

Longhair option Blue Tabby Persian Longhair	Temperament Placid and friendly

Country of origin Great Britain	Ancestry Non-pedigree Shorthairs	Origins 1880s

SILVER SPOTTED

"M"-shape on forehead •

One of the most popular of the spotted varieties, the Silver shows an attractive contrast between its silvery fur and the darker black markings.

• **FEATURES** The spots must be distinct, and must not merge into each other, a fault known as brindling.

• **REMARK** The breed came to prominence by winning Top Shorthair entry at a show in Cheltenham, England, in 1965.

• *black tail tip corresponding with body markings*

• *silver ground colour*

FUR TYPE: short, dense, and crisp

• *round paws*

Longhair option Silver Tabby Persian Longhair	Temperament Placid and friendly

Country of origin Great Britain	Ancestry Non-pedigree Shorthairs	Origins 1880s

BROWN CLASSIC TABBY

It appears that all the early Brown Tabbies exhibited in Victorian times originated from non-pedigree stock, and little is known about their origins. They now tend to be less common than other forms of the tabby.

points of "M" extend from above eyes to between ears •

• **FEATURES** The basic coloration should be a rich, coppery brown, often difficult to achieve; the tabby markings must be black.
• **REMARK** The Tabby Cat Club, which helps to develop the breed, was set up in 1968.

FUR TYPE: short, dense, and crisp

• ground colour rich and even in all areas

Longhair option Brown Classic Tabby Persian Longhair	Temperament Placid and friendly

Country of origin Great Britain	Ancestry Non-pedigree Shorthairs	Origins 1880s

RED SPOTTED

Although the spots on the back of a Spotted British Shorthair will not be confused with the broken bars of a mackerel tabby, this breed retains the "M"-shaped tabby head markings.

• "M"-shape on head

deep orange eyes •

• **FEATURES** Good contrast between the two distinctive shades of red in the coat is important. The type of these cats is distinctly British, with their massive round heads and cobby bodies.
• **REMARK** In Egyptian mythology, the god *Ra* is portrayed in the form of a spotted cat killing *Apep*, the serpent of darkness.

• spots follow the typical distribution of tabby patternings

narrow tail rings •

FUR TYPE: short, dense, and crisp

• dark red spots clearly visible

Longhair option Red Tabby Persian Longhair	Temperament Placid and friendly

Country of origin Great Britain	Ancestry Non-pedigree Shorthairs	Origins 1880s

CREAM SPOTTED

Although it is possible to have spotted cats in any of the recognized solid colours, the Cream Spotted shown here is one of the more unusual forms.

broad skull •

strong, short neck •

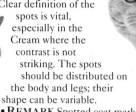

FUR TYPE: short, dense, and crisp

- **FEATURES** Clear definition of the spots is vital, especially in the Cream where the contrast is not striking. The spots should be distributed on the body and legs; their shape can be variable.
- **REMARK** Spotted coat markings are common in wild cats; they also occur naturally in non-pedigree cats, particularly in the eastern Mediterranean area.

• oval or round spots or rosettes

• relatively short legs, terminating in firm, round paws

Longhair option Cream Tabby Persian Longhair	Temperament Placid and friendly

Country of origin Great Britain	Ancestry Non-pedigree Shorthairs	Origins 1880s

RED MACKEREL TABBY

The only distinction between the Red mackerel tabby and the classic is in the pattern of markings on the body.

- **FEATURES** In the mackerel tabby, a dark line runs down the centre of the back, with a broken line on each side. Lines resembling a fish's skeleton run down the sides of the body, hence the name "mackerel". Body coloration is red rather than orange, with the tabby markings of a darker shade of red.
- **REMARK** The name "tabby" is derived from *al Attabiya*, a district of Baghdad, Iraq, where a black and white, "watered" silk was produced.

large, rounded eyes, set wide apart and level •

brick-red nose •

• deep red markings, offset against paler body colour, evident as narrow lines down the sides of the body

rings on tail should be numerous and narrow •

• dark tip to tail

FUR TYPE: short, dense, and crisp

Longhair option Red Mackerel Tabby Persian Longhair	Temperament Placid and friendly

| Country of origin Great Britain | Ancestry Non-pedigree Shorthairs | Origins 1880s |

BLUE-CREAM

This breed came to prominence after World War II, but it is still relatively scarce. The earliest Blue-cream individuals appeared in Tortoiseshell litters and from matings between Blues and Creams.
• **FEATURES** There should be no pronounced patches of one or other colour in the coat, the aim being to produce cats with evenly mixed cream and blue coloration.
• **REMARK** Regular grooming is most important when a Blue-cream is moulting.

small, round-tipped ears

orange eyes

blue nose leather

round face

coloration clearly defined over entire body

FUR TYPE: short, dense, and crisp

colour on paws evenly mixed

| Longhair option Blue-cream Persian Longhair | Temperament Placid and friendly |

| Country of origin Great Britain | Ancestry Non-pedigree Shorthairs | Origins 1880s |

TORTOISESHELL

Tortoiseshell cats are invariably female; males occur only because of a genetic abnormality and are usually sterile.
• **FEATURES** Tortoiseshell coloration results from a combination of black, and light and dark red hairs. The darkest kittens in a litter often prove to be the best adults.
• **REMARK** Tortoiseshell patterning is believed to have emerged early in the domestication process, possibly in North Africa and Turkey where such cats still abound. There is a high incidence of non-pedigree tortoiseshells in the western isles of Scotland, possibly brought by the Vikings.

black pads

cobby body shape

short, strong legs

coat colours evenly intermingled

FUR TYPE: short, dense, and crisp

thick tail with rounded tip

| Longhair option Tortoiseshell Persian Longhair | Temperament Placid and friendly |

Country of origin Great Britain	Ancestry Non-pedigree Shorthairs	Origins 1880s

BLUE AND WHITE

The bi-coloured appearance is common in non-pedigree cats, but producing exhibition British Shorthairs with the right pattern of markings invariably proves difficult.

• **FEATURES** The aim is to produce cats showing just one third white fur, with the remainder being a solid, even shade of blue. Ideally, coloration should be distributed along the top of the head and ears, back, and down the sides, with the underparts white; in practice, however, this is difficult to achieve.

• **REMARK** Originally, only combinations of white with red, black, blue, or cream were permitted but now any of the solid colours, combined with white, is generally acceptable.

• *any tabby markings should soon disappear*

FUR TYPE: short, dense, and crisp

• *thick base to tail*

• *no white hairs marring blue coloration*

Longhair option Blue and White Persian Longhair	Temperament Placid and friendly

Country of origin Great Britain	Ancestry Non-pedigree Shorthairs	Origins 1880s

BLACK AND WHITE

Black and White British Shorthairs were the most highly prized bi-colours in Victorian times, although never numerous. They have proved valuable in the development of Tortoiseshell and Whites.

• **FEATURES** As well as having the typical stocky British Shorthair shape, these cats must show a very clear contrast between black and white areas of fur.

• **REMARK** In the early cat shows, the markings on the Black and White had to be even, with white chest and feet, and a white blaze on the face.

• *white blaze between eyes*

FUR TYPE: short, dense, and crisp

• *jet black*

Longhair option Black and White Persian Longhair	Temperament Placid and friendly

Country of origin Great Britain	Ancestry Non-pedigree Shorthairs	Origins 1880s

RED CLASSIC TABBY

Like other British Shorthairs, these cats are affectionate, hardy, and usually very healthy.
• **FEATURES** In the classic tabby, the markings must be clearly defined and perfectly symmetrical. Any trace of white is a serious fault in these tabbies. The classic tabby form is distinguished from its mackerel counterpart by the pattern of the markings; these extend in swirls in the classic tabby, but form vertical stripes running down the body in the mackerel.
• **REMARK** Only since the advent of cat shows have attempts been made to breed tabbies with a particular patterning.

line runs from corner of each eye •

butterfly markings on shoulder •

• legs ringed with darker fur

FUR TYPE: short, dense, and crisp

typical oyster-shaped markings surrounded by rings •

Longhair option Red Classic Tabby Persian Longhair	Temperament Placid and friendly

Country of origin Great Britain	Ancestry Non-pedigree Shorthairs	Origins 1880s

BLUE CLASSIC TABBY

These tabbies are becoming increasingly popular, their markings making an attractive contrast against the paler ground colour.
• **FEATURES** In classic tabby patterning, an "M" shape is visible on the forehead. Darker lines extend to the shoulders, forming butterfly shapes. An unbroken line continues down the back to the tail, with oyster-shaped patches on each flank. Small narrow rings of darker fur encircle the tail, which has a dark tip.
• **REMARK** Producing tabbies with the ideal pattern of markings is a difficult task for the breeder.

• short, straight nose

• darker blue markings stand out clearly against bluish fawn ground colour

FUR TYPE: short, dense, and crisp

pink pads •

Longhair option Blue Classic Tabby Persian Longhair	Temperament Placid and friendly

Country of origin Great Britain	Ancestry Non-pedigree Shorthairs	Origins 1880s

BLACK SMOKE

The silver undercoat and contrasting top-coat of these cats produce an unusual, shimmering effect.

• **FEATURES** When sitting still, Black Smokes are indistinguishable from solid Black Shorthairs but, when moving, the silver undercoat becomes apparent, to wonderful effect. Odd white hairs in the coat are considered to be a fault.

• **REMARK** Smokes derive from matings of Silver Tabbies and self British Shorthairs.

typical rounded face

FUR TYPE: short, dense, and crisp

eye colour varies from deep gold to orange or copper

black top-coat conceals silver undercoat

black pads

relatively short legs

Longhair option Black Smoke Persian Longhair	Temperament Placid and friendly

Country of origin Great Britain	Ancestry Non-pedigree Shorthairs	Origins 1880s

TORTIE SMOKE

The distinctive qualities of the Smoke result from a gene that inhibits coloration of the undercoat. Another gene emphasizes coloration along the full length of the guard hairs, creating a rippling effect.

• **FEATURES** Characteristic tortoiseshell patterning should be distributed evenly throughout the coat. The silver undercoat contributes to the breed's soft, hazy appearance.

• **REMARK** Any British breed can be produced in a Smoke equivalent, but the darker colour forms have proved most popular.

well-spaced eyes

short, strong neck

cobby body

good mix of colours visible

round paws

FUR TYPE: short, dense, and crisp

Longhair option Tortie Smoke Persian Longhair	Temperament Placid and friendly

| Country of origin | Great Britain | Ancestry | Non-pedigree Shorthairs | Origins | 1880s |

BLACK TIPPED

Originally known as Chinchilla Shorthairs, these cats have been officially recognized under their present name only since 1978.
• FEATURES Only the tips of the outer coat should show dark markings; this coloration is evident on the upper part of the body, and extends down the flanks, legs, and tail. The underparts, from the chin to the tail, should be pure white, and free from any sign of tipping.
• REMARK The Chinchilla Longhair legacy may still be apparent in kittens before they acquire their adult coats.

green eyes essential •

FUR TYPE: short, dense, and crisp

tipping creates sparkling effect •

• red nose

no barring on legs •

| Longhair option | Chinchilla Persian Longhair | Temperament | Placid and friendly |

| Country of origin | Great Britain | Ancestry | Non-pedigree Shorthairs | Origins | 1880s |

RED TIPPED

British Shorthairs in any of the self and tortoiseshell colours can be bred in a tipped form.
• FEATURES Here the tipping to the fur is red, offset against the white undercoat and otherwise predominantly white hairs. All forms, apart from the Black Tipped, can have eye coloration ranging from deep gold to orange or copper.
• REMARK Some cats show heavier tipping than others, and these are preferred to the paler individuals provided that they show no evidence of tabby markings.

red skin encircles eyes •

tipping evident on tail •

• white underparts contrast with tipping elsewhere

• short red nose

FUR TYPE: short, dense, and crisp

• evenly distributed red tipping

tipping less prominent towards paws •

| Longhair option | Red Shell Cameo Persian Longhair | Temperament | Placid and friendly |

COLOUR POINTED BRITISH SHORTHAIR

T HESE CATS, which have been recognized as a breed in Britain only since 1991, have been developed to conform in type to British Shorthairs while displaying Siamese-type coloured points. Unfortunately, the name given to this breed is similar to that of the Colorpoint Shorthair grouping in the United States: the latter is quite separate from Colour Pointed British Shorthairs, however, being comprised only of cats of distinctly Siamese type.

Country of origin	Great Britain	Ancestry	British Shorthairs x Himalayan	Origins	1980s

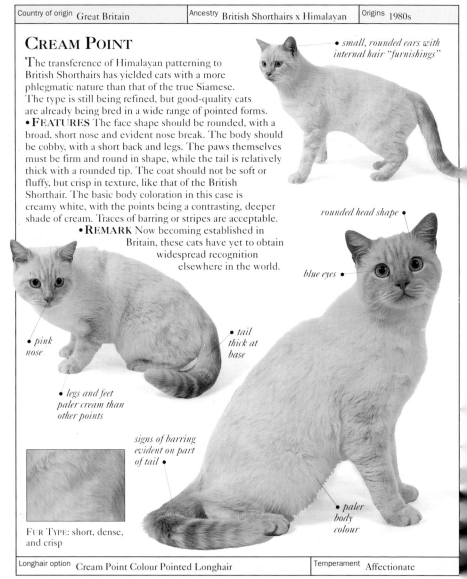

CREAM POINT

The transference of Himalayan patterning to British Shorthairs has yielded cats with a more phlegmatic nature than that of the true Siamese. The type is still being refined, but good-quality cats are already being bred in a wide range of pointed forms.

• **FEATURES** The face shape should be rounded, with a broad, short nose and evident nose break. The body should be cobby, with a short back and legs. The paws themselves must be firm and round in shape, while the tail is relatively thick with a rounded tip. The coat should not be soft or fluffy, but crisp in texture, like that of the British Shorthair. The basic body coloration in this case is creamy white, with the points being a contrasting, deeper shade of cream. Traces of barring or stripes are acceptable.

• **REMARK** Now becoming established in Britain, these cats have yet to obtain widespread recognition elsewhere in the world.

• *small, rounded ears with internal hair "furnishings"*

• *rounded head shape*

• *blue eyes*

• *pink nose*

• *tail thick at base*

• *legs and feet paler cream than other points*

signs of barring evident on part of tail •

• *paler body colour*

FUR TYPE: short, dense, and crisp

Longhair option	Cream Point Colour Pointed Longhair	Temperament	Affectionate

| Country of origin | Great Britain | Ancestry | British Shorthairs x Himalayan | Origins | 1980s |

BLUE POINT

The popularity of these cats is likely to increase rapidly as the potential within the group is explored further by breeders.
• **FEATURES** The body coloration of the Blue Point should be a glacial shade of white, contrasting with the medium blue coloration of the points themselves.
• **REMARK** Coat quality is a vital feature of these cats; it must be short, and any tendency towards a soft or woolly coat is a fault.

thick neck

FUR TYPE: short, dense, and crisp

good contrast between points and coat colour •

medium blue •

• firm, round paws

| Longhair option | Blue Point Colour Pointed Longhair | Temperament | Affectionate |

| Country of origin | Great Britain | Ancestry | British Shorthairs x Himalayan | Origins | 1980s |

SEAL POINT

The blue eyes that are characteristic of Colour Pointed British Shorthairs must be round in shape and set wide apart on the head, revealing no trace of the Siamese ancestry of these cats. In the case of the Seal Point, though, heavier dark shading on the flanks is quite common, especially as the young cat starts to mature.
• **FEATURES** The coloration of the body should create an overall impression of light, warm fawn. The points are a contrasting and significantly darker shade of seal-brown.
• **REMARK** The shape of the head may alter somewhat in mature males, which develop noticeable jowls.

clearly defined mask •

• point coloration of even depth

• pale fawn

FUR TYPE: short, dense, and crisp

• deep, broad chest

| Longhair option | Seal Point Colour Pointed Longhair | Temperament | Affectionate |

Country of origin Great Britain	Ancestry British Shorthairs x Himalayan	Origins 1980s

RED POINT

These cats are easy to care for, a weekly combing being adequate to maintain their coats in good condition when they are not moulting. Regular stroking also helps to remove dead hairs.
• **FEATURES** The apricot-white body is offset by the red points; however, the contrast between the points and the body coloration is less distinctive in this case than in the darker coloured varieties.
• **REMARK** Internal ear furnishings should not be excessive in these cats.

pink nose pad •

• *blue eyes*

• *rounded tip to tail*

tabby markings may be present, especially on legs and feet •

FUR TYPE: short, dense, and crisp

Longhair option Red Point Colour Pointed Longhair	Temperament Affectionate

Country of origin Great Britain	Ancestry British Shorthairs x Himalayan	Origins 1980s

CHOCOLATE POINT

The large eyes of British Shorthairs are always expressive, but the contrasting colour of the mask emphasizes this feature. The eyes should be quite widely spaced, so that there is at least the width of an eye between them.
• **FEATURES** Another of the more darkly pointed forms, the Chocolate has an ivory body colour and contrasting milk-chocolate points. These should be of an even colour, and clearly defined against the body.
• **REMARK** A level bite is essential in these cats, as in other British Shorthairs.

FUR TYPE: short, dense, and crisp

• *mask clearly marked against body coloration*

small ears with rounded tips •

tail thick at base •

• *solid coloured tail*

Longhair option Chocolate Point Colour Pointed Longhair	Temperament Affectionate

Country of origin Great Britain	Ancestry British Shorthairs x Himalayan	Origins 1980s

BLUE-CREAM POINT

The dilute form of the Tortie, the Blue-cream Point is essentially a female-only variety, as in the case of other tortoiseshell breeds.

• **FEATURES** There may be signs of pale blue or cream coloration on the back and down the sides of an otherwise whitish body. Paw pads may be blue, pink or a combination.

• **REMARK** Blue points are broken by cream markings.

blue and cream coloration most apparent on back •

round face with full cheeks

• blue and cream areas

FUR TYPE: short, dense, and crisp

• blue points should be broken with cream markings

round, firm paws •

Longhair option Blue-cream Point Colour Pointed Longhair	Temperament Affectionate

Country of origin Great Britain	Ancestry British Shorthairs x Himalayan	Origins 1980s

SEAL TORTIE POINT

Another tortoiseshell variant, again showing the characteristic blue eyes of this group. These friendly cats invariably prove good mothers.

• **FEATURES** The basic body coloration is fawn, with shadings of warm brown and red on the sides and over the back. All the points should be seal-brown in colour, broken with various areas of differing shades of red.

• **REMARK** The highly individual markings of these cats also extend to the nose and pads.

short, level back, contributing to breed's cobby appearance •

• short, broad nose

• points broken with varying shades of red

FUR TYPE: short, dense, and crisp

• mottled seal colour

Longhair option Seal Tortie Point Colour Pointed Longhair	Temperament Affectionate

EXOTIC

THE ORIGINS of these cats date back to the attempts of American Shorthair breeders to introduce the coat-texture qualities of the Longhair into their cats. Some fanciers liked the resulting hybrids and decided to use them as the basis for a new breed. The Exotic Shorthair was first recognized in 1967. Although Burmese were used in the early days, out-crosses with only Persian or American Shorthairs are permitted in American pedigrees today.

Country of origin USA	Ancestry American Shorthair x Longhair	Origins 1960s

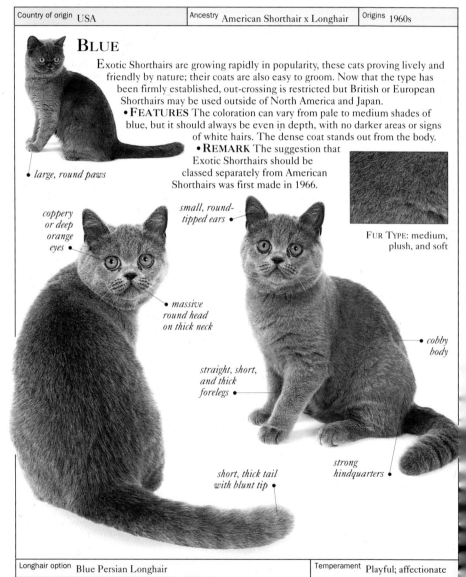

BLUE

Exotic Shorthairs are growing rapidly in popularity, these cats proving lively and friendly by nature; their coats are also easy to groom. Now that the type has been firmly established, out-crossing is restricted but British or European Shorthairs may be used outside of North America and Japan.
• **FEATURES** The coloration can vary from pale to medium shades of blue, but it should always be even in depth, with no darker areas or signs of white hairs. The dense coat stands out from the body.
• **REMARK** The suggestion that Exotic Shorthairs should be classed separately from American Shorthairs was first made in 1966.

• *large, round paws*

FUR TYPE: medium, plush, and soft

coppery or deep orange eyes •

small, round-tipped ears •

• *massive round head on thick neck*

• *cobby body*

straight, short, and thick forelegs •

short, thick tail with blunt tip •

strong hindquarters •

Longhair option Blue Persian Longhair	Temperament Playful; affectionate

Country of origin USA	Ancestry American Shorthair x Longhair	Origins 1960s

BLACK

These cats resemble Longhairs in all but coat length; their well-spaced ears are small with rounded tips and set so they tilt slightly forwards.
• **FEATURES** The black coloration should be of a deep, lustrous shade, with no hint of a rusty hue in adult cats. There must be no signs of barring or white hairs.
• **REMARK** The coloration of kittens may be slightly grey or rusty, but this improves with age.

FUR TYPE: medium, plush, and soft

• broad, short, snub nose, with noticeable break in profile

thick tail •

• deep-chested body, set low on legs

• tight, round paws

strong legs •

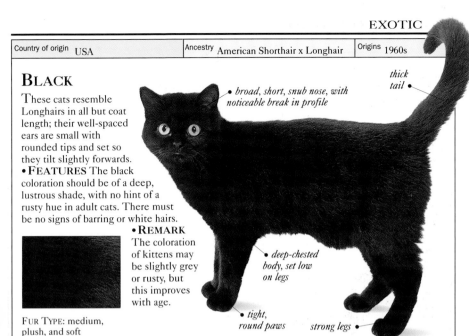

Longhair option Black Persian Longhair		Temperament Playful; affectionate

Country of origin USA	Ancestry American Shorthair x Longhair	Origins 1960s

BLUE POINT COLOURPOINT

These attractive colourpoints, sometimes dubbed "panda bears" because of their large, round eyes and cuddly appearance, have yet to receive wide recognition, but they are growing in numbers. They should have a good undercoat, combined with guard hairs of medium length.
• **FEATURES** The Blue Point is characterized by the colour of its points, contrasting with an off-white body colour and lighter underparts.
• **REMARK** The massive head and short, stubby nose distinguish these cats from other short-haired colourpoints.

• well-spaced, large, round, appealing eyes

• no kink in tail

FUR TYPE: medium, plush, and soft

• blue tail

• blue nose complements point colour

• dense fur stands out

Longhair option Blue Point Colour Pointed Longhair	Temperament Playful; affectionate

Country of origin USA	Ancestry American Shorthair x Longhair	Origins 1960s

SHADED GOLDEN

Selective breeding has helped to ensure that the type of these cats matches that of their long-haired ancestors. They are also similarly good-natured. Their dense fur must be free-standing and never so long that it hangs down like that of the Longhair.

• **FEATURES** The shading results from either seal-brown or black tipping on the golden yellow fur. The undercoat varies from apricot to light gold.

• **REMARK** It is quite usual for exotic kittens to appear rather indolent, compared with those of other breeds.

• *broad and powerful jaws, with full cheeks*

FUR TYPE: medium, plush, and soft

• *short, thick legs*

Longhair option Shaded Golden Persian Longhair	Temperament Playful; affectionate

Country of origin USA	Ancestry American Shorthair x Longhair	Origins 1960s

SILVER TORTIE CLASSIC TABBY

Both tabby and tortie patterning should be clearly apparent in these cats. The Silver Tabby combination is one of the most striking, offset in this case with shades of red.

• **FEATURES** The dense black tabby markings should stand out well against the clear silver ground colour. The underparts tend to be paler than other areas of the body, while unbroken black lines, or "necklaces", extend across the neck and top of the chest.

• **REMARK** The description "exotic" was chosen for these cats to distinguish them from the American Shorthair and to emphasize their link with the imported Longhair.

• *ears set low on head*

• *deep chest and massive shoulders*

• *black tip to tail*

• *oyster-shaped tabby patterning*

FUR TYPE: medium, plush, and soft

Longhair option Silver Tortie Classic Tabby Persian Longhair	Temperament Playful; affectionate

Country of origin USA	Ancestry American Shorthair x Longhair	Origins 1960s

LILAC TABBY POINT COLOURPOINT

This particular variety has not become widely recognized yet, although it is a very attractive combination. The coat in this case, as in other Exotics, should be dense and stand out from the body. The nose is broader and shorter than in other shorthairs, reflecting the breed's Longhair ancestry.

• **FEATURES** The warm, lilac tabby markings, contrasting with a magnolia-white body colour, are offset in this case by the frosty grey of the points. Darker shading on the back and sides of the body may be present.

• **REMARK** The tail of the Exotic Shorthair is normally kept straight and beneath the level of the back when the cat is moving.

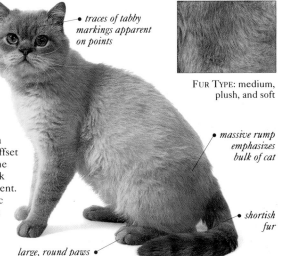

traces of tabby markings apparent on points

FUR TYPE: medium, plush, and soft

massive rump emphasizes bulk of cat

shortish fur

large, round paws

Longhair option Lilac Tabby Point Colour Pointed Longhair	Temperament Playful; affectionate

Country of origin USA	Ancestry American Shorthair x Longhair	Origins 1960s

BROWN SPOTTED

The "M"-shaped tabby marking is clearly apparent on the head, with lines running backwards down to the shoulders. The ears, edged with black, have a central, coppery brown "thumb-print".

• **FEATURES** The dense, black, spotted pattern contrasts with a coppery brown agouti ground colour. The round, oval, or rosette-shaped spots should be well defined, extending over the body and legs. Spots can be present on the tail, though this usually shows a ringed pattern.

• **REMARK** The Exotic Shorthair is sometimes described as a "Longhair in its petticoat", and certainly, these cats moult quite heavily compared with other shorthairs.

ears are directed forwards on the head

eye colour can be deep gold, orange, or copper

very dense hair stands away from body

spotted tail

FUR TYPE: medium, plush, and soft

Longhair option Brown Spotted Persian Longhair	Temperament Playful; affectionate

MANX

IT HAS BEEN SUGGESTED that the Manx breed may be descended from cats that swam ashore to the Isle of Man, off England's west coast, from a shipwrecked Spanish galleon in 1588. It is more likely, however, that the breed arose from cats native to the island. Although absolute absence of tail is essential in a true Manx (the Rumpy), cats with varying degrees of tail (Risers, Stumpies, and Longies) are useful in Manx breeding programmes.

Country of origin Great Britain	Ancestry Non-pedigree Shorthairs	Origins 1600s

WHITE

There is no trace of a tail in the Rumpy Manx, just a hollow where the tail would normally start. In the Rumpy Riser, however, some vertebrae can be discerned in this region. The vertebral column of the Manx tends to differ from that of other cats, the shortened vertebrae giving the breed a curved profile.
• **FEATURES** Manx are powerfully built cats that do not appear to suffer greatly from the lack of a tail. They have been bred in a vast range of colours, although those showing Siamese-type markings are not recognized by all associations. The coat in this case should be pure white. The "double coat" consists of a dense, short undercoat, with a coarser, slightly longer top-coat. During the summer months, the undercoat is shed, resulting in a sleeker appearance.
• **REMARK** Manx are traditionally long-lived cats and show few signs of ageing.

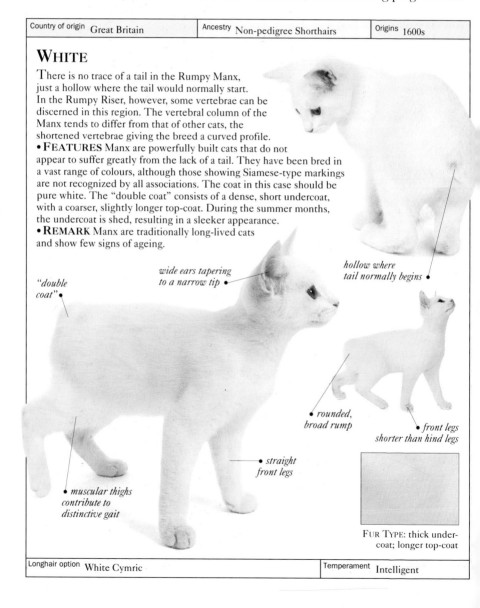

"double coat"

wide ears tapering to a narrow tip

hollow where tail normally begins

rounded, broad rump

front legs shorter than hind legs

straight front legs

muscular thighs contribute to distinctive gait

FUR TYPE: thick under-coat; longer top-coat

Longhair option White Cymric	Temperament Intelligent

| Country of origin Great Britain | Ancestry Non-pedigree Shorthairs | Origins 1600s |

BLACK AND WHITE

Manx have always been popular, and have become something of a symbol of their native Isle of Man, featuring on the coinage of the island.

• **FEATURES** The quality of the double coat is considered to be more important in Manx than their colour or markings.

• **REMARK** With their longer hind legs, Manx have an unusual hopping walk; this is deemed a fault in all but kittens in the United States.

• curved back with rump higher than shoulder

• clearly defined coloured areas

FUR TYPE: thick under-coat; longer top-coat

| Longhair option Black and White Cymric | Temperament Intelligent |

| Country of origin Great Britain | Ancestry Non-pedigree Shorthairs | Origins 1600s |

RED CLASSIC TABBY

Tabby markings are not uncommon in the Manx; in fact, the first Manx champion was actually a Silver Tabby called *Bonhaki*.

• **FEATURES** The basic coloration of these cats is red rather than orange, with the tabby patterning clearly discernible against the ground colour. The markings on each of the different forms of tabby should be dense and clearly defined.

• **REMARK** Breeding Manx cats is a slow and frustrating process. The litter sizes are small and some of the kittens are likely to show traces of tail of variable length. It is important to check that the anal opening is properly formed in newly born Manx kittens.

rounded rump •

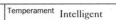

compact body shape •

• darker tabby markings

tabby rings •

• rabbit-like posture

FUR TYPE: thick under-coat; longer top-coat

| Longhair option Red Classic Tabby Cymric | Temperament Intelligent |

Country of origin Great Britain	Ancestry Non-pedigree Shorthairs	Origins 1600s

RED CLASSIC TABBY AND WHITE

Rumpy Manx are paired to cats showing at least a trace of a tail because the gene responsible for taillessness is also linked to defects in kittens bred from like-to-like pairings; these tend to result in the death of the kittens, either before or just after birth.

• **FEATURES** In this case, there is a combination of red and white coloration, with the darker red, classic pattern, tabby markings superimposed on the red areas.

• **REMARK** The hair beneath the hocks on the hind legs of Manx may be rather thin, as they often rest on their legs rather than on their paws.

medium ears, tapering to rounded tip

large, round, expressive eyes

great depth to flanks

clear delineation between red and white areas

no trace of tail

FUR TYPE: thick under-coat; longer top-coat

Longhair option Red Classic Tabby and White Cymric	Temperament Intelligent

Country of origin Great Britain	Ancestry Non-pedigree Shorthairs	Origins 1600s

TORTOISESHELL

Manx kittens are at risk from *spina bifida*, and possibly from constipation in later life, because of their particular spinal structure.

• **FEATURES** This cat shows the typical tortoiseshell coloration of black and light and dark red. This Stumpy's tail is long enough to be moved, but is not as long as that of a Longie. These cats are useful in breeding programmes, although not always accepted for exhibiting.

• **REMARK** A cattery has been set up on the Isle of Man, to preserve the Manx on their native island.

furnishings of hair within ears

clear evidence of short tail visible here

solid body profile

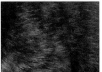

FUR TYPE: thick under-coat; longer top-coat

Longhair option Tortoiseshell Cymric	Temperament Intelligent

JAPANESE BOBTAIL

CATS WITH DEFORMED TAILS are well documented in various parts of Asia; the genes responsible for this mutation were probably introduced with the early cats taken to Japan from China about 1,000 years ago. Asian cats with stubby and kinked tails may share a common ancestry with the Japanese Bobtail, but there is no connection between the Bobtail and the Manx: these are now known to be entirely separate mutations. This breed has a long history in its native Japan, but is still scarce in other parts of the world. The tail of the Japanese Bobtail is about 10 cm (4 in) long and is relatively inflexible; the joints are virtually fused. It is usually kept curled close to the body when the cat is resting, but when walking, the tail may be held upright.

Country of origin Japan	Ancestry Non-pedigree Shorthairs	Origins 1000s

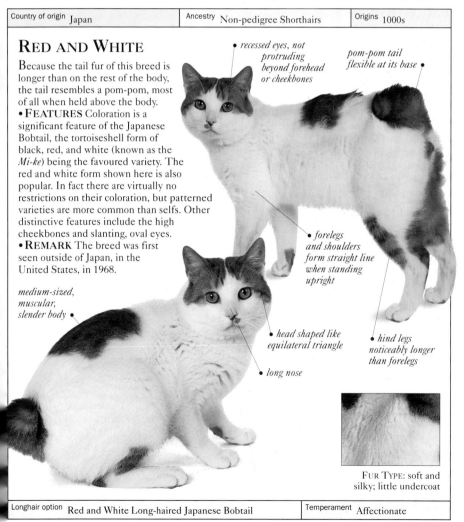

RED AND WHITE

Because the tail fur of this breed is longer than on the rest of the body, the tail resembles a pom-pom, most of all when held above the body.
• **FEATURES** Coloration is a significant feature of the Japanese Bobtail, the tortoiseshell form of black, red, and white (known as the *Mi-ke*) being the favoured variety. The red and white form shown here is also popular. In fact there are virtually no restrictions on their coloration, but patterned varieties are more common than selfs. Other distinctive features include the high cheekbones and slanting, oval eyes.
• **REMARK** The breed was first seen outside of Japan, in the United States, in 1968.

medium-sized, muscular, slender body •

• *recessed eyes, not protruding beyond forehead or cheekbones*

pom-pom tail flexible at its base •

• *forelegs and shoulders form straight line when standing upright*

• *head shaped like equilateral triangle*

• *hind legs noticeably longer than forelegs*

• *long nose*

FUR TYPE: soft and silky; little undercoat

Longhair option Red and White Long-haired Japanese Bobtail	Temperament Affectionate

SCOTTISH FOLD

I N 1951, A KITTEN with folded ears appeared in a litter born to a farm cat. Originating close to Coupar Angus in Scotland, these cats have since become known as Scottish Folds. The original cat, christened *Susie*, gave birth to another white kitten with folded ears. It was then that a local shepherd, named William Ross, decided to try and establish a whole new breed with the folded ear characteristic. He started with this kitten, who was called *Snooks*.

Country of origin Scotland	Ancestry Non-pedigree Shorthairs	Origins 1951

BLACK AND WHITE

During the early days of the breed's development, in the 1950's, crossings were undertaken with other non-pedigree shorthairs, and only later were British Shorthair cats introduced to help develop the Scottish Fold bloodline.
• **FEATURES** The folded ears are directed forwards but, because the flaps are also folded down, the tips of the ears point in the direction of the nose. A less obvious feature of the breed today is its thickened, short legs, which have been actively discouraged by out-crossings to other cat breeds.
• **REMARK** Fears that the ear shape would encourage ear infections have proved to be false.

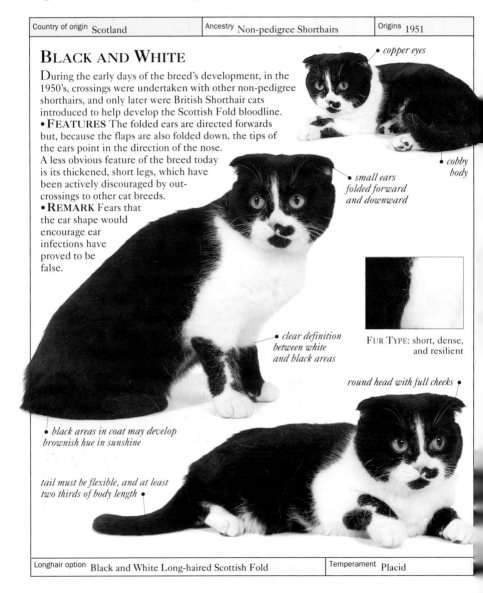

• *copper eyes*

• *cobby body*

• *small ears folded forward and downward*

• *clear definition between white and black areas*

FUR TYPE: short, dense, and resilient

round head with full cheeks •

• *black areas in coat may develop brownish hue in sunshine*

tail must be flexible, and at least two thirds of body length •

Longhair option Black and White Long-haired Scottish Fold	Temperament Placid

Country of origin Scotland	Ancestry Non-pedigree Shorthairs	Origins 1951

BLUE AND WHITE

The appearance of these distinctive cats attracts great interest although, ironically, they are now far more common outside Great Britain than in their Scottish homeland. This has arisen largely because the breed was not recognized by the GCCF, with the result that it attracted little interest from breeders within the United Kingdom.

• **FEATURES** In this case, the blue coloration may vary from a pale to a medium shade, depending on the individual cat, and contrasts with the white areas in the coat. The blue fur may become slightly rusty in colour before a moult. Bi-coloured forms of the Scottish Fold tend to be the most popular, especially where there is good contrast in coloration, as seen in this case.

• **REMARK** This breed was accepted for registration in the United States in 1973, and by the CA of Britain in 1984.

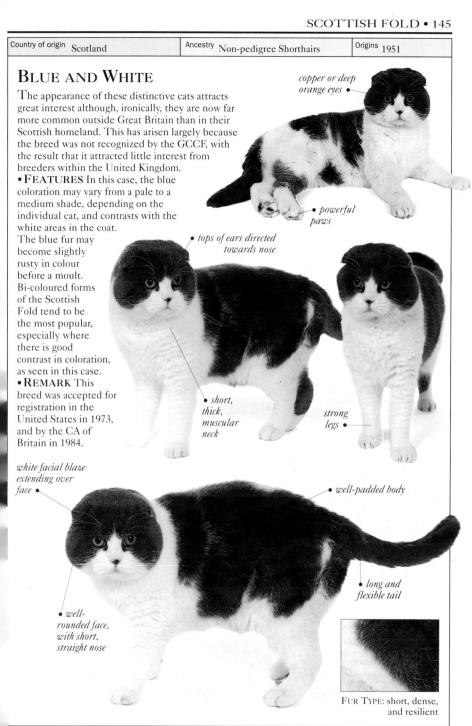

copper or deep orange eyes

powerful paws

tops of ears directed towards nose

short, thick, muscular neck

strong legs

white facial blaze extending over face

well-padded body

long and flexible tail

well-rounded face, with short, straight nose

FUR TYPE: short, dense, and resilient

Longhair option Blue and White Long-haired Scottish Fold	Temperament Placid

Country of origin Scotland	Ancestry Non-pedigree Shorthairs	Origins 1951

TORTIE AND WHITE

Scottish Folds have been bred in a wide range of colours and patterns. It has been relatively easy to produce so many forms because this is a dominant mutation: only one Scottish Fold parent is needed to produce a proportion of similar offspring.

• **FEATURES** The typical tortoiseshell patterning is clearly evident here, being broken by white areas of fur.

• **REMARK** All the kittens in a litter have normal ears at first, but the Folds become recognizable by their ears when they are about two to three weeks old.

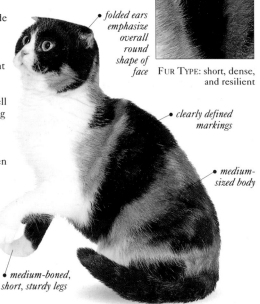

• *folded ears emphasize overall round shape of face*

FUR TYPE: short, dense, and resilient

• *clearly defined markings*

• *medium-sized body*

• *long, flexible tail tapering along length*

• *medium-boned, short, sturdy legs*

Longhair option Tortie and White Long-haired Scottish Fold	Temperament Placid

Country of origin Scotland	Ancestry Non-pedigree Shorthairs	Origins 1951

BLACK SMOKE AND WHITE

The careful registration policy adopted by the Cat Association of Britain insists that one parent must be a non-Fold. Further checks have been made in the standard which penalizes short, inflexible tails or excessively thick limbs.

• **FEATURES** The mainly white under-coat and black guard hairs contrast with the variable pure white areas, depending on the individual cat.

• **REMARK** British Shorthair pairings tend to produce Scottish Folds with rounder eyes and thicker coats than those that result from American Shorthair crosses.

• *full, rounded cheeks and muzzle*

FUR TYPE: short, dense, and resilient

Longhair option Black Smoke and White Long-haired Scottish Fold	Temperament Placid

SNOWSHOE

THIS BREED WAS developed during the 1960s by Dorothy Hinds-Daugherty, a breeder of Siamese cats from Philadelphia. She faced some opposition at first because of fears that the characteristic white markings of the Snowshoe could become widespread in	Siamese bloodlines as a result of ill-judged crossings. Progress was rather slow until the 1980s, but now these cats are bred in various countries around the world. In spite of the white paws, which give the breed its name, their ancestry does not include Birmans.

Country of origin	USA	Ancestry	American Shorthairs x Siamese	Origins	1960s

SEAL AND WHITE POINT

The muscular, relatively large body of the Snowshoe stems from its American Shorthair ancestry, whereas the body length is a reflection of the Siamese stock. Males are often distinctly larger than females, weighing up to 5.4 kg (12 lb).

• **FEATURES** With white areas superimposed on the traditional Siamese patterning, an ever-increasing range of colours is being bred displaying these markings. The white boots on the forelegs must reach the ankles and extend just below the hocks on the hind legs. In older cats, the coloration tends to darken, but contrast between the point and body colour is vital.

• **REMARK** Kittens are white at birth, and it may take two years for the markings to become fully apparent.

tail tapers to tip •

• white paws

• strong, muscular body

FUR TYPE: glossy and quite short

seal-coloured points •

outline of head shaped like equilateral triangle •

• blue eyes

• medium-length muzzle and high cheekbones

• tail length should equal distance from shoulders to base of tail

Longhair option	None		Temperament	Active

AMERICAN SHORTHAIR

T HE AMERICAN SHORTHAIR has evolved from European cats taken to North America during the early years of exploration and settlement. Ships' cats, highly valued as a means of controlling the rodent population on board, travelled the world and, not surprisingly, some were occasionally left at ports-of-call. Also, the early settlers would almost certainly have taken cats with them, not just as pets, but also for their hunting skills.

Prior to the first European voyages of exploration in the 1500s, there was no indigenous domestic cat population in North America, but the number of cats increased as permanent settlements were established. As these cats have evolved, they have acquired a slightly different appearance from their British and European counterparts, with less rounded faces and slightly larger bodies.

Country of origin USA	Ancestry Non-pedigree Shorthairs	Origins 1600s

BLACK

American Shorthairs were allowed to evolve without undue human interference, particularly in the early days, and they have developed into a versatile, hardy breed with a friendly and intelligent disposition. Their dense coats provide them with good protection especially if they are hunting in undergrowth.

• **FEATURES** The most significant distinction between American and European Shorthairs is the shape of the face, which is less rounded, and with a slightly longer nose. Overall, the American Shorthairs are also slightly larger than their European counterparts.

• **REMARK** With their robust natures, American Shorthairs do not thrive in an indoor environment and will benefit from being able to to explore out-of-doors, even in a relatively small garden.

• *medium ears*

• *striking, round eyes*

• *dense, coal-black coat with no rusty hues*

muscular chest and shoulders •

• *black nose*

• *firm, round paws*

• *medium-to-large body*

broad tail tapers to blunt tip •

FUR TYPE: short and thick, with hard texture

Longhair option Black Maine Coon	Temperament Independent

Country of origin USA	Ancestry Non-pedigree Shorthairs	Origins 1600s

ODD-EYED WHITE

The White American Shorthair can be bred in three varieties, differing only in eye coloration. However, deafness is associated with the blue-eyed form and, in this case, the ear on the side of the blue eye may be afflicted.
• **FEATURES** Overall, these cats should give the impression of being feline athletes, with their muscular bodies clearly outlined beneath the short fur.
• **REMARK** Despite existing for centuries in an unrefined state, the first American Shorthair was registered in about 1900; even this, however, was actually a cat born in Great Britain.

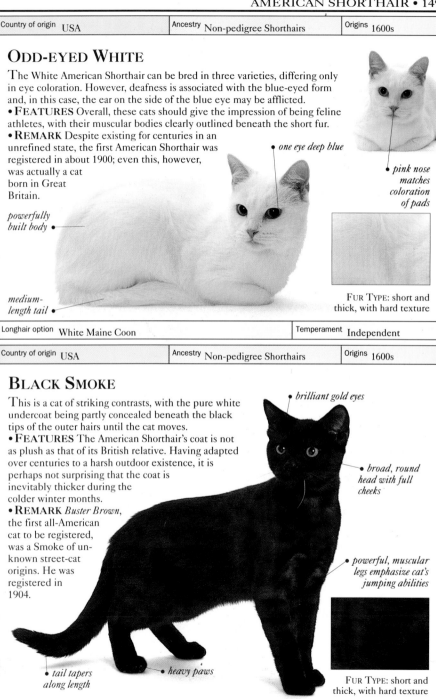

one eye deep blue

pink nose matches coloration of pads

powerfully built body

medium-length tail

FUR TYPE: short and thick, with hard texture

Longhair option White Maine Coon	Temperament Independent

Country of origin USA	Ancestry Non-pedigree Shorthairs	Origins 1600s

BLACK SMOKE

This is a cat of striking contrasts, with the pure white undercoat being partly concealed beneath the black tips of the outer hairs until the cat moves.
• **FEATURES** The American Shorthair's coat is not as plush as that of its British relative. Having adapted over centuries to a harsh outdoor existence, it is perhaps not surprising that the coat is inevitably thicker during the colder winter months.
• **REMARK** *Buster Brown*, the first all-American cat to be registered, was a Smoke of unknown street-cat origins. He was registered in 1904.

brilliant gold eyes

broad, round head with full cheeks

powerful, muscular legs emphasize cat's jumping abilities

tail tapers along length

heavy paws

FUR TYPE: short and thick, with hard texture

Longhair option Black Smoke Maine Coon	Temperament Independent

| Country of origin USA | Ancestry Non-pedigree Shorthairs | Origins 1600s |

RED CLASSIC TABBY

unbroken line extends from corner of each eye

This form of the American Shorthair tends to be slightly larger than its British counterpart. The Red is always popular, with the deep, rich red markings displayed against a paler, red ground colour.
• **FEATURES** When viewed from above, the shoulder markings should appear rather like a butterfly, with the outline of the wings clearly visible. A dark line runs through the centre of the "butterfly" down to the tail, with two darker stripes on either side, separated by areas of the paler ground colour.

brilliant gold eyes

• **REMARK** Grooming is simple, and helps to emphasize contrasts in the coat.

blotched patterning

FUR TYPE: short and thick, with hard texture

| Longhair option Red Classic Tabby Maine Coon | Temperament Independent |

| Country of origin USA | Ancestry Non-pedigree Shorthairs | Origins 1600s |

BROWN CLASSIC TABBY

stripes along back

The Brown Classic Tabby tends to be less popular than other, more striking tabby forms of American Shorthair, although some top examples of this form have come to prominence within the American cat fancy.
• **FEATURES** This variety is characterized by a coppery brown ground colour, broken by a dense black pattern of markings, the latter surrounded by a lighter ring of of coppery brown.
• **REMARK** The development of this breed was placed in jeopardy in the 1960s by matings with Longhairs and Burmese. Such pairings have now been outlawed, and American Shorthairs once more conform to their traditional type.

shortish, muscular neck

muscular legs emphasize cat's athletic nature

leg length should correspond to depth of body

FUR TYPE: short and thick, with hard texture

| Longhair option Brown Classic Tabby Maine Coon | Temperament Independent |

Country of origin	USA	Ancestry	Non-pedigree Shorthairs	Origins	1600s

BROWN PATCHED TABBY

The American Shorthair is a breed well equipped for survival: its muzzle length is ideally suited to catching prey, and its moderately short and square shape means that there is considerable strength in the cat's jaws.

• **FEATURES** The unusual patterning of these tabbies results from the presence of tortoiseshell markings superimposed both on their basic coloration and on the tabby markings. "Patching" describes the appearance of red or cream areas of colour, or sometimes both, in the coat.

• **REMARK** These cats are sometimes known as "torbies" which is simply an abbreviated form of "tortie tabby".

cheeks less well developed in kittens

random patterning, varying from one individual to another

tabby markings apparent

FUR TYPE: short and thick with hard texture

Longhair option	Brown Patched Tabby Maine Coon	Temperament	Independent

Country of origin	USA	Ancestry	Non-pedigree Shorthairs	Origins	1600s

RED AND WHITE VAN TABBY

muscular shoulders

The excellent temperament of the American Shorthair, coupled with its healthy disposition and wide range of colours, gives plenty of choice to the intending exhibitor or pet owner. Years of fending for themselves in the wild have endowed this breed with a natural intelligence.

• **FEATURES** While these tabbies do not differ in type from other American Shorthairs, their pattern of markings is distinctive. Mainly white, their darker colouring and tabby markings are restricted to the head, legs, and tail.

• **REMARK** The description "Van" originated from the Turkish Van breed (*see pp.78–79*), which shows this patterning.

predominantly white body

brilliant blue eyes

FUR TYPE: short and thick with hard texture

tabby barring on legs

pink pads

even tabby rings apparent on tail

Longhair option	Red and White Van Tabby Maine Coon	Temperament	Independent

Country of origin USA	Ancestry Non-pedigree Shorthairs	Origins 1600s

CREAM MACKEREL TABBY

Tabby forms of the American Shorthair are among the most popular; their coat texture emphasizes the pattern of markings with excellent contrast. The mackerel tabby is sometimes described as the "natural" or "wild" type, because it occurs in wild cats.

• **FEATURES** The markings in this case are dark buff against a pale cream ground colour.

• **REMARK** In the mackerel tabby, two broken lines run parallel with an unbroken line along the spine; narrow lines run down the body.

dark buff-cream markings on pale cream ground colour •

• characteristic "M"-shaped marking on head

• mackerel striping

• even barring on legs

barred tail •

FUR TYPE: short and thick, with hard texture

Longhair option Cream Mackerel Tabby Maine Coon	Temperament Independent

Country of origin USA	Ancestry Non-pedigree Shorthairs	Origins 1600s

BLUE MACKEREL TABBY

The pattern of markings should be symmetrical. The underparts are spotted, as in the classic tabby form, and well-marked individuals show a number of darker rings on the neck and upper chest. The mackerel lines should be numerous, but should not overlap.

• **FEATURES** This variety is characterized by a pale ground colour, which extends to the lips and the chin, with corresponding darker blue tabby markings. In this case, both the cat's nose and paw pads are a subtle, contrasting shade of rose-red.

• **REMARK** The tabby markings should be well defined, with good contrast between the light and dark fur.

FUR TYPE: short and thick, with hard texture

• thick neck

barred legs •

deep blue markings encircle tail •

"necklaces" •

Longhair option Blue Mackerel Tabby Maine Coon	Temperament Independent

Country of origin USA	Ancestry Non-pedigree Shorthairs	Origins 1600s

BLUE-CREAM

This is the dilute form of the tortoiseshell, some-times described as the Blue Tortie. In type, these shorthairs should not differ from other colours although, being an essentially female-only form like other torties, they will not show as much development of the cheeks as can be seen in some male American Shorthairs.

• **FEATURES** No tabby markings should be apparent in this case. The muzzle must be square, and a dip in the nose profile is essential. Nose coloration can be blue, pink, or a combination of both colours.

• **REMARK** The leg length of the American Shorthair should correspond to the body depth.

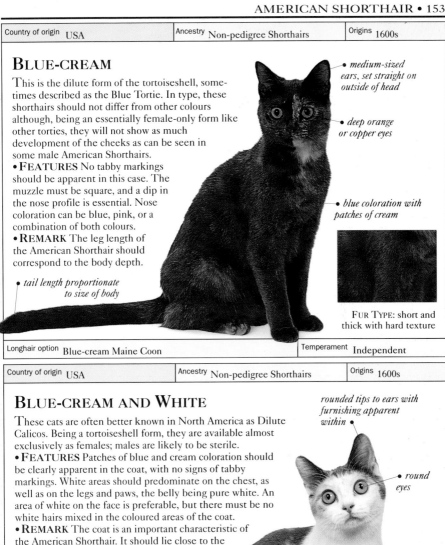

medium-sized ears, set straight on outside of head

deep orange or copper eyes

blue coloration with patches of cream

tail length proportionate to size of body

FUR TYPE: short and thick with hard texture

Longhair option Blue-cream Maine Coon	Temperament Independent

Country of origin USA	Ancestry Non-pedigree Shorthairs	Origins 1600s

BLUE-CREAM AND WHITE

These cats are often better known in North America as Dilute Calicos. Being a tortoiseshell form, they are available almost exclusively as females; males are likely to be sterile.

• **FEATURES** Patches of blue and cream coloration should be clearly apparent in the coat, with no signs of tabby markings. White areas should predominate on the chest, as well as on the legs and paws, the belly being pure white. An area of white on the face is preferable, but there must be no white hairs mixed in the coloured areas of the coat.

• **REMARK** The coat is an important characteristic of the American Shorthair. It should lie close to the body with no signs of a fluffy undercoat.

rounded tips to ears with furnishing apparent within

round eyes

muscular chest

clearly defined patches of colour

feet should be white with no trace of blue or cream

FUR TYPE: short and thick, with hard texture

Longhair option Blue-cream and White Maine Coon	Temperament Independent

Country of origin	USA	Ancestry	Non-pedigree Shorthairs	Origins	1600s

CREAM CLASSIC TABBY

American Shorthairs are popular in their homeland but are not common elsewhere. The tabby forms were among the notable winners of the 1960s, and helped to promote the breed.

• **FEATURES** Clear definition is vital: in this case the buff cream markings stand out well against the pale cream ground colour. Markings must be symmetrical.

• **REMARK** Having evolved through a process of natural selection, the urge to hunt is still very strong in these cats.

orange eyes

widely spaced ears with rounded tips

barring on legs

ground colour paler than markings

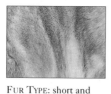

unbroken "necklaces" on chest

FUR TYPE: short and thick, with hard texture

darker rings on tail

Longhair option	Cream Classic Tabby Maine Coon	Temperament	Independent

Country of origin	USA	Ancestry	Non-pedigree Shorthairs	Origins	1600s

SILVER CLASSIC TABBY

The stunning appearance of these cats results partly from the way in which the coat lies close to the body.

• **FEATURES** The ground colour is an attractive silvery white, offset by dense black markings. Great efforts have been made by breeders to eliminate traces of tarnished coloration in these cats.

• **REMARK** The name for this entire group of cats was changed from "Domestic Shorthair" to "American Shorthair" after a Silver Tabby won the US Cat of the Year title in 1965.

"M"-shaped marking on head clearly visible

brick-red nose

FUR TYPE: short and thick, with hard texture

"necklaces" encircle neck

dark rings

symmetrical black blotch on each side of body

Longhair option	Silver Classic Tabby Maine Coon	Temperament	Independent

Country of origin USA	Ancestry Non-pedigree Shorthairs	Origins 1600s

CHOCOLATE SHADED

Although grooming these cats is straightforward, it should be carried out regularly in order to help emphasize the distinctive markings.

• **FEATURES** The undercoat of the Chocolate Shaded is whitish, with chocolate tipping to the individual hairs creating a variance of shading over the body. The shading is darkest over the back, becoming paler on the flanks, and whitish underneath.

• **REMARK** The coat of the American Shorthair may vary throughout the year, becoming thicker and heavier in the winter.

thick, medium-length neck and full, muscular chest •

• round green eyes, slanted just slightly at outer edges

FUR TYPE: short and thick with hard texture

• whitish underparts contrast with chocolate tipping elsewhere on body

Longhair option Chocolate Shaded Maine Coon	Temperament Independent

Country of origin USA	Ancestry Non-pedigree Shorthairs	Origins 1600s

SILVER SHADED

tipping on face should correspond in depth to that on legs •

The presence of more extensive tipping means that the Silver Shaded is darker than the Chinchilla. In this case, a distinctly blackish shade can be seen.

• ears positioned on outside of head; rounded at tips

• **FEATURES** The depth of the coloration is most pronounced on the upper parts, shading to white on the lower parts of the body. The eye coloration can be either bluish green or pure green, and the brick-red nose is clearly outlined with a black edging. The pads should be entirely black.

muscular body •

• **REMARK** The short hair of these cats does not allow such a noticeable contrast as in long-haired breeds, but the tipping is still clearly evident.

under surface of tail white; no tipping evident •

FUR TYPE: short and thick with hard texture

Longhair option Silver Shaded Maine Coon	Temperament Independent

AMERICAN WIREHAIR

ALTHOUGH CATS with wiry coats were reported in Britain and elsewhere following World War II, none was established, and the origins of today's wirehairs can be traced back to a red and white kitten born on a farm in Verona, New York State, in the 1960s. News of this kitten reached a local rex-breeder, Mrs O'Shea, who obtained both the male kitten and his normally coated sister. The breeding programme then undertaken by Mrs O'Shea to establish the wire-haired mutation first entailed pairing brother and sister together. It soon emerged that this characteristic is dominant and provided one parent is wire-haired then a proportion of wire-haired kittens will occur in the litter. Crossings with American Shorthairs were later used to develop the breed.

Country of origin USA	Ancestry Non-pedigree Shorthairs	Origins 1966

TORTIE AND WHITE

The hair of the American Wirehair is crimped, the individual guard hairs being hooked or bent at their ends, even in the ears. The hairs making up the coat are also thinner than normal.
• **FEATURES** The thickness of the coat should result in the appearance of ringlets, which are especially noticeable on the head, as well as a more open wave pattern. Overall, the coats of these cats look and feel rather like lamb's wool, being somewhat less coarse on the underparts, including on the underside of the chin. The whiskers themselves are also normally curled.
• **REMARK** These cats can be bred in any colour or pattern, with only the addition of American Shorthairs permitted in their bloodlines. Their eye coloration should always correspond to their coat colour. Wire-haired kittens have tight, curly coats at birth, but the full potential of their coats is unlikely to be apparent until they are at least four or five months old.

• *round, medium-sized head, with prominent cheekbones*

springy coat •

• *good definition of tortie markings*

muscular body •

• *compact feet*

• *hair on tail corresponds to that on body*

• *medium, well-muscled legs*

FUR TYPE: medium; crimped and coarse

Longhair option None	Temperament Playful and active

Country of origin USA	Ancestry Non-pedigree Shorthairs	Origins 1966

BROWN MACKEREL TABBY

These cats require very little grooming, just brushing once a week to remove loose hairs. If it should be necessary to bath them, possibly before a show, this should be carried out several days in advance. Once the cat's coat has dried completely, its springy character will return naturally.

• **FEATURES** Tabby markings are still clearly discernible despite the unusual texture of the coat, and a good contrast between the tabby markings and the ground colour is desirable.

• **REMARK** Although healthy and long-lived cats, American Wirehairs are still quite scarce outside of North America.

crimped hair within ear

large, round eyes

tabby "necklaces"

medium-length tail tapers to rounded tip •

FUR TYPE: medium; crimped and coarse

Longhair option None		Temperament Playful and active

Country of origin USA	Ancestry Non-pedigree Shorthairs	Origins 1966

TORTIE AND WHITE VAN

American Wirehairs generally resemble the American Shorthair in all but the coat characteristics. Recently, however, some breeders have been choosing to breed Wirehairs of a slightly smaller size.

• **FEATURES** The "Van" patterning of this tortoiseshell and white, female-only variety has been introduced from the American Shorthair.

• **REMARK** Although the first pure-bred American Wirehairs were born in 1969, no unrelated cats of this type have been recorded. All of today's American Wirehairs must be descended directly, therefore, from *Adam*, the cat that originally gave rise to this highly distinctive breed.

FUR TYPE: medium; crimped and coarse

coloured areas ideally confined to head and tail, and body itself white

tortie markings •

tail carried level with body

medium, strong-boned legs

oval paws •

Longhair option None		Temperament Playful and active

AMERICAN CURL

T HE DISTINCTIVE curled ears of this breed are a relatively new mutation in the cat world, having been first documented in 1981. In that year, a long-haired kitten showing this characteristic feature was noticed by Joe and Grace Ruga, of Lakewood, California. In turn, two of this cat's kittens also had curly ears, and so it became clear that this was likely to be a dominant mutation, which would occur independently of coat length. The first time that the American Curls were displayed at a show was in 1983, at Palm Springs, California, where they attracted immediate interest. Joe and Grace Ruga, and a friend called Nancy Kiester, set out to establish the breed, which occurs in both a long-haired (*see p.112*) and a short-haired form.

Country of origin USA	Ancestry Non-pedigree Curl	Origins 1981

BROWN CLASSIC TORTIE TABBY

The development of the short-haired American Curl has been relatively slow, largely because the original curly eared kittens were long-haired. But they are now gaining in popularity and can be bred in any colour, offering great scope for breeders.
• **FEATURES** The extent of the curling of the ears can vary, and those cats showing the greatest degree of curling are preferred, provided that the ears point to the centre of the base of the skull. Little emphasis is placed on the colour and markings of the coat for judging purposes but, in this case, both tortie and tabby patterning should be clearly apparent.
• **REMARK** Because the American Curl Shorthair has not been established for long, ordinary, unregistered cats may feature in some of their pedigrees.

curl extends backwards from face •

• ears firm, and relatively large, with rounded tips

straight nose •

• straight legs

• relatively long tail

• round feet

hind legs slightly longer than front legs •

moderately long body •

tail tapers along length •

FUR TYPE: short and silky; little undercoat

Longhair option Brown Classic Tortie Tabby Long-haired American Curl	Temperament Gentle

| Country of origin | USA | Ancestry | Non-pedigree Curl | Origins | 1981 |

BLACK

In spite of their unusual appearance, American Curls are playful, healthy cats. Grooming is minimal, apart from combing to remove dead hairs from the coat.
• **FEATURES** Black coloration should be solid, with no white hairs in the coat. The shape of the ears and the proportions of the body are the most significant features. The overall type is semi-foreign, with the face of greater length than width. The relatively large eyes are shaped like walnuts, and positioned so that they slant towards the nose.
• **REMARK** The flexible ear tips are able to swivel.

broad-based ears with furnishings within

FUR TYPE: short and silky; little undercoat

smooth coat

medium-length legs

tail should correspond to length of body

medium-sized cat

tapering tip

| Longhair option | Black Long-haired American Curl | Temperament | Gentle |

| Country of origin | USA | Ancestry | Non-pedigree Curl | Origins | 1981 |

SEAL TABBY POINT

The introduction of Siamese colour characteristics into the American Curl bloodlines has already taken place, so pointed variants now exist. However, it is important that these cats remain true to their type, midway between that of the Oriental breeds and the cobby outlines of British Shorthairs.
• **FEATURES** The points should show characteristic seal-brown coloration, with tabby markings apparent on the legs and tail. Stripes, notably below the eyes, must also be in evidence.
• **REMARK** Kittens are invariably paler than the adults.

erect, open ears curve gently back from face

"M"-shaped tabby marking

blue eyes essential

clearly defined rings of various sizes evident along tail

various broken tabby stripes apparent on legs

dark tip to tail

round feet

FUR TYPE: short and silky; little undercoat

| Longhair option | Seal Tabby Point Long-haired American Curl | Temperament | Gentle |

EUROPEAN SHORTHAIR

IT IS ONLY RECENTLY that moves have been made to establish European Shorthairs as a recognized group in their own right. Before 1982 they were classed alongside British Shorthairs, and even today these two groups of cats are similar in many respects. The divergence in type is becoming more pronounced, however, because the European Shorthairs are now being selectively bred, with no British Shorthair crosses permitted in their pedigrees. However, these cats are available in a similarly wide range of colours, including self, bi-coloured, tabby, and tortoiseshell forms. Since the European division was first established, such cats have tended to become less cobby than their British relatives, with marginally longer faces.

Country of origin Italy	Ancestry Non-pedigree Shorthairs	Origins 1982

CREAM

European Shorthairs are hardy, adaptable cats. Paler colours, such as the Cream, tend to be quite rare and overall European Shorthairs are far less well known than either their British or American relatives. It is difficult to persuade breeders to support these shorthairs, when similar breeds are already well established.
• **FEATURES** The depth of coloration in the Cream is variable. The "hotter" shades, which show a reddish hue, are frowned upon, as are cats showing clear evidence of tabby markings. This latter fault is very difficult to overcome, however, and even litter-mates may differ in this respect.
• **REMARK** There is a rare, pure white European Shorthair, which is not deaf, in spite of having blue eyes.

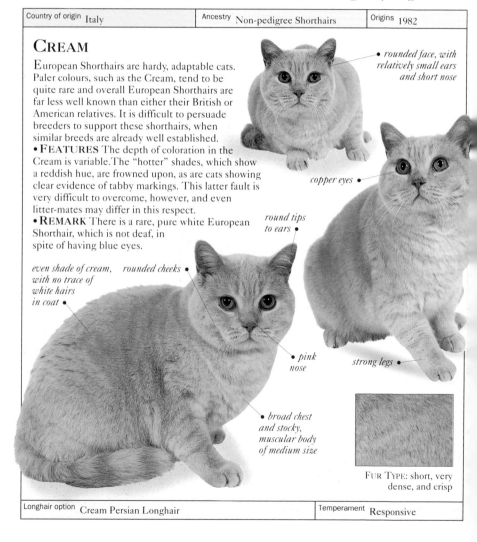

• *rounded face, with relatively small ears and short nose*

copper eyes •

round tips to ears •

even shade of cream, with no trace of white hairs in coat •   *rounded cheeks* •

• *pink nose*

strong legs •

• *broad chest and stocky, muscular body of medium size*

FUR TYPE: short, very dense, and crisp

Longhair option Cream Persian Longhair	Temperament Responsive

Country of origin Italy	Ancestry Non-pedigree Shorthairs	Origins 1982

RED SHADED CAMEO MACKEREL TABBY

Cats have been kept on mainland Europe for millennia, and a large number of colour forms and patterns have arisen without selective breeding. Emphasis is now being placed on establishing a clearly defined type for the European Shorthair.

• **FEATURES** The undercoat in this case is white, with red tipping on the longer guard hairs being most pronounced on the back. The red coloration becomes paler on the sides of the body, and fades out to white on the underparts.

• **REMARK** Like other native breeds, European Shorthairs are hardy and healthy cats.

round tips to ears, which show furnishings inside

well-spaced, large, round eyes

thick tail, broadest at base •

FUR TYPE: short, very dense, and crisp

Longhair option Red Shaded Cameo Mackerel Tabby Persian Longhair	Temperament Responsive

Country of origin Italy	Ancestry Non-pedigree Shorthairs	Origins 1982

TORTIE SMOKE

The Tortoiseshell and Smoke features combine, in this case, to produce a cat showing a good contrast in its outer coloration, but which also differs from that of the undercoat.

• **FEATURES** While the undercoat itself should be as white as possible, the cream, red, and black tipping on the guard hairs form the tortoiseshell coloration. These coloured areas should be broken into clearly defined, distinct patches.

• **REMARK** If these cats spend long periods outdoors, the black coloration in their patterning may become slightly discoloured by the sun, and take on a brownish hue.

round facial shape •

FUR TYPE: short, very dense, and crisp

medium to large body

lighter smoke coloration most apparent when cat moves

round-tipped, well-proportioned tail •

Longhair option Tortie Smoke Persian Longhair	Temperament Responsive

Country of origin Italy	Ancestry Non-pedigree Shorthairs	Origins 1982

CREAM SHADED CAMEO TABBY

A characteristic type is now apparent in top European Shorthairs, separating them from their British counterparts: the heads of the former are slightly longer, and they are less cobby in overall shape.

• **FEATURES** The guard hairs are tipped with cream, and superimposed on this light patterning are the tabby markings in a darker shade of cream; both of these contrast with the ground colour.

• **REMARK** With their easily cared for short coats and their amenable natures, these cats make a good choice as pets. They do retain a strong hunting instinct, however.

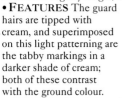

"M"-shaped tabby markings on head

FUR TYPE: short, very dense, and crisp

• tabby markings in darker shade of cream

firm, round paws •

Longhair option Cream Shaded Cameo Tabby Persian Longhair	Temperament Responsive

Country of origin Italy	Ancestry Non-pedigree Shorthairs	1982

RED SILVER MACKEREL TABBY

Tabby combinations are commonly seen in short-haired British and American breeds. European Shorthairs have also been bred in many colours, and in a similarly wide range of tabby patterns.

• **FEATURES** The red tabby markings are here set against a silvery ground colour, creating an attractive contrast. There must be stripes running back from the corner of each eye, with narrow lines across the cheeks. The ears are the same colour as the markings, apart from a central area about the size of a thumb-print, which is silver.

• **REMARK** During a moult, the tabby markings tend to become less distinctive.

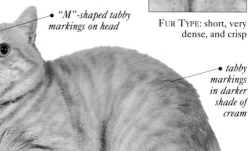

• rings on tail

mackerel tabby markings on body •

• rings of darker coloration, or "necklaces", around neck

• solid coloured tip to tail

• barring on legs

• medium-long tail

FUR TYPE: short, very dense, and crisp

Longhair option Red Silver Mackerel Tabby Persian Longhair	Temperament Responsive

Country of origin Italy	Ancestry Non-pedigree Shorthairs	Origins 1982

BLACK SILVER TABBY

All three basic forms of tabby markings – classic, mackerel, and spotted – occur in the European Shorthair, and do not differ essentially in patterning from those of other related short-haired breeds. The characteristic "M"-shaped marking on the head is common to all three, while the body patterning serves to distinguish them.

• **FEATURES** The Black Silver is one of the most strikingly marked of all tabbies, its dense black markings contrasting with the silver ground colour. There should be a narrow black line running down the centre of the back, with broken lines on either side. The vertical stripes radiate from these down the sides of the body. They should be narrow and evenly distributed, with both sides of the body appearing to be symmetrically marked. The tail must be ringed.

• **REMARK** The tabby patterning is usually less apparent in kittens, compared with adult cats, and kittens are also typically darker overall.

ear furnishings

strong, round paws

mackerel tabby patterning

barring "bracelets" clearly apparent on legs

dense black markings on silver ground colour

muscular neck

well-spaced, large, round, green eyes

narrow stripe running down spine clearly visible

rings on tail may be either complete or broken

unbroken black "necklaces" present on upper neck and chest

firm, tight paws

FUR TYPE: short, very dense, and crisp

black markings on hind legs reach up to hock joint

black tip to tail

Longhair option Black Silver Tabby Persian Longhair	Temperament Responsive

COLOUR POINTED EUROPEAN SHORTHAIR

T HE POINTED APPEARANCE of cats such as the Siamese has been superimposed here on the European Shorthair to produce cats that should be identical in terms of type to other European Shorthairs, apart from the coat. As in the Siamese, the production of the colour pigment responsible for the coloration of the points is influenced by the temperature; the cat's body is slightly colder at its extremities, and so greater pigment production occurs here. In a warm climate, such as southern Europe, it is likely that such cats will be slightly paler than those kept further north.

Country of origin Italy	Ancestry Non-pedigree Shorthairs	Origins 1982

BLUE POINT

Contrast is obviously a significant feature with these cats and, ideally, the points should show an even depth of coloration against the coat. Try to avoid binding the paw if the cat injures it, as the bandage will cause the paw to retain heat and the coloration of the point will be lightened. The body coloration tends to darken with age, so the show career of such cats is usually quite limited, but they will still be valuable afterwards for stud purposes.

• **FEATURES** The points, comprising the mask, ears, legs, paws, and tail, should be a light shade of blue, contrasting with the glacial white body coloration, which becomes blue over the back.

• **REMARK** The full range of pointed colours can be developed in these cats.

• blue ears

blue tail •

blue eyes •

shading on back •

• rounded face

stop between eyes •

FUR TYPE: short, very dense, and crisp

medium-length, stocky, well-muscled body •

• even depth of coloration on legs and paws

• thick, medium-length tail

Longhair option Blue Point Colour Pointed Longhair	Temperament Responsive

CHARTREUX

I T IS BELIEVED that this old French breed was developed by Carthusian monks in the monastery of La Grande Chartreuse, near Grenoble. The monastery is believed to date from the 1300s, or even earlier, but the actual origins of the breed are unknown. Legend has it that such cats were brought back from the Crusades by knights. They passed them to the care of the monks who controlled the breed by selling only neutered animals. The coloration of these cats is distinctive; indeed, no other colours are recognized.

| Country of origin | France | Ancestry | Non-pedigree Shorthairs | Origins | 1300s |

BLUE-GREY

The Chartreux used to be bred partly for its unique fur, which would fetch a high price. By the 1920s, however, the breed had declined in numbers; it survived largely through the efforts of two sisters who had been attracted by the bluish grey cats roaming in hospital grounds at Belle-Ile-sur-Mer. These cats formed the nucleus of their breeding programme; subsequent crosses involving both non-pedigree and pedigree Blues, and especially British Shorthairs, were used to maintain and refine the traditional French breed.
• **FEATURES** The solid, bluish grey coat coloration can vary from ash to slate-grey; the silver tipping helps to give the coat a sheen.
• **REMARK** This breed was imported to the United States in 1970.

large, broad, trapezoid head

coloration should be even in tone

round paws

clear, brilliant orange eyes may fade as cat grows older

blue nose

FUR TYPE: medium-short, dense, and glossy

dense fur with woolly resilient undercoat

muscular body

kitten's eye colour changes from blue to brownish-grey, then to orange

blue coat

medium-length tail with round tip

| Longhair option | None | Temperament | Friendly |

CORNISH REX

THESE CATS originated from a kitten born in Cornwall, England, in 1950. They have since been bred to a relatively foreign, or Oriental, body type in a wide range of colours. The distinctive coat lacks the outer, primary guard hairs, whereas the remaining, secondary guard hairs and the down hairs are wavy and reduced in length. Because of their relatively short hair, Cornish Rexes may not be comfortable outdoors if the weather is cold or wet.

Country of origin Great Britain	Ancestry Non-pedigree Shorthairs	Origins 1950

WHITE

Named "rex" after a similar mutation found in rabbits, the first rex kitten, *Kallibunker*, was paired back to his mother, and in due course further rexes were produced.
• FEATURES Although *Kallibunker* himself had a reasonably Oriental appearance, the use of short-haired cats in the early breeding programme produced a more cobby type, which is now considered to be a fault in this breed.
• REMARK The first Cornish Rexes were exported to the United States in 1957; since then the breed has attracted a substantial following throughout the world.

ears well-covered with fine fur •

straight nose •

• large ears, wide at base and tapering to rounded tips

long, straight legs give impression of height •

oval-shaped eyes •

pure white wavy coat •

slender, hard, muscular body •

• long, fine tail, well covered with curly fur

• pink pads

FUR TYPE: short, plush, and wavy or curled

Longhair option None	Temperament Playful

Country of origin Great Britain	Ancestry Non-pedigree Shorthairs	Origins 1950

CREAM

Cream coloration was apparent
almost at the start of the breed's
development: *Kallibunker*, the original
Cornish Rex, sired two male kittens,
one of whom was cream and white.
• **FEATURES** These cats usually have
a fairly dense coat, without long guard
hairs, but a coat that is shaggy or too
short is considered to be a fault. Whiskers
and eyebrows should be crinkled.
• **REMARK** Most Cornish Rex owners
groom their pets by stroking them firmly
from head to tail. This helps to emphasize
the distinctive, wavy
pattern of the coat.

flat-topped head

coat particularly wavy on back

pink nose

long, straight legs

wavy hair on legs

long, tapering tail

FUR TYPE: short, plush,
and wavy or curled

Longhair option None	Temperament Playful

Country of origin Great Britain	Ancestry Non-pedigree Shorthairs	Origins 1950

BLUE AND WHITE

Mutations identical to the Cornish Rex have occurred in
Germany and in the United States: the German Rex first
appeared in 1931 but is now very rare, even in Germany. In
North America various rex mutations have been recorded but
are not widely kept at present. The Cornish Rex became
established in the 1960s and was recognized in 1967.
• **FEATURES** The blue coloration in this case should
be even and clearly defined. Breeders
often aim to produce a
symmetrical pattern
of markings, but
this is not
compulsory.
• **REMARK**
Rexes can
benefit from
a bran bath
to remove
grease from
the coat.

eyebrows and whiskers long and crinkled

good covering of fur over whole body

silky feel to coat

curly or wavy hair

FUR TYPE: short, plush,
and wavy or curled

Longhair option None	Temperament Playful

Country of origin Great Britain	Ancestry Non-pedigree Shorthairs	Origins 1950

TORTOISESHELL

The markings of the Tortoiseshell Cornish Rex can vary from one cat to another but the type should be consistent in every individual.
• **FEATURES** The black patches evident in the coat should be well broken by shades of red, creating good contrast. Younger cats may show traces of grey rather than black hairs but these will usually be replaced when the cat moults. The coloration within the coat should be evenly distributed. In some cases, a lighter blaze of colour may be present on the forehead.
• **REMARK** The short fur covering the underparts should be clearly wavy.

oval eyes

FUR TYPE: short, plush, and wavy or curled

very long legs

arched back and rounded rump

Longhair option None	Temperament Playful

Country of origin Great Britain	Ancestry Non-pedigree Shorthairs	Origins 1950

TORTIE AND WHITE VAN

The somewhat tubular appearance of the Cornish Rex stems from its fine-boned yet muscular body. It stands quite tall, and males are generally larger than females.
• **FEATURES** These cats are predominantly white; the Van pattern is a characteristic of the Turkish Van (pp.78–79), with coloration mainly restricted to the tail and odd patches on the head.
• **REMARK** When resting, the Cornish Rex usually curls up the tip of its flexible tail.

tortoiseshell patterning most apparent on head

crinkled whiskers

extremely flexible tail

dainty paws emphasize length of legs

FUR TYPE: short, plush, and wavy or curled

tapering tail

Longhair option None	Temperament Playful

| Country of origin | Great Britain | Ancestry | Non-pedigree Shorthairs | Origins | 1950 |

CINNAMON SILVER

The quality of the coat is a vital feature in all Cornish Rexes, with no hairless patches nor very short areas of fur. The distinctive curly-coated patterning should be evident over the entire body, down to the paws.

• **FEATURES** The coloration consists of a white undercoat with cinnamon ticking. The ticking should be most prominent running from the head to the tail along the spine and down on to the cat's flanks.

flat skull •

• **REMARK** The cinnamon ticking creates a light, sparkling effect.

• slender, muscular body and arched back

FUR TYPE: short, plush, and wavy or curled

| Longhair option | None | Temperament | Playful |

| Country of origin | Great Britain | Ancestry | Non-pedigree Shorthairs | Origins | 1950 |

CHOCOLATE POINT SI-REX

The pointed versions of the Cornish Rex are quite a recent development and have yet to receive widespread recognition. In the case of this breed, however, coloration is generally of little significance; the type of these cats and their distinctive coats are important for judging.

body shading most pronounced over back and flanks •

• **FEATURES** The body coloration should be basically ivory-white; the relatively little dark shading should correspond to the milk-chocolate-coloured points. Nose and pads are of a similar shade.

• chocolate mask

• good quality coat with clear signs of curls, waves, and ripples

• **REMARK** Pointed Cornish Rexes should be identical in type to other rexes.

FUR TYPE: short, plush, and wavy or curled

long, fine tail, with good covering of curly, milk-chocolate-coloured fur •

| Longhair option | None | Temperament | Playful |

Country of origin Great Britain	Ancestry Non-pedigree Shorthairs	Origins 1950

RED SMOKE

Rexes can be bred in any coat colour or pattern, but the most controversial are the Si-rexes, which show Siamese markings.
• **FEATURES** A deep, rich shade of red, free from tabby markings, is desirable with the lighter Smoke patterning most apparent when the cat moves. The fur itself has a silky texture.
• **REMARK** A shaggy coat is regarded as a serious flaw in this breed, and recent attempts to produce a long-haired form have not met with great interest.

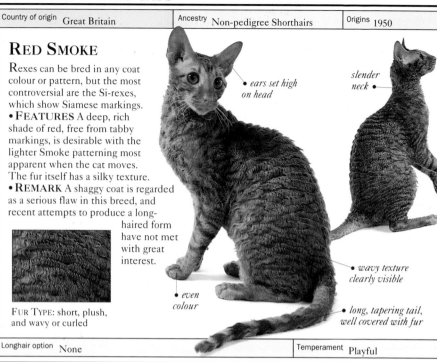

ears set high on head

slender neck

wavy texture clearly visible

even colour

long, tapering tail, well covered with fur

FUR TYPE: short, plush, and wavy or curled

Longhair option None		Temperament Playful

Country of origin Great Britain	Ancestry Non-pedigree Shorthairs	Origins 1950

BLUE SMOKE

Cornish Rexes can show a tendency to obesity, which spoils their slender body shape, and may be harmful. It is best, therefore, to avoid overfeeding them.
• **FEATURES** In this case, the blue predominates against a white background. Rex kittens may have a sparse coat, but it usually becomes more profuse as they get older. In adults, however, bare patches are considered to be a serious fault.
• **REMARK** A blue female called *Riovista Kismet* was one of the most famous early rexes, being a direct descendant of the original Cornish Rex *Kallibunker*.

curl, ripple, or wave effect most noticeable over back and tail

muscular thighs

long, straight legs

FUR TYPE: short, plush, and wavy or curled

Longhair option None		Temperament Playful

Country of origin	Great Britain	Ancestry	Non-pedigree Shorthairs	Origins	1950

BLUE-CREAM SMOKE

It is said that one of the earliest Cornish Rexes was a Blue-cream male, but this is unlikely as the colour is a dilute form of tortoiseshell, and such males are invariably sterile. It is more likely that the cat in question was a Blue Tabby.

• **FEATURES** Although males are larger and heavier than females, they must be lean and muscular in build.

• **REMARK** Cornish Rexes usually prove to be very healthy, and the females make good mothers.

even mixing of medium blue and pale cream coloration

fine-boned, well-muscled appearance

FUR TYPE: short, plush, and wavy or curled

small oval paws •

Longhair option	None	Temperament	Playful

Country of origin	Great Britain	Ancestry	Non-pedigree Shorthairs	Origins	1950

BLACK SMOKE AND WHITE

The quality of the coat, rather than its coloration or markings, is the most important feature of the Cornish Rex. The tight, marcel waves are vital, as is the cat's type. In this case the white markings can be asymmetrical, but they are not allowed in Si-rexes.

• **FEATURES** The silvery undercoat shows clearly in the Smoke Cornish Rexes because of the absence of the long guard hairs. Darker coloration is restricted to the awn hairs, the down being silver.

• **REMARK** The greasy coat of Cornish Rexes can lead to a condition known as stud tail.

oval eyes; colour in keeping with coat colour

length of head one third greater than maximum width

long slender legs •

• *tail tip carried upwards when tail is low*

• *dainty paws*

FUR TYPE: short, plush, and wavy or curled

Longhair option	None	Temperament	Playful

DEVON REX

T HIS SECOND rex mutation, which appeared in 1960, was originally thought to be a form of the Cornish Rex, but no rex kittens resulted when these cats were mated, confirming that they were genetically different. The coat of the Devon Rex is distinctive, in that both sets of guard hairs and down hairs are present, these being more twisted than in the Cornish mutation.

Country of origin Great Britain	Ancestry Non-pedigree Shorthairs	Origins 1960

WHITE

But for the publicity surrounding the appearance of the Cornish Rex at cat shows in 1960, the Devon Rex might have gone unrecorded. A woman in Devon, England, had noticed a large, curly-coated male cat near her home. It mated with her cat, and one of the kittens had a similar, curly coat. Fortunately, having heard about the Cornish Rex, she realized the potential significance of her pet.
• FEATURES The coat in this case is pure white, and it may be necessary to wash these particular rexes before a show if the fur becomes dirty. Like all Devon Rexes, they are muscular cats with a distinctly foreign appearance.
• REMARK The pixie-like ears, which help to distinguish these cats from Cornish Rexes, are large and set low; they need regular cleaning with cotton-wool.

• oval eyes, set well apart

FUR TYPE: short, fine, soft, wavy, and curly

large broad ears •

coat less wavy than on Cornish Rex •

pure white coloration •

• small, oval paws

• long, tapering tail with good covering of fur

• pink pads

Longhair option None	Temperament Playful

Country of origin Great Britain	Ancestry Non-pedigree Shorthairs	Origins 1960

CREAM

With their wedge-shaped faces and broad ears giving them a mischievous appearance, these rexes make lively and affectionate companions. They should not be exposed outdoors to prolonged periods of cold or wet weather.

• FEATURES The coat of a Devon Rex kitten is less profuse than an adult's. In this case, it should be an even depth of cream.

• REMARK The Devon Rex was first recognized in 1967.

• *hard, muscular body*

• *slender neck*

down present on underparts •

• *coat must be short and wavy*

FUR TYPE: short, fine, soft, wavy, and curly

Longhair option None	Temperament Playful

Country of origin Great Britain	Ancestry Non-pedigree Shorthairs	Origins 1960

BLUE

Kirlee, the forerunner of this breed, was smokey-grey in colour; the Blue is the variant closest in coloration to the original.

• FEATURES The "stop" in the nose of this breed is an important feature, being clearly visible between the eyes.

• REMARK While most cats wag their tails from side to side as a sign of disapproval, the Devon Rex does this when it is contented. This behaviour, coupled with their curled fur and devoted personalities, has led to their being called "poodle cats".

• *eyes slope towards outer edges of ears*

• *even coloration*

• *short wedge-shaped face with prominent cheeks*

• *shorter coat on underparts*

FUR TYPE: short, fine, soft, wavy, and curly

Longhair option None	Temperament Playful

Country of origin Great Britain	Ancestry Non-pedigree Shorthairs	Origins 1960

CREAM TABBY POINT SI-REX

Out-crossings with a range of other breeds, including Burmese, Bombay, and Siamese, have led to the wide range of colours now seen in the Devon Rex. Matings with the Cornish Rex have not been encouraged since it became clear that the breeds were separate mutations.
• FEATURES Coat quality is vitally important in this breed, but kittens do not develop a full coat until they are around 18 months of age. Cream coloration with darker tabby markings on the points distinguishes this variety.
• REMARK The Devon Rex is now becoming more widely available overseas.

flat skull

small, oval paws

slim legs

coat more profuse in adult

FUR TYPE: short, fine, soft, wavy, and curly

Longhair option None	Temperament Playful

Country of origin Great Britain	Ancestry Non-pedigree Shorthairs	Origins 1960

SILVER TORTIE TABBY

One of the many interesting patterned combinations now available, this Devon Rex shows the potential variety within the breed. As with all tortoiseshell forms, these cats are almost invariably female.
• FEATURES In Tortie Tabbies, the tabby markings usually replace the black present in the coat of a tortoiseshell, the white undercoat being essentially unaffected.
• REMARK In North America, these cats are known as "torbies" or as "patched tabbies".

ears set low

strong chin and prominent whisker pads

muscular yet slender body

tail must show no sign of kink

FUR TYPE: short, fine, soft, wavy, and curly

Longhair option None	Temperament Playful

| Country of origin Great Britain | Ancestry Non-pedigree Shorthairs | Origins 1960 |

CREAM AND WHITE

Although bi-colour forms of the Devon Rex have not always been popular in show circles, these attractive cats possess the affectionate and devoted nature that is typical of the breed.

• **FEATURES** The distribution of the cream and white patches is less significant than the quality of the coat.

• **REMARK** There should be no tabby markings in the cream areas in adults, although there may still be traces visible in the case of kittens.

• even cream coloration

FUR TYPE: short, fine, soft, wavy, and curly

slender oval paws •

| Longhair option None | Temperament Playful |

| Country of origin Great Britain | Ancestry Non-pedigree Shorthairs | Origins 1960 |

WHITE AND BLACK SMOKE

Although the mother of the original Devon Rex kitten was Tortoiseshell and White, other bi-colour forms have not been generally favoured.

• **FEATURES** The ears of the Devon Rex are its most distinctive feature, although the face shape also distinguishes these cats from Cornish Rexes. There should be a good contrast between the black and white areas.

• **REMARK** Breeders have tended to concentrate on improving the quality of the Devon Rex's coat, with less emphasis on the markings, which can be variable.

large ears, well covered with fine fur; may be tufted at tips •

• hard, slender, muscular body which can be extended in an elongated fashion, as here

• white undercoat visible in black areas

good covering of fur on tail •

FUR TYPE: short, fine, soft, wavy, and curly

| Longhair option None | Temperament Playful |

Country of origin Great Britain	Ancestry Non-pedigree Shorthairs	Origins 1960

BLUE-CREAM AND WHITE

As a member of the tortoiseshell group, the Blue-cream and White Devon Rex is essentially a female-only variant; any males are likely to be sterile.
• **FEATURES** While baldness is a serious fault in these cats, it is accepted that their whiskers are fragile and may therefore break off quite easily.
• **REMARK** Devon Rexes may shed a considerable amount of fur when moulting, resulting in bald patches. This is not a cause for concern, but an isolated area of hair loss at other times might indicate the presence of a ringworm infection.

short muzzle

long tail •

characteristic stop in facial profile •

• *long hind legs*

• *body carried high on legs*

FUR TYPE: short, fine, soft, wavy, and curly

Longhair option None		Temperament Playful

Country of origin Great Britain	Ancestry Non-pedigree Shorthairs	Origins 1960

BLACK SMOKE

The coat of the Devon Rex has a slightly coarser feel than that of its Cornish relative, as well as being less consistent in both the length of the hair and in its wavy patterning.
• **FEATURES** Although coloration is not considered to be as significant in the Smoke as type and quality of the coat, the Black is often preferred because of its striking contrasts. In some cats the front legs may appear to be bowed but this is an illusion, resulting from the broad chest, rather than being due to an inherent weakness.
• **REMARK** Grooming by hand, and using a piece of silk, help to emphasize the arrangement of the hairs.

• *fur-covered ears*

• *wavy coat*

tail well covered with fur, but not bushy •

FUR TYPE: short, fine, soft, wavy, and curly

Longhair option None		Temperament Playful

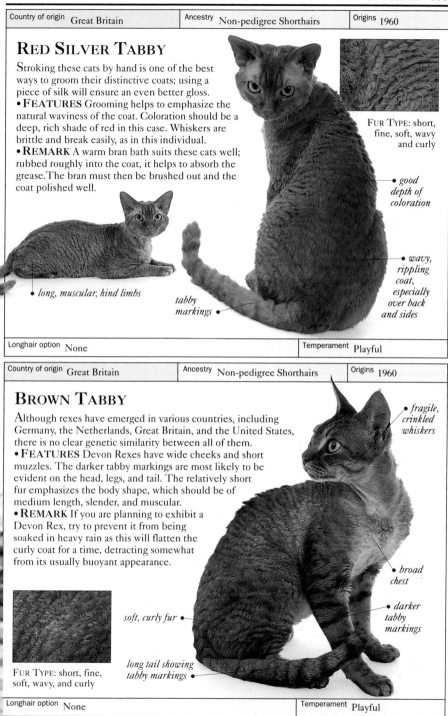

| Country of origin | Great Britain | Ancestry | Non-pedigree Shorthairs | Origins | 1960 |

RED SILVER TABBY

Stroking these cats by hand is one of the best ways to groom their distinctive coats; using a piece of silk will ensure an even better gloss.
• **FEATURES** Grooming helps to emphasize the natural waviness of the coat. Coloration should be a deep, rich shade of red in this case. Whiskers are brittle and break easily, as in this individual.
• **REMARK** A warm bran bath suits these cats well; rubbed roughly into the coat, it helps to absorb the grease. The bran must then be brushed out and the coat polished well.

FUR TYPE: short, fine, soft, wavy and curly

• *good depth of coloration*

• *wavy, rippling coat, especially over back and sides*

• *long, muscular, hind limbs*

tabby markings •

| Longhair option | None | Temperament | Playful |

| Country of origin | Great Britain | Ancestry | Non-pedigree Shorthairs | Origins | 1960 |

BROWN TABBY

Although rexes have emerged in various countries, including Germany, the Netherlands, Great Britain, and the United States, there is no clear genetic similarity between all of them.
• **FEATURES** Devon Rexes have wide cheeks and short muzzles. The darker tabby markings are most likely to be evident on the head, legs, and tail. The relatively short fur emphasizes the body shape, which should be of medium length, slender, and muscular.
• **REMARK** If you are planning to exhibit a Devon Rex, try to prevent it from being soaked in heavy rain as this will flatten the curly coat for a time, detracting somewhat from its usually buoyant appearance.

• *fragile, crinkled whiskers*

• *broad chest*

• *darker tabby markings*

soft, curly fur •

FUR TYPE: short, fine, soft, wavy, and curly

long tail showing tabby markings •

| Longhair option | None | Temperament | Playful |

SPHINX

T HE SPHINX may not appeal to everyone, but it always attracts attention. Some cat organizations do not recognize the breed, believing that the lack of hair may be potentially harmful to the cats' well-being. This is not unique, however; similar mutations have occurred in dogs and in mice.

Country of origin Canada	Ancestry Non-pedigree Shorthairs	Origins 1966

BROWN AND WHITE

One of a litter of kittens born in Ontario, Canada, was hairless, and that individual has since been used to develop the breed in a wide range of colours. Earlier forms of "hairless" cat had been recorded in France and Mexico, but were not developed.

• **FEATURES** In spite of sometimes being described as "hairless", Sphynx cats do retain a variable amount of short, downy fur that is most noticeable at the extremities of the body.

• **REMARK** During recent years, there appears to have been a growing interest in these cats, and they are now being bred in Europe as well as in North America.

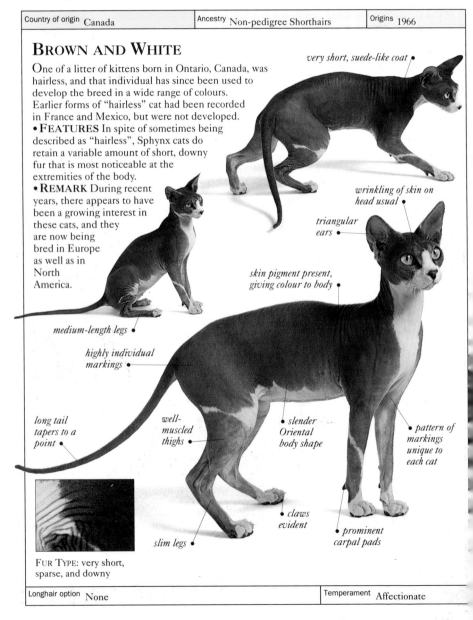

very short, suede-like coat

wrinkling of skin on head usual

triangular ears

skin pigment present, giving colour to body

medium-length legs

highly individual markings

long tail tapers to a point

well-muscled thighs

slender Oriental body shape

pattern of markings unique to each cat

claws evident

slim legs

prominent carpal pads

FUR TYPE: very short, sparse, and downy

Longhair option None	Temperament Affectionate

Country of origin Canada	Ancestry Non-pedigree Shorthairs	Origins 1966

BLACK AND WHITE

The first Sphynx was actually born to a Black and White cat. Now, however, the breed has been developed in a wide range of colours and markings. In all cases, eye coloration should correspond with that of the body. The relative lack of coat means that these cats are not only vulnerable to the cold, but are also at risk in hot weather, the white areas being susceptible to sunburn.

• **FEATURES** The coloration of each individual cat is evident from its skin; this colour is also emphasized by the sparse coating of fur. Kittens are usually born with a denser covering of fur, which becomes thinner as they grow older.

• **REMARK** It is now clear that the Sphynx's lack of hair is a recessive mutation, which means these cats need to be paired together in order to ensure that the offspring will have a similar, "hairless" appearance.

ears rounded at tip •

whiskers may be absent •

rounded, barrel-shaped chest •

• body typically feels warm to touch

• characteristic stance with front paw raised and curled back under body

• face slightly angular, with broad ears

• body muscular, and not excessively wrinkled

• clear contrast between white and black areas

FUR TYPE: very short, sparse, and downy

• powerful paws

"lion tail" of slightly longer hair close to tip •

Longhair option None	Temperament Affectionate

SELKIRK REX

THERE IS ALWAYS the possibility that new mutations will arise unexpectedly and, if there is sufficient interest, breeds may be developed from them. The Selkirk Rex is one of the latest additions to the list of cat breeds and originated in the United States in 1987. In that year, Peggy Voorhees, of the Bozeman Humane Society, saw a blue-cream and white kitten in a litter of non-pedigree cats born in Wyoming. It had green eyes and an unusual coat; its hair was curly, like its whiskers, and its ear hairs resembled steel-wool.

Country of origin USA	Ancestry Non-pedigree Shorthairs	Origins 1987

BLUE-CREAM

The original curly-coated kitten was mated at 14 months of age with a pedigree Black Longhair, owned by Jeri Newman, a breeder of Longhairs. Of the six kittens that resulted, three had curly coats like that of their mother.
• **FEATURES** There is no restriction on colour in this breed; the coat is a much more significant feature for exhibition purposes. The clarity of coloration is important, however, with the eye colour matching that of the coat. In this case the coat is blue and cream; the eyes can vary from deep gold to copper.
• **REMARK** The curly coat indicates that this is a rex-type breed, but it differs from the previously established forms, being a genetically dominant feature.

curls most evident around neck •

• rounded head

medium-sized ears with rounded tips, well spaced on head

• large paws

• rectangular, muscular body, showing good colour

medium-length, thick tail, tapering to tip •

• loose curls clearly apparent on tail

• well-boned, muscular legs, contributing to somewhat bulky appearance

FUR TYPE: thick, plush, and curly

Longhair option Blue-cream Long-haired Selkirk Rex	Temperament Friendly

| Country of origin | USA | Ancestry | Non-pedigree Shorthairs | Origins | 1987 |

TORTOISESHELL

Although kittens are born with the curled type of coat, these hairs are shed around the age of six months and the coat then becomes rather sparse and wiry for a period. It will not be until they are between eight and ten months old that these rexes actually develop their characteristic thick, plush coats.

• **FEATURES** The curling effect is evident in both the rather coarse outer guard hairs and in the underlying down and awn hairs. The whiskers are also curled.

• **REMARK** The distribution of tortoiseshell patterning is random, as is the case in other breeds.

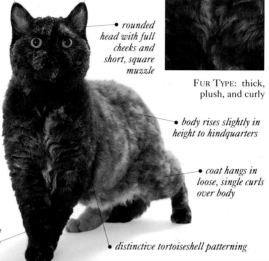

rounded head with full cheeks and short, square muzzle

FUR TYPE: thick, plush, and curly

body rises slightly in height to hindquarters

coat hangs in loose, single curls over body

coat shows good density and soft texture

distinctive tortoiseshell patterning

| Longhair option | Tortoiseshell Long-haired Selkirk Rex | Temperament | Friendly |

| Country of origin | USA | Ancestry | Non-pedigree Shorthairs | Origins | 1987 |

BLACK TORTIE SMOKE

Various breeds are being used as out-crosses in the development of the Selkirk Rex, including British, American, and Exotic Shorthairs, as well as Longhairs. The use of other rexes, such as the Cornish or Devon forms, is not permitted. In August 1990, two American cat associations agreed to accept the breed; its supporters had formed the Selkirk Rex Society to guide its development.

• **FEATURES** The white undercoat contrasts with black tipping and tortie areas in the coat.

• **REMARK** Both sexes have jowls.

ear tuft

furnishings visible in well-spaced ears

round, widely separated eyes

FUR TYPE: thick, plush, and curly

females invariably smaller than males

kitten's coat develops from eight to ten months

rounded tip to tail

| Longhair option | Black Tortie Smoke Long-haired Selkirk Rex | Temperament | Friendly |

RUSSIAN SHORTHAIR

THESE CATS were originally known as "Archangel Blues" after the Russian port from which they were first brought to Britain, perhaps as early as the 1600s. They were exhibited at the early cat shows in the same class as the British Shorthair, the latter usually winning, but from 1912 they were grouped separately as "Foreign Blues". In recent years, black and white forms of this breed have been developed, mainly in Australia and New Zealand.

Country of origin Russian	Ancestry Non-pedigree Shorthairs	Origins 1800s

BLUE

The numbers of Russian Blues declined drastically after World War II. In order to preserve the breed, crosses involving Blue Point Siamese were used, but this resulted in these cats developing a more foreign type. In recent years, breeders have worked hard to re-establish their distinctive traditional appearance.

• **FEATURES** The fur of the Russian Shorthair has a unique, seal-like texture. It should be a solid, medium shade of blue with a distinctive silvery sheen. The nose and paw pads are also blue, except in the case of kittens, while the almond-shaped eyes should be a vivid emerald-green.

• **REMARK** Pure lines of Russia Blues still exist in the former USSR and some of these cats are now entering breeding programmes elsewhere.

large, pointed, upright ears •

• *long, graceful body shape*

short, wedge-shaped head with forehead and nose aligned •

prominent whisker pads •

• *ears wide at base*

FUR TYPE: short, thick, fine, and silky

double coat with silvery sheen •

plush coat •

• *soft, blue-grey coat*

• *long, tapering tail*

Longhair option None	Temperament Affectionate; docile

KORAT

NAMED AFTER the province of Korat in north-east Thailand, these cats appear to have a very long history in that part of the world. The breed was first seen in the West in 1896, with modern bloodlines dating from as recently as 1959 when an American breeder obtained a pair. These were bred together, and others followed, and now Korats are kept by cat fanciers around the world. A breed association was established in 1965.

Country of origin Thailand	Ancestry Unknown	Origins 1300–1700s

BLUE

This breed has been prized in Thailand for centuries, and is recorded in the *Cat Book Poems* of the Ayutthaya kingdom (1350–1767).
• **FEATURES** In the *Cat Book Poems*, the Korat is described as having "smooth hairs with tips like clouds and roots like silver, and eyes that shine like dewdrops on a lotus leaf". Since its introduction to the West, breeders have been careful to preserve the traditional appearance of the Korat.
• **REMARK** Although the Korat was recognized in the United States in 1966, this was not achieved in Great Britain until 1975.

• round, luminous, green eyes

• medium legs, with small, oval paws

large, round-tipped ears •

• heart-shaped head

• broad forehead with gently curving face

tapering tail, heavier at base •

• medium-length tail with round tip

silvery sheen to coat •

• medium-sized, muscular body

FUR TYPE: short, fine, and close-lying

Longhair option None	Temperament Playful

SIAMESE

WITH ITS ANGULAR FACE and svelte outline, the Siamese is one of the best known of pedigree cats. Ironically, however, it seems to have lost some of its popularity to the newer breeds that have been developed from it over recent years. Siamese are described as a pointed breed, meaning that on the extremities of their body, or points, the coloration is darker than elsewhere.

Country of origin	Thailand	Ancestry	Non-pedigree Asiatics	Origins	1300s

CREAM POINT

The temperature at which these cats are kept has a direct influence on their pigmentation: relatively warm surroundings are likely to result in paler coloration of the points. All Siamese are born pure white; the darker shade of the points becomes apparent only gradually, and the full contrast is not apparent until they are one year old.
- **FEATURES** The back and sides of the body are pale cream in this case, the remainder of the body being white. The points are a darker shade of cream, most notably on the ears, mask, and tail.
- **REMARK** Slight signs of darker freckling on the pink coloration of the nose and pads are not penalized. Cream points breed true when they are mated together.

FUR TYPE: very short, fine, and glossy

bright blue eyes

elegant neck and long, svelte body

fine muzzle

hind legs longer than front legs

eyes slant towards nose

alert, intelligent expression

pink paw pads

long, tapering tail with no trace of kink

Longhair option	Cream Point Balinese	Temperament	Affectionate

| Country of origin | Thailand | Ancestry | Non-pedigree Asiatics | Origins | 1300s |

RED POINT

Red Point Siamese, originally described as "Orange Points" were first shown in Britain in 1934 when they aroused controversy because they did not correspond to the traditional Siamese coloration. Red Tabby Persian pairings were used to introduce the red coloration.

• **FEATURES** Apricot coloration on the back and sides of the body, toning to white, contrasts with the bright reddish-gold points. Ghost tabby markings may be apparent on the mask, as well as on the legs and tail.

• **REMARK** In North America, these cats are traditionally viewed as Colourpoint Shorthairs.

pointed ears

wedge-shaped head

sleek, close-lying fur

long body

long, slender legs

FUR TYPE: very short, fine, and glossy

| Longhair option | Red Point Balinese | Temperament | Affectionate |

| Country of origin | Thailand | Ancestry | Non-pedigree Asiatics | Origins | 1300s |

LILAC POINT

The earliest Lilac Point may have been seen in Britain in 1896 when a Siamese which was described as being "not quite blue" was disqualified from a show.

• **FEATURES** The pinkish grey points contrast with an off-white magnolia body coloration. The eyes are bright blue. There must be no heavy ringing around the tail.

• **REMARK** In the United States, Lilac Points should have a glacial white body with no signs of body shading as is permitted in Great Britain.

large ears, with wide bases

FUR TYPE: very short, fine, and glossy

mask is complete in all but kittens, connecting to ears by tracings

pale bib and chest

fine bone structure

small, oval paws

slight ringing

| Longhair option | Lilac Point Balinese | Temperament | Affectionate |

Country of origin Thailand	Ancestry Non-pedigree Asiatics	Origins 1300s

BLUE POINT

One of the traditional forms of the Siamese, Blue Points began to gain a strong following in the 1930s, which they have maintained to the present day.
• FEATURES Coloration is very important, but achieving the correct balance is difficult. Breeding other Siamese with existing bloodlines may darken the white body, and the points may become slate-grey.
• REMARK This is said to be the most affectionate and gentle Siamese.

• *vivid blue eyes*

• *wide ears*

• *light blue points*

• *white body coloration, shading to light blue on back*

FUR TYPE: very short, fine, and glossy

Longhair option Blue Point Balinese	Temperament Affectionate

Country of origin Thailand	Ancestry Non-pedigree Asiatics	Origins 1300s

CHOCOLATE POINT

Siamese kittens are mostly white at birth. Coloration appears first on the ears and tail, with the chocolate points often not fully coloured until the kittens are one year old. Kittens that develop early will often have points that are too dark as adults.
• FEATURES The points should be a milk-chocolate shade, against ivory body coloration. The ears must be the same shade as other points, whereas the legs may be slightly paler. However, this is not desirable.
• REMARK The chocolate gene was present in early Seal Points, but these cats were not recognized for showing until the 1950s.

• *bright blue eyes*

• *slim legs, with small, oval paws*

• *milk-chocolate-coloured tail*

• *coat lies close to body, emphasizing sleek appearance*

• *long, tapering tail*

FUR TYPE: very short, fine, and glossy

Longhair option Chocolate Point Balinese	Temperament Affectionate

Country of origin Thailand	Ancestry Non-pedigree Asiatics	Origins 1300s

SEAL POINT

wedge-shaped head

This is the traditional colour of the Siamese, first seen in Europe during the 1880s. Siamese mature early, and females may be sexually active from six months of age, although they are not normally bred until they are older.
• **FEATURES** This is an example of an older cat, showing the darker colour on the back and flanks that comes with age. In this case, the points are deep seal-brown, contrasting with the bright blue eyes.

coloration darker on back

• **REMARK** The original Siamese cats, first described in 1793 by the German explorer Peter Simon Pallas, had rounder faces than those of today.

FUR TYPE: very short, fine, and glossy

Longhair option Seal Point Balinese	Temperament Affectionate

Country of origin Thailand	Ancestry Non-pedigree Asiatics	Origins 1300s

BLUE TORTIE POINT

large, pointed ears

Tortoiseshell patterning was introduced into Siamese lines by the use of shorthairs; Siamese features were then maintained by selective breeding.
• **FEATURES** Here, the basic body colour is white, with a mixture of pale blue and pale cream along the back and sides. The mask, ears, legs, feet, and tail are blue, with areas of cream. Each of the points should show some break in colour, irrespective of the extent of the cream markings.

almond-shaped eyes

• **REMARK** Tortie Point Siamese are a combination of Siamese with Tortoiseshell. As with other Torties, they are almost exclusively female.

long, svelte body

hind legs longer than front legs

FUR TYPE: very short, fine, and glossy

Longhair option Blue Tortie Point Balinese	Temperament Affectionate

Country of origin Thailand	Ancestry Non-pedigree Asiatics	Origins 1300s

CHOCOLATE TORTIE POINT

These cats are recognized separately, as Colorpoint Shorthairs, by some North American registries; in the United Kingdom, however, they are classified as Siamese, differing only in their markings from other Siamese.
• **FEATURES** The ivory body colour darkens to apricot and pale chocolate on the back and sides of the body. The milk-chocolate points must be broken by paler areas, which may be variable in coloration.
• **REMARK** The various forms of Tortie Point developed slowly, but are now well established.

darker coloration on back

long, tapering wedge-shaped head

long, tapering tail with no kink

milk-chocolate points broken with red

FUR TYPE: very short, fine, and glossy

Longhair option Chocolate Tortie Point Balinese	Temperament Affectionate

Country of origin Thailand	Ancestry Non-pedigree Asiatics	Origins 1300s

SEAL TORTIE POINT

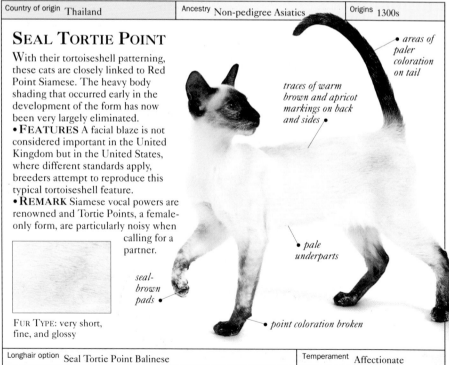

With their tortoiseshell patterning, these cats are closely linked to Red Point Siamese. The heavy body shading that occurred early in the development of the form has now been very largely eliminated.
• **FEATURES** A facial blaze is not considered important in the United Kingdom but in the United States, where different standards apply, breeders attempt to reproduce this typical tortoiseshell feature.
• **REMARK** Siamese vocal powers are renowned and Tortie Points, a female-only form, are particularly noisy when calling for a partner.

areas of paler coloration on tail

traces of warm brown and apricot markings on back and sides

pale underparts

seal-brown pads

point coloration broken

FUR TYPE: very short, fine, and glossy

Longhair option Seal Tortie Point Balinese	Temperament Affectionate

| Country of origin Thailand | Ancestry Non-pedigree Asiatics | Origins 1300s |

RED TABBY POINT

Siamese cats with tabby markings on their points were first described as "Shadow-pointed Siamese" and, later, as "Lynx-pointed". Their present name was recognized in Britain in 1966.
• **FEATURES** The body coloration in the case of the Red Tabby Point is white, with a hint of apricot on the back and sides. The mask, ears, and tail have bright, reddish gold markings; those on the legs and feet may be slightly paler.
• **REMARK** Odd Tabby Points have been known since the early days of the breed in Britain, the first example having been described in 1902; they have become well known only relatively recently, however.

clearly defined tail rings

tapering tail with no kink

pink pads

small, oval paws

FUR TYPE: very short, fine, and glossy

| Longhair option Red Tabby Point Balinese | Temperament Affectionate |

| Country of origin Thailand | Ancestry Non-pedigree Asiatics | Origins 1300s |

SEAL TABBY POINT

Better known in North America as "Lynx Point Siamese", these cats have been developed in all the Siamese colours. Whatever the cat's coloration, the pattern of markings should be constant.
• **FEATURES** The body shading tends to be more pronounced in the case of the Seal Tabby Point, which is the darkest form, than in other instances.
• **REMARK** These cats became popular after the accidental mating of a Seal Point female in 1960. One of the kittens with tabby markings was then crossed back to a Siamese.

characteristic stripes around eyes and nose

darkly marked whisker pads

FUR TYPE: very short, fine, and glossy

dark rings on tail

clearly defined, striped patterning on legs

solid coloration present on back of hind legs

seal pads

| Longhair option Seal Tabby Point Balinese | Temperament Affectionate |

Country of origin	Thailand	Ancestry	Non-pedigree Asiatics	Origins	1300s

CREAM TABBY POINT

The attractive appearance of Tabby Point Siamese led to their being known by a variety of names, such as Silver Point Siamese, Attabiya, and Lynx Pointed, before their present name became accepted.

• **FEATURES** The back and upper sides are pale cream, with the remainder of the body white; the points have deeper, buff-cream barring.

• **REMARK** The Cream is the palest of the Tabby Points.

pink nose corresponding in colour to paw pads

clearly defined rings along tail

well-proportioned body

white underparts

solid coloration on back of hind legs

FUR TYPE: very short, fine, and glossy

Longhair option	Cream Tabby Point Balinese	Temperament	Affectionate

Country of origin	Thailand	Ancestry	Non-pedigree Asiatics	Origins	1300s

LILAC TABBY POINT

Mating a Tabby Point with any Siamese should result in Tabby Point kittens, but achieving the desired patterning of tabby markings is extremely difficult.

• **FEATURES** The tabby markings should be apparent on all the points, with the pinkish grey shade broken by paler coloration. The ears, as in other Tabby Points, are solid coloured, apart from a paler "thumb-print" marking at the centre.

• **REMARK** Blue eye coloration is a characteristic feature of all Siamese cats.

solid-coloured ears

tabby markings apparent on forehead

nose lavender-pink, with lavender border

firm, athletic body

long, graceful neck

long, fine legs

FUR TYPE: very short, fine, and glossy

Longhair option	Lilac Tabby Point Balinese	Temperament	Affectionate

Country of origin	Thailand	Ancestry	Non-pedigree Asiatics	Origins	1300s

BLUE TABBY POINT

Once the Tabby Point feature was established, it was not difficult to combine this with all the point colours of the Siamese. Good contrast is most likely in the darker pointed forms, although excessive shading can also then be apparent.

• **FEATURES** The body coloration varies from bluish white to platinum-grey, the underparts being much lighter. The points should be blue-grey, broken by paler areas.

• **REMARK** As Tabby Points grow older, body coloration is likely to shows markings such as large spots or wide bands.

long, tapering tail

• slightly convex profile; long nose with no break

clearly defined striping on legs •

solid coloration at back of hind legs •

FUR TYPE: very short, fine, and glossy

Longhair option	Blue Tabby Point Balinese	Temperament	Affectionate

Country of origin	Thailand	Ancestry	Non-pedigree Asiatics	Origins	1300s

CHOCOLATE TABBY POINT

The unmistakable "M"-shaped tabby marking on the head is a feature of all Tabby Points, but it is most prominent in cats with the darker coloured points. Other tabby characteristics must also be apparent, such as the "pencil" lines on either side of the face, extending from the eyes.

• **FEATURES** The ivory-coloured body may darken with age. The points, in this case, are a warm, milk-chocolate colour broken by lighter coloration, and take the form of striped legs and rings around the tail. The eyes are a brilliant clear blue, with dark rims.

• **REMARK** Tabby Point Siamese were recognized in Great Britain in 1966.

• large ears

• pinkish nose, edged by chocolate

tabby markings and point colours not evident in young kitten

• tinted ivory on back and sides of body

markings on legs paler than on other points •

FUR TYPE: very short, fine, and glossy

dark tip to tail •

Longhair option	Chocolate Tabby Point Balinese	Temperament	Affectionate

Country of origin Thailand	Ancestry Non-pedigree Asiatics	Origins 1300s

LILAC TORTIE TABBY POINT

It can be difficult to distinguish between Tortie
Tabby Point and Tortie Point kittens as both
varieties can show tabby markings on the points;
these may not become clear for six or eight weeks
and, in the case of Torties, can take as long as six
months to disappear; this is, therefore, the stage
when identification does become possible.
• **FEATURES** The tortie patching is
cream in this case but Tortie Tabby
Points, in general, are more
similar to Tabby Points than
they are to Tortie Points.
• **REMARK** These cats
are also known in the
United States as
"Tortie Lynx
Points".

*wide base
to ears*

*patching
over tabby
pattern on
points*

*clearly defined
tail-rings*

*small,
oval feet*

FUR TYPE: very short,
fine, and glossy

Longhair option Lilac Tortie Tabby Point Balinese	Temperament Affectionate

Country of origin Thailand	Ancestry Non-pedigree Asiatics	Origins 1300s

BLUE TORTIE TABBY POINT

The tabby markings are fairly prominent in this case, especially on the cream
areas of the body. The distinctive mottling on the ears is a means by which
this variety can be distinguished from the Blue Tortie Point.
• **FEATURES** As in other Siamese, the eyes should be deep blue and
of Oriental shape, slanting in towards the nose. The coat is pale, with
few body markings. The underparts are paler than the rest of the body.
The nose and pads should be mottled with pink, rather than pure blue.
• **REMARK** The tabby ancestry of these
cats means that they are sometimes
described as "Blue Tortie Lynx
Points", as in the case of
other Tabby Points.

*striping
evident
on head*

*broken darker
rings on legs*

FUR TYPE: very short,
fine, and glossy

solid markings at rear of hind legs

Longhair option Blue Tortie Tabby Point Balinese	Temperament Affectionate

Country of origin Thailand	Ancestry Non-pedigree Asiatics	Origins 1300s

CHOCOLATE TORTIE TABBY POINT

These cats are precocious, like other Siamese, and may be sexually mature by six months of age. Females make good mothers, but do not like unnecessary disturbance, especially cats that have not bred before.
• **FEATURES** The warm, chocolate markings associated with the tabby are broken by characteristic red or cream mottling on the points. The basic body shade is ivory, with some shading. As in other cases, there should be a paler thumb-print of colour in the centre of the ears, which is more prominent in this darker form.
• **REMARK** In North America these cats are regarded by some registries as Colorpoint Shorthairs, because of their more varied ancestry.

• *long, angular head with no clear nose break*

typically svelte, Siamese body shape •

FUR TYPE: very short, fine, and glossy

• *tail shows tabby rings and solid tip*

Longhair option Chocolate Tortie Tabby Point Balinese	Temperament Affectionate

Country of origin Thailand	Ancestry Non-pedigree Asiatics	Origins 1300s

SEAL TORTIE TABBY POINT

The sleek appearance of Siamese is easily maintained; brushing and combing about twice a week is adequate, while rubbing the coat occasionally with a chamois leather emphasizes its natural gloss. Tortie Tabby Points are often quieter and less demanding than traditional forms, making them a good choice of pet.
• **FEATURES** As with other Siamese, the markings of these cats tend to be highly individual, with none showing identical patterning. The tabby pattern on the points is broken with cream. The body coloration in the Seal is more pronounced than in the lighter forms.
• **REMARK** The appearance of this form resulted from combining Tabby Point and Tortie Point with Seal Point coloration.

deep blue eyes •

• *cream breaks up tabby markings*

darker shading on body and flanks •

FUR TYPE: very short, fine, and glossy

Longhair option Seal Tortie Tabby Point Balinese	Temperament Affectionate

BURMESE

THE SLEEK SHAPE of these cats, coupled with their good nature, as well as the ever-increasing range of colours, has ensured their popularity. Burmese display neither the extreme svelte type of the Siamese nor the cobby shape of the British Shorthair. Those bred in North America usually have a more stocky build, which is emphasized by the slightly shorter legs.

Country of origin Thailand	Ancestry Non-pedigree Shorthairs	Origins 1400s

CREAM

Young Burmese kittens of all varieties tend to be quite pale in colour, and may also display slight tabby markings. In the case of adult Cream Burmese, some tabby traces may still be apparent on the face. Other slight markings are permitted, provided they are not on the sides of the body or the underparts; a white patch is considered a serious flaw.

• **FEATURES** Adults should be a rich shade of cream. The ears should be slightly darker in coloration than the back.

• **REMARK** An unplanned mating in 1964 between a Red Tabby and a Blue Burmese began the breeding programme that led to the development of these cats. They finally achieved recognition in Britain in 1970.

FUR TYPE: short and glossy, with satin feel

• outer line of ear continues that of face

• upper eyelid slants towards nose; lower eyelid rounded

• well-spaced, golden yellow eyes •

• strong, rounded chest

• slender legs

• muscular body •

straight tail tapering to tip •

hind legs slightly longer than forelegs •

• pink pads •

Longhair option Cream Tiffanie	Temperament Playful

Country of origin	Thailand	Ancestry	Non-pedigree Shorthairs	Origins	1400s

RED

While the development of colours such as the Red has forged ahead in Britain, American breeders regard the Brown as the only true form of the Burmese, other colours being grouped separately as Malayans.
• **FEATURES** The coat colour should be a light tangerine shade with traces of tabby face markings accepted.
• **REMARK** The Red has yet to achieve widespread recognition in North America, even in the Malayan category.

• *ears darker in coloration than back*

• *amber eyes*

FUR TYPE: short and glossy, with satin feel

• *muscular body*

• *pink nose*

• *wide cheekbones*

medium length tail •

Longhair option	Red Tiffanie	Temperament	Playful

Country of origin	Thailand	Ancestry	Non-pedigree Shorthairs	Origins	1400s

CHOCOLATE

Not to be confused with the Brown Burmese, the Chocolate form is better known in America as the "Champagne". These cats were first imported to Britain from the United States in the late 1960s.
• **FEATURES** The overall colour in the case of the Chocolate Burmese is a warm milk-chocolate, which should be slightly paler on the underparts. The coloration should be even with no markings. The mask and ears, on the other hand, may be slightly darker than the other points.
• **REMARK** The sleek coat of these cats, like others of this breed, needs very little attention to keep it immaculate.

• *mask darker than points*

• *warm, chocolate-brown nose*

• *medium tail tapering to rounded tip*

rounded chest •

• *tail lighter in colour than face*

neat, oval paws •

FUR TYPE: short and glossy, with satin feel

Longhair option	Chocolate Tiffanie	Temperament	Playful

Country of origin Thailand	Ancestry Non-pedigree Shorthairs	Origins 1400s

LILAC

Chocolate and Brown Burmese were imported from the United States to Britain in 1969, laying the foundations for the development of this form.
• **FEATURES** Pale as kittens, these cats gradually change colour to a delicate shade of dove-grey. The pads change from shell-pink to lavender-pink. The ears and mask may show deeper coloration than the rest of the body.
• **REMARK** Known in the United States as the "Platinum Malayan".

round-tipped ears tilt slightly forwards •

• muscular, yet elegant neck

• pink pads

FUR TYPE: short and glossy, with satin feel

hind legs slightly longer than front legs •

Longhair option Lilac Tiffanie	Temperament Playful

Country of origin Thailand	Ancestry Non-pedigree Shorthairs	Origins 1400s

BLUE

The appearance of this colour in a litter of Burmese in 1955 aroused considerable interest, the kitten herself being appropriately named *Sealcoat Blue Surprise*.
• **FEATURES** The blue coloration in Burmese is actually a soft shade of silvery grey, sometimes spoken of as being "antique silver". The silvery sheen should be most pronounced on the feet, face, and ears. A slightly darker shade is permitted on the back and tail.
• **REMARK** Recognized in Britain in 1970, Blues were slower to gain a following in the United States.

• glossy coat indicates good health

• silvery sheen on feet

FUR TYPE: short and glossy, with satin feel

dark grey nose •

• high, wide cheekbones taper to form short, blunt wedge

Longhair option Blue Tiffanie	Temperament Playful

Country of origin Thailand	Ancestry Non-pedigree Shorthairs	Origins 1400s

BROWN

Although cats with a similar appearance to the Burmese have been known in Thailand for centuries, the development of the line in the West began with the mating of *Wong Mau*, a brown cat brought from Burma (Myanmar) to the United States in 1930, with a Siamese male.

• **FEATURES** Mature cats should be a rich, warm shade of seal-brown, and just slightly paler on the underparts.

• **REMARK** This is the original form of the Burmese, known in North America as the "Sable".

FUR TYPE: short and glossy, with satin feel

mask and ears slightly darker than body •

• *even depth of coloration*

• *no kink along tail*

Longhair option Brown Tiffanie		Temperament Playful

Country of origin Thailand	Ancestry Non-pedigree Shorthairs	Origins 1400s

CHOCOLATE TORTIE

Like other tortoiseshell forms, Chocolate Tortie Burmese are almost exclusively female, and any males that are produced will almost inevitably be sterile.

• **FEATURES** Type is of paramount importance in these Burmese; the coat has chocolate and red coloration, with no barring.

• **REMARK** The first Chocolate Tortie Burmese were bred in the late 1960s, and are still comparatively scarce; Blue Torties are more numerous.

top of head slightly rounded •

amber eyes •

red blotches •

• *rounded tip to tail*

• *chocolate areas*

tail tapers slightly along length •

• *medium-length, muscular, rounded body*

FUR TYPE: short and glossy, with satin feel

• *neat, oval pads*

Longhair option Chocolate Tortie Tiffanie		Temperament Playful

Country of origin Thailand	Ancestry Non-pedigree Shorthairs	Origins 1400s

LILAC TORTIE

In this case, as with other Burmese, the underparts are a lighter shade than the coloration on the back. Although odd white hairs in the cat's coat may be overlooked by judges, any real evidence of white patches is deemed a serious fault. The coat itself is naturally glossy, and helps to emphasize the elegant outline of the Burmese.

• FEATURES The coloration of the Lilac Tortie should be a combination of lilac and cream, which gives rise to its alternative description of Lilac-cream. There should be no trace of barring on the coat, but considerable variation is permitted in terms of the coloration itself. As with other tortoiseshell forms, the variance in shades may make the coat appear to consist of several distinct colours.

• REMARK Less emphasis is placed on coloration in the Tortie Burmese than on the type.

head slightly rounded on top

well-spaced eyes, with upper lid slanting towards nose; lower lid rounded

FUR TYPE: short and glossy, with satin feel

medium-length, muscular body

straight tail with no kink

attractive intermingling of colours

round ear tips

nose break clearly visible in profile

medium-length tail

relatively long neck

wide cheekbones, narrowing to short wedge

sleek coat

strong, rounded chest

tail tapers along length to rounded tip

slender legs

hind legs longer than front

neat, oval paws

Longhair option Lilac Tortie Tiffanie	Temperament Playful

Country of origin Thailand	Ancestry Non-pedigree Shorthairs	Origins 1400s

BLUE TORTIE

The coloration of these cats as kittens is relatively pale, often showing traces of tabby markings.
• **FEATURES** This Blue-cream has patches of blue and cream fur, without any obvious barring. Nose leather should be plain or blotched, blue and pink.
• **REMARK** Like all torties, this breed is almost always female, and any males born are likely to prove sterile.

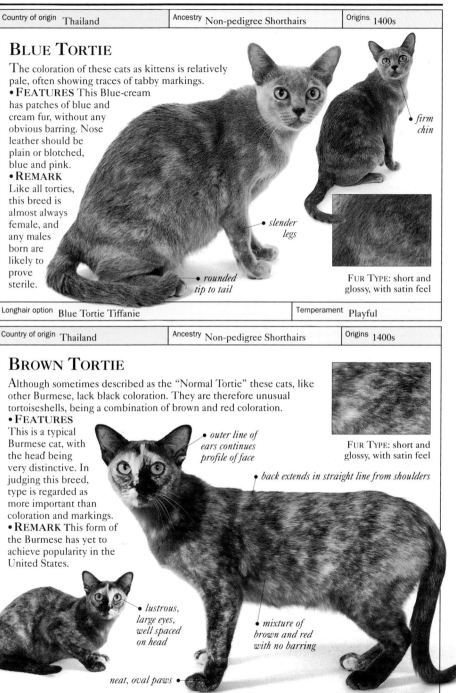

• *firm chin*

• *slender legs*

• *rounded tip to tail*

FUR TYPE: short and glossy, with satin feel

Longhair option Blue Tortie Tiffanie	Temperament Playful

Country of origin Thailand	Ancestry Non-pedigree Shorthairs	Origins 1400s

BROWN TORTIE

Although sometimes described as the "Normal Tortie" these cats, like other Burmese, lack black coloration. They are therefore unusual tortoiseshells, being a combination of brown and red coloration.
• **FEATURES** This is a typical Burmese cat, with the head being very distinctive. In judging this breed, type is regarded as more important than coloration and markings.
• **REMARK** This form of the Burmese has yet to achieve popularity in the United States.

• *outer line of ears continues profile of face*

FUR TYPE: short and glossy, with satin feel

• *back extends in straight line from shoulders*

• *lustrous, large eyes, well spaced on head*

• *mixture of brown and red with no barring*

neat, oval paws •

Longhair option Brown Tortie Tiffanie	Temperament Playful

TONKINESE

THERE IS EVIDENCE to suggest that the first Tonkinese seen in the West was actually accepted as being the founder of the Burmese line. There is certainly a close relationship between Tonkinese and Burmese, the Tonkinese being accepted as a Burmese x Siamese hybrid. In the 1960s, during the early development of the Tonkinese, they became known as Golden Siamese because they had the distinctive golden bronze-sepia coloration of the Burmese, offset against the point patterning of the Siamese. The Tonkinese was first recognized in Canada, and then later accepted in the United States in 1972.

Country of origin Burma (Myanmar)	Ancestry Burmese x Siamese	Origins 1930s

CREAM

The breeding of these cats now revolves around Tonkinese bloodlines, and a percentage of both Burmese and Siamese kittens can be anticipated in each litter. The Tonkinese is now accepted by all registering bodies in the United States.
• **FEATURES** There is considerable variation in the acceptance of colours. In Great Britain, for instance, the Cat Association has now chosen to accept Tonkinese in the range of colours that already exist within the Burmese breed.
• **REMARK** The points are slightly darker than the body.

lithe, muscular, medium-sized body

widely spaced ears; broad at base and with oval tips

blue-green eyes

cream-coloured coat, lighter on underparts, with darker points

relatively long, slim legs

FUR TYPE: short, glossy, soft, and close-lying

long, tapering tail

Longhair option Cream Tiffanie	Temperament Active; affectionate

| Country of origin | Burma (Myanmar) | Ancestry | Burmese x Siamese | Origins | 1930s |

LILAC

In a litter of four kittens bred from Tonkinese parents there will be, on average, two Tonkinese kittens, one Siamese, and one Burmese. But some Tonkinese parents may produce litters containing no Tonkinese offspring at all.
• **FEATURES** The body colour is a delicate shade of dove-grey, between the dark coloration of the Burmese and the lighter shade of the Siamese. The points are a dark pinkish grey.
• **REMARK** The kittens are lighter in colour than adults, but have distinct points.

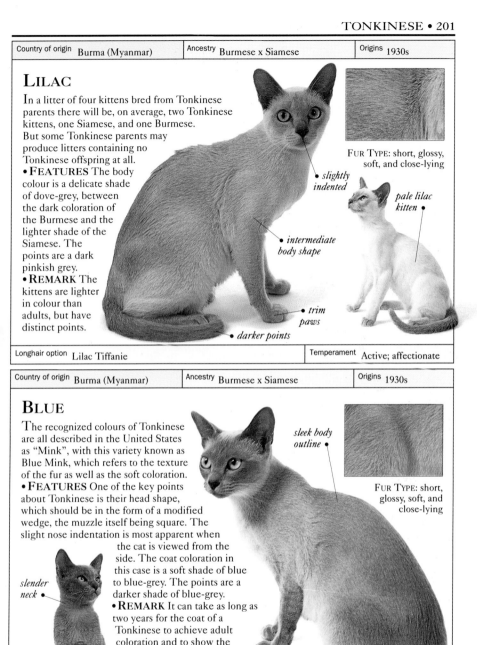

FUR TYPE: short, glossy, soft, and close-lying

slightly indented

pale lilac kitten

intermediate body shape

trim paws

darker points

| Longhair option | Lilac Tiffanie | Temperament | Active; affectionate |

| Country of origin | Burma (Myanmar) | Ancestry | Burmese x Siamese | Origins | 1930s |

BLUE

The recognized colours of Tonkinese are all described in the United States as "Mink", with this variety known as Blue Mink, which refers to the texture of the fur as well as the soft coloration.
• **FEATURES** One of the key points about Tonkinese is their head shape, which should be in the form of a modified wedge, the muzzle itself being square. The slight nose indentation is most apparent when the cat is viewed from the side. The coat coloration in this case is a soft shade of blue to blue-grey. The points are a darker shade of blue-grey.
• **REMARK** It can take as long as two years for the coat of a Tonkinese to achieve adult coloration and to show the ideal, low level of contrast.

sleek body outline

FUR TYPE: short, glossy, soft, and close-lying

slender neck

kitten's colour will alter

hind legs are somewhat longer than front legs

| Longhair option | Blue Tiffanie | Temperament | Active; affectionate |

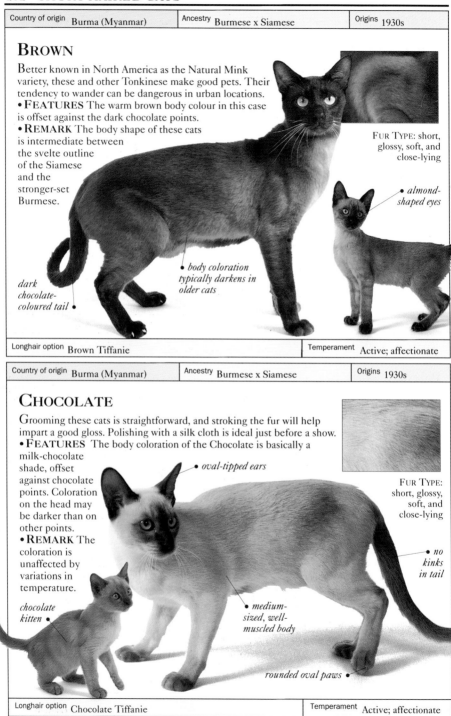

Country of origin Burma (Myanmar)	Ancestry Burmese x Siamese	Origins 1930s

BROWN

Better known in North America as the Natural Mink variety, these and other Tonkinese make good pets. Their tendency to wander can be dangerous in urban locations.
• **FEATURES** The warm brown body colour in this case is offset against the dark chocolate points.
• **REMARK** The body shape of these cats is intermediate between the svelte outline of the Siamese and the stronger-set Burmese.

FUR TYPE: short, glossy, soft, and close-lying

• *almond-shaped eyes*

dark chocolate-coloured tail •

• *body coloration typically darkens in older cats*

Longhair option Brown Tiffanie	Temperament Active; affectionate

Country of origin Burma (Myanmar)	Ancestry Burmese x Siamese	Origins 1930s

CHOCOLATE

Grooming these cats is straightforward, and stroking the fur will help impart a good gloss. Polishing with a silk cloth is ideal just before a show.
• **FEATURES** The body coloration of the Chocolate is basically a milk-chocolate shade, offset against chocolate points. Coloration on the head may be darker than on other points.
• **REMARK** The coloration is unaffected by variations in temperature.

• *oval-tipped ears*

FUR TYPE: short, glossy, soft, and close-lying

• *no kinks in tail*

chocolate kitten •

• *medium-sized, well-muscled body*

rounded oval paws •

Longhair option Chocolate Tiffanie	Temperament Active; affectionate

Country of origin Burma (Myanmar)	Ancestry Burmese x Siamese	Origins 1930s

LILAC TORTIE

One of the most distinctive features of the Tonkinese is their eye coloration, which should ideally be of a blue-green shade, sometimes referred to as aquamarine.

• **FEATURES** In these cats, the lilac points are broken by cream markings, which vary considerably in size and extent. There should be no sign of a facial blaze.

• **REMARK** Depth of colour, clarity, and brilliance are important factors in assessing the eye coloration in these cats.

oval tips to ears •

eyes rounded at lower edge, slanting towards outer corner of ear •

FUR TYPE: short, glossy, soft, and close-lying

straight tail •

Longhair option Lilac Tortie Tiffanie	Temperament Active; affectionate

Country of origin Burma (Myanmar)	Ancestry Burmese x Siamese	Origins 1930s

BROWN TORTIE

Although Tonkinese may appear light, they are much heavier than their Siamese relatives. There must be a clear distinction between the points and the body coloration. Kittens do not reach their true adult coloration until they are about one year old.

• **FEATURES** The coloration on the body should be an even shade of warm brown; the points are slightly darker, broken by cream patches.

• **REMARK** Barring is most likely in the case of young cats, and should disappear within one year. Kittens also lack the tracings that link the mask and ears in adults.

elegant, well-muscled body •

high cheekbones •

tight abdomen •

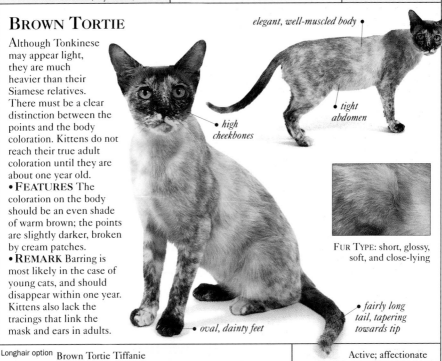

FUR TYPE: short, glossy, soft, and close-lying

fairly long tail, tapering towards tip •

oval, dainty feet •

Longhair option Brown Tortie Tiffanie	Active; affectionate

BURMILLA

THIS FAIRLY RECENT introduction to the cat scene is best known in Great Britain, where its development began in the early 1980s. It is an agouti breed, and is bred in both silver and golden forms, with tipping or shading on the coat. Careful in-breeding has emphasized the short, dense, soft coat.

Country of origin Great Britain		Ancestry Burmese x Chinchilla Longhair	Origins 1981

CHOCOLATE TIPPED

The kittens produced from the unplanned mating of a Silver Chinchilla Longhair with a Lilac Burmese formed the original stock for the Burmilla. Their owner, Baroness Miranda von Kirchberg, developed a breeding programme with the aim of producing cats with the type of the Burmese and the tipping of the Silver Chinchilla. Burmillas first appeared at a Cat Association show in 1983.
• FEATURES The tipping in this case is chocolate, with a silver undercoat. The deepest coloration should be along the back, continuing down the tail, and becoming paler on the flanks.
• REMARK Some light spotting on the belly of these cats is permitted.

"necklets" of darker fur should be broken

"M"-shaped outline clearly visible on head

distinct nose break •

• tail carried proud

tipping should be even and symmetrical •

well-muscled body •

FUR TYPE: short, fine, soft, and close-lying

• chocolate area extends from feet up to hocks

• body shading should be as free from tabby markings as possible

• lightly barred tail with dark tip

Longhair option None		Temperament Active and friendly

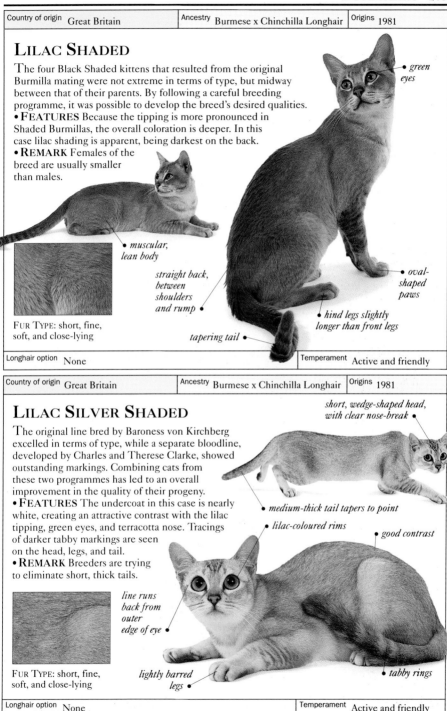

| Country of origin | Great Britain | Ancestry | Burmese x Chinchilla Longhair | Origins | 1981 |

LILAC SHADED

The four Black Shaded kittens that resulted from the original Burmilla mating were not extreme in terms of type, but midway between that of their parents. By following a careful breeding programme, it was possible to develop the breed's desired qualities.
• **FEATURES** Because the tipping is more pronounced in Shaded Burmillas, the overall coloration is deeper. In this case lilac shading is apparent, being darkest on the back.
• **REMARK** Females of the breed are usually smaller than males.

green eyes •

• muscular, lean body

straight back, between shoulders and rump •

• oval-shaped paws

• hind legs slightly longer than front legs

FUR TYPE: short, fine, soft, and close-lying

tapering tail •

| Longhair option | None | | Temperament | Active and friendly |

| Country of origin | Great Britain | Ancestry | Burmese x Chinchilla Longhair | Origins | 1981 |

LILAC SILVER SHADED

short, wedge-shaped head, with clear nose-break •

The original line bred by Baroness von Kirchberg excelled in terms of type, while a separate bloodline, developed by Charles and Therese Clarke, showed outstanding markings. Combining cats from these two programmes has led to an overall improvement in the quality of their progeny.
• **FEATURES** The undercoat in this case is nearly white, creating an attractive contrast with the lilac tipping, green eyes, and terracotta nose. Tracings of darker tabby markings are seen on the head, legs, and tail.
• **REMARK** Breeders are trying to eliminate short, thick tails.

• medium-thick tail tapers to point

• lilac-coloured rims

• good contrast

line runs back from outer edge of eye •

FUR TYPE: short, fine, soft, and close-lying

lightly barred legs •

• tabby rings

| Longhair option | None | | Temperament | Active and friendly |

Country of origin Great Britain	Ancestry Burmese x Chinchilla Longhair	Origins 1981

LIGHT CHOCOLATE TIPPED

The depth of tipping (or shading) is not a consistent feature throughout the cat's life, the coloration tending to darken as the cat matures.

• **FEATURES** The shape of the eyes is an important characteristic; they must be of intermediate shape between round and almond. They are set rather like those of an Oriental, with a slight slope towards the nose. The tipping in this case corresponds to the rich chocolate coloration of the Burmese.

• **REMARK** Burmilla kittens are relatively light in coloration at birth.

"M"-shaped marking

FUR TYPE: short, fine, soft, and close-lying

chocolate tipping

• tabby markings

• muscular legs reflect Burmese ancestry

• tail terminates in solid tip

None	Temperament Active and friendly

Country of origin Great Britain	Ancestry Burmese x Chinchilla Longhair	Origins 1981

BROWN TIPPED

One of the most important features of the Asian group, including the Burmilla, is temperament, and this is reflected in the breed standards used for judging purposes – a relatively new departure for the cat fancy.

• **FEATURES** Brown tipping, offset against the silver undercoat, typifies these cats. The depth of tipping is not especially significant, provided that it is even. Very pale tipping is considered undesirable, as it results in a virtually white appearance.

• **REMARK** The Burmilla was granted recognition by the Cat Association of Britain in November 1983.

green eyes •

• well-spaced ears, creating a butterfly-wing impression when viewed from front

FUR TYPE: short, fine, soft, and close-lying

• tabby markings

Longhair option None	Temperament Active and friendly

ASIAN

THE DESCRIPTION "Asian" is used to describe cats of traditional Burmese type that differ in terms of coloration, patterning, or coat length. However the name itself is used only for the Asian Smokes and Tabbies, which have been developed in classic, mackerel, spotted, and ticked forms; in contrast the Asian group, as drawn up by the GCCF in Britain, includes a much wider range of breeds, including the Burmilla, Bombay, and Tiffanie, which are all of similar type to these other Asians. The Singapura may be added to the group once these cats are more widely established.

Country of origin Great Britain	Ancestry Burmese x Chinchilla Longhair	Origins 1981

BROWN MACKEREL TABBY

There is tremendous potential for breeders within the Asian tabby group, for such cats can be bred in all four tabby patterns, a wide range of colours, and even a variety of tortie combinations are possible.

• **FEATURES** The Asian mackerel tabby has more discrete markings than the classic form. Like the classic, it shows a line running down the back to the tip of the tail, but in this case, narrow vertical lines also extend down the sides of the body, with no blotches on the flanks. Asian ticked tabbies show a great reduction in the number of markings on their coat, their fur being mainly ticked, while the spotted form can similarly be distinguished quite easily.

• **REMARK** Good contrast between the black tabby markings and the paler ground colour is important in this Asian mackerel tabby.

ears tilt slightly forward

well-spaced eyes

distinct nose break

"M"-shaped marking on head

oval paws

medium-length body

elegant, medium-thick tail

tail carried proud

neat, tight paws

hind legs longer than front legs

FUR TYPE: short, fine, soft, and close-lying

Longhair option Brown Mackerel Tabby Tiffanie	Temperament Active and friendly

Country of origin Great Britain	Ancestry Burmese x Chinchilla Longhair	Origins 1981

RED (CORNELIAN)

The Asian category of short-haired cats provides a means of categorizing cats of medium-foreign appearance that are similar in type to the Burmese.
• **FEATURES** Self-coloured Asians, such as this individual, have currently received only preliminary recognition in the United Kingdom.
• **REMARK** "Cornelian" is the name proposed for this self-coloured Asian when it is formally recognized.

long tail

straight back •

FUR TYPE: short, fine, soft, and close-lying

pink nose •

neat, oval paws •

powerful hind legs •

Longhair option Red Tiffanie	Temperament Active and friendly

Country of origin Great Britain	Ancestry Burmese x Chinchilla Longhair	Origins 1981

BURMESE-BROWN SMOKE

The Asian Smoke group includes cats showing Burmese colouring, as in the case of this individual. The undercoat of Smokes should be white or whitish.
• **FEATURES** The brown tipping here should extend to between one third and one half of the entire hair length. Pale tabby markings should be apparent over the body, with silvery traces on the head.
• **REMARK** In some cats, slight tufts of longer hair may be evident on the ears.

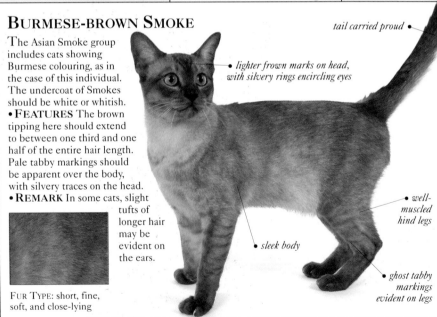

tail carried proud •

• *lighter frown marks on head, with silvery rings encircling eyes*

• *well-muscled hind legs*

• *sleek body*

• *ghost tabby markings evident on legs*

FUR TYPE: short, fine, soft, and close-lying

Longhair option Brown Smoke Tiffanie	Temperament Active and friendly

Country of origin Great Britain	Ancestry Burmese x Chinchilla Longhair	Origins 1981

CHOCOLATE SMOKE

These Asian breeds tend to be slightly quieter by nature than their Burmese relatives, but their voices can still be quite loud; this is especially true when a female in oestrus is calling for a mate.

• **FEATURES** The contrast in this case between the chocolate outer coat and the whitish ground colour can be seen when the fur is parted. Very slight tabby markings are apparent on the coat. The relatively large, widely spaced eyes add to the appealing appearance of these friendly cats.

• **REMARK** Paler areas in the coat are acceptable but actual white areas are viewed as a fault.

FUR TYPE: short, fine, soft, and close-lying

• *strong, rounded, medium-width chest*

• *contrast of Smoke patterning becomes more evident as cat walks*

• *tapering tail*

Longhair option Chocolate Smoke Tiffanie	Temperament Active and friendly

Country of origin Great Britain	Ancestry Burmese x Chinchilla Longhair	Origins 1981

BLACK SMOKE

Contrast between the different colours in the coat is most pronounced in this Smoke variety. As in other Asians, the coloration of the nose, pads, and eye-rims matches that of the outer coat.

• **FEATURES** The Smoke effect, created by the contrast between the whitish ground colour and the jet-black hair, is clearly discernible here. The pale tabby markings should give the shimmering effect of watered silk over the body.

• **REMARK** The silvery markings around the eyes of Asians are known as "clown marks", because of their resemblance to the make-up of circus clowns.

• *gently rounded skull between large ears*

• *medium-thick tapering tail*

• *lighter undercoat less apparent along back than on underparts*

FUR TYPE: short, fine, soft, and close-lying

oval-shaped paws •

Longhair option Black Smoke Tiffanie	Temperament Active and friendly

BOMBAY

THIS HIGHLY DISTINCTIVE breed was created in 1958 by Nikki Horner of Kentucky. The intention was to produce a cat that resembled a miniature black panther. The breed is of intermediate type, but a noticeable difference is now emerging between the original cats, developed in the United States, and those being bred in Britain, resulting from the difference in type of their Burmese ancestors. First recognized in the United States in 1976, the Bombay has yet to receive universal recognition. The GCCF include it in the Asian group because of its similarity in type to the Burmese.

Country of origin USA	Ancestry Burmese x American Shorthair	Origins 1950s

BLACK

The Bombay is a cat that craves human attention, as well as being tolerant of children and dogs. It is therefore ideal as a family pet.

• **FEATURES** The short, "patent-leather" coat is a distinctive feature of the breed, and is offset by the brightly coloured eyes. Kittens may prove quite slow to develop, with tabby markings often present in their coat. Their eyes are blue at first, like those of all kittens. They then turn grey, and finally turn a gold or deep copper colour.

• **REMARK** The Bombay was developed from the combination of a Sable Burmese and a Black American Shorthair. Today, while the breed retains the coloration of the American Shorthair, it also closely resembles the Burmese in type.

FUR TYPE: short and sleek; discernible sheen

• *muscular, medium-sized body*

• *straight tail with no kinks*

• *dense, jet-black fur*

• *deep copper eyes preferred, but can be gold*

• *round-tipped ears*

• *short, wedge face*

• *neat, oval paw pads*

• *strong, firm body*

• *medium, tapering tail*

Longhair option Black Tiffanie	Temperament Assertive

SINGAPURA

T HE NAME "SINGAPURA" originates from the Malaysian name for Singapore, where development of this breed began during the mid-1970s. The ancestors of these cats, often living feral lives in south-eastern Asia, and known as the "Drain Cat of Singapore", show an Abyssinian-type coat pattern.

Country of origin Singapore	Ancestry Non-pedigree Ticked Shorthairs	Origins 1974

SEPIA AGOUTI

Tommy Meadow took five of the local Singapore cats back to the United States in 1975. These five cats, plus another individual taken out of the Singapore SPCA in 1980, provided the foundation for the breed.
• **FEATURES** The Singapura is a small breed, and may weigh less than 2.7 kg (6 lb). Traditionally sable-brown in colour with warm brown, wavy ticking over much of the body and the muzzle, the chin and chest are usually lighter.
• **REMARK** The Singapura was first exhibited in the United States during 1975, and the breed was awarded championship status there soon afterwards.

slightly pointed, large ears

dark, seal-brown ticking on warm, "old ivory" ground colour

dark blackish brown tip on tail

underparts paler than sides of body

barring present on inside of front legs

kittens' eye colour changes up to the age of 9 weeks

individual hairs show at least two bands of dark ticking with light roots and dark tips

kittens' coats look longer as bodies are smaller

FUR TYPE: short, silky, and sleek

Longhair option None	Temperament Inquisitive

ORIENTAL SHORTHAIR

SOME OF THE FIRST Siamese cats seen in the West had a solid body colour and no Siamese markings. These cats gradually died out, however, as only typical Siamese with blue eyes were recognized for exhibiting at that time. Successful attempts to recreate the type began in the 1950s. The category includes both self colours and marked varieties such as the tabbies; they can be bred in any colour and with any markings except in a pointed form.

Country of origin Great Britain	Ancestry Siamese crosses	Origins 1950s

FOREIGN WHITE

Following the successful development of the Havana (*p.216*), the quest for this colour began in Britain by crossing Siamese with short-haired whites. This led to white cats with either orange or blue eyes. The breed was then developed by mating those with blue eyes back to Siamese. Although two of the three original lines had problems with deafness, this has now been carefully eliminated.

• **FEATURES** In type, these cats are now indistinguishable from their Siamese ancestors in all but fur coloration.

• **REMARK** This breed was accepted for show purposes in Britain under the name of Foreign White, but they have become better known internationally as Oriental Whites.

blue eyes

FUR TYPE: short, fine, and glossy

• *long, slender legs terminate in small, oval paws*

very long, thin, tapering tail •

• *pure white coat emphasizes svelte shape*

• *pink nose with no trace of darker markings*

• *pink pads on feet*

Longhair option White Oriental Longhair	Temperament Lively

Country of origin Great Britain	Ancestry Siamese crosses	Origins 1950s

CREAM

• *angular, flat-topped head*

tapering tail with no kink •

The prefix Foreign has been dropped from all breeds but the Foreign White since the early 1990's.
• **FEATURES** The coat in this case should be pale cream and should display little or no evidence of tabby markings.
  • **REMARK** A geneticist has worked out that within this group there are almost 400 possible colour forms.

• *lithe, tubular body*

hind legs slightly longer than forelegs •

FUR TYPE: short, fine, and glossy

Longhair option Cream Oriental Longhair	Temperament Lively

Country of origin Great Britain	Ancestry Siamese crosses	Origins 1950s

LILAC

Although the earliest examples of the Lilac appeared during the development of the Havana in the 1950s, no serious attempt was made to develop the colour until the 1960s.
• **FEATURES** Lilac kittens may have tabby markings on their coat and tail but these soon disappear. Faint markings may also appear along the flanks of older cats during the summer months, but these will vanish when the cat moults in the autumn. Bluish or fawn tones in the coat are viewed as serious faults.
• **REMARK** This colour was known in its early days as the "Oriental Lavender".

• *long, straight nose emphasizes shape of head*

frosty grey coat with distinctive pinkish tone •

• *green, almond-shaped eyes*

• *slim, elegant legs*

FUR TYPE: short, fine, and glossy

Longhair option Lilac Oriental Longhair	Temperament Lively

Country of origin	Great Britain	Ancestry	Siamese crosses	Origins	1950s

RED

The sleek appearance of these cats is emphasized by their long, slender profile and fine, glossy fur. In Great Britain, the solid-coloured varieties were known as Foreign Shorthair, and only the patterned forms, such as the Red Tabby, were called Oriental Shorthairs.

• **FEATURES** In this case, the red coloration should be of a rich, warm, even shade. Any white hairs evident in the coat are considered to be a serious fault.

• **REMARK** It is not unusual for tabby markings to be apparent in these cats, and especially in the case of kittens, as a result of the breeding programme.

pink pads •

even red coloration •

FUR TYPE: short, fine, and glossy

Longhair option	Red Oriental Longhair	Temperament	Lively

Country of origin	Great Britain	Ancestry	Siamese crosses	Origins	1950s

FAWN

Another recent addition, the Fawn is in every way a typical Oriental cat. Their short coats are easy to maintain in top condition and, in personality, they make affectionate and often quite demanding companions.

• **FEATURES** The coloration should be even and consistent in depth to the roots of each hair. The coat should have a pinkish rather than blue tinge, with no white hairs.

• **REMARK** The development of the Caramel was an important breakthrough in the breeding of this and other Oriental self colours.

• green eyes with no flecks of other colours

long slender legs •

• elegant neck

• warm, rosy mushroom shade

oval paws •

• very long, tapering tail

FUR TYPE: short, fine, and glossy

Longhair option	Fawn Oriental Longhair	Temperament	Lively

| Country of origin | Great Britain | Ancestry | Siamese crosses | Origins | 1950s |

RED AND WHITE

There is tremendous scope within the Oriental group, with the possibility of superimposing virtually any colour or pattern on to cats of Oriental type.

- **FEATURES** In this breed, poise and balance are significant with all parts of the body in proportion. The head should take the form of a well-balanced triangle.
- **REMARK** Oriental bi-colours with solid coloured tails contributed to the development of the Seychellois breed.

- *large ears*

FUR TYPE: short, fine, and glossy

- *white and coloured areas clearly defined*

- *slanting eyes*

- *hind legs longer than front legs*

| Longhair option | Red and White Oriental Longhair | Temperament | Lively |

| Country of origin | Great Britain | Ancestry | Siamese crosses | Origins | 1950s |

CINNAMON

- *vivid green eyes*

In Britain, the term "foreign" was used for self-coloured forms of these cats, but they are now generally viewed simply as Orientals, as has always been the case with patterned varieties. This colour was known as the "Oriental Caramel" in the United States, and as the "Blonde Havana" in the Netherlands, but is now generally known as the "Oriental Cinnamon".

- *cinnamon-brown nose*

- **FEATURES** Coloration should be a solid shade of cinnamon-brown, with no trace of white. Eye colour must be bright green.
- **REMARK** These cats emerged from crossings between Havanas and Sorrel Abyssinians during the 1960s, initially in the Netherlands, and subsequently in Great Britain.

- *long, tapering tail*

- *long, slender, svelte body with firm abdomen*

- *slender legs*

- *fine feet, with small, oval-shaped paws*

FUR TYPE: short, fine, and glossy

| Longhair option | Cinnamon Oriental Longhair | Temperament | Lively |

Country of origin Great Britain	Ancestry Siamese crosses	Origins 1950s

CARAMEL

These cats emerged during the development of
Oriental Shaded cats and have contributed in turn
to newer self colours such as the Apricot.
• **FEATURES** With a typical Siamese profile,
these cats are entirely bluish fawn in colour; the
coloration extends to nose, pads, and eye rims.
• **REMARK** This variety originated from the
mating of a Silver Chinchilla
Longhair and a Siamese.

• *medium-sized body*

angular head •

pure green eyes •

FUR TYPE: short, fine,
and glossy

• *small oval paws*

Longhair option Caramel Oriental Longhair	Temperament Lively

Country of origin Great Britain	Ancestry Siamese crosses	Origins 1950s

HAVANA

Originally described under this name in the United States, the breed was
known in Great Britain, until 1970, as the Chestnut Brown Foreign.
• **FEATURES** The Havana in Europe is now more similar to the Oriental
Self Brown being bred in North America, with a discernible Siamese type.
The American form of the Havana Brown has developed a more rounded face
shape and shorter nose, however, as out-crossings to Siamese are outlawed.
• **REMARK** The
development of the
Havana began in 1951
when a Chocolate
Point Siamese was
mated with a black
non-pedigree cat.

• *bright green eyes*

rich, warm, chestnut-brown coloration •

• *triangular head*

FUR TYPE: short, fine,
and glossy

long, slim legs •

long, tapering tail •

Longhair option Brown Oriental Longhair	Temperament Lively

Country of origin	Great Britain	Ancestry	Siamese crosses	Origins	1950s

BLUE

These and other Orientals tend to be somewhat quieter than their Siamese ancestors, yet they can be just as affectionate and demanding.
• **FEATURES** Pure blue coloration without any traces of white is required. The eyes must be entirely green with no flecking.
• **REMARK** Blue cats of oriental type cropped up occasionally in litters of Siamese but did not attract great attention until the development of the Havana and Lilac.

FUR TYPE: short, fine, and glossy

• *eyes slant towards nose*

• *colour consistent to base of hairs*

Longhair option	Blue Oriental Longhair	Temperament	Lively

Country of origin	Great Britain	Ancestry	Siamese crosses	Origins	1950s

BLACK

Also known as the Oriental Ebony, this is the oldest of the Oriental forms now being bred. It came to prominence in the 1980s.
• **FEATURES** The coloration in this case must be pure black with no hint of a rusty hue in adults.
• **REMARK** The first Oriental Blacks were bred from Siamese mated to Russian Blues during the development of the Havana. Their sleek coats give them a very striking appearance.

• *wedge-shaped head*

• *long nose with no stop*

large, pricked ears •

• *shiny, jet-black coat*

• *long, slender legs*

• *fur lies close to body, emphasizing sleek shape*

FUR TYPE: short, fine, and glossy

• *very long, tapering tail*

Black Oriental Longhair	Temperament	Lively

| Country of origin Great Britain | Ancestry Siamese crosses | Origins 1950s |

CARAMEL SILVER TICKED TABBY

Ticked Oriental tabbies are distinguished by their sparkling body appearance, with none of the usual blotches, stripes, or spots, apart from a darker area of colouring running along the back.
• **FEATURES** In this case, the body is a combination of cool bluish fawn and a paler silvery fawn ground colour. There should be one or two necklaces visible in the vicinity of the upper chest, with bluish fawn tabby stripes on the head, legs, and tail.
• **REMARK** In this case, the silver gene gives a cool tone to the coloration, which is acceptable for show purposes.

bluish fawn "frown" lines forming tabby "M" on head

FUR TYPE: short, fine, and glossy

two or three bands of ticking on each hair

dark tip to tail

| Longhair option Caramel Silver Ticked Tabby Oriental Longhair | Temperament Lively |

| Country of origin Great Britain | Ancestry Siamese crosses | Origins 1950s |

CINNAMON TORTIE

Oriental torties, as with all other tortie forms, are almost exclusively female. They were originally bred from pairings of Havanas or Blacks with Red Point Siamese cats.
• **FEATURES** The warm cinnamon shade associated with the Oriental Cinnamon is here combined with dark or pale red, or with both of these colours. Again, there must be no white hairs evident in the coat, nor are any signs of tabby markings permitted.
• **REMARK** These cats are known sometimes as "Oriental Parti-colours".

green eyes

FUR TYPE: short, fine, and glossy

some breaks in coloration with shades of red also apparent in coat

legs vary in coloration

long, elegant legs emphasize height

| Cinnamon Tortie Oriental Longhair | Temperament Lively |

Country of origin	Great Britain	Ancestry	Siamese crosses	Origins	1950s

CHOCOLATE TORTIE

The pattern of markings in these cats is entirely random but it is nevertheless important that the coloured areas on the head, body, and extremities show the characteristic tortie markings.
• **FEATURES** The basic appearance of these cats is a warm shade of chestnut-brown, offset by either dark or pale red patterning, or a combination of both colours. A red facial blaze, although not considered essential, is preferred.
• **REMARK**
Green eyes are characteristic of all Oriental torties.

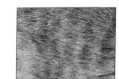

chocolate and red coloration

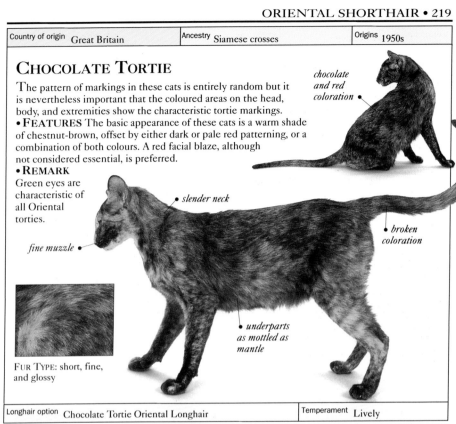

• *slender neck*

• *broken coloration*

fine muzzle •

• *underparts as mottled as mantle*

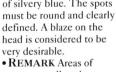

FUR TYPE: short, fine, and glossy

Longhair option	Chocolate Tortie Oriental Longhair	Temperament	Lively

Country of origin	Great Britain	Ancestry	Siamese crosses	Origins	1950s

TORTIE BLACK SILVER SPOTTED

These cats show a closer similarity to Oriental Silver Spotteds than to torties. Tabby markings, coupled with good Oriental body type, are seen as more significant than the quality of the tortie patterning.
• **FEATURES** The blue markings are offset against a paler shade of silvery blue. The spots must be round and clearly defined. A blaze on the head is considered to be very desirable.
• **REMARK** Areas of cream, as well as the patterning, identify these cats as tortie tabbies.

"M"-shaped scarab marking •

• *marking extends behind ears*

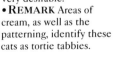

FUR TYPE: short, fine, and glossy

facial blaze •

bars apparent on legs •

Longhair option	Tortie Black Silver Spotted Oriental Longhair	Temperament	Lively

Country of origin Great Britain	Ancestry Siamese crosses	Origins 1950s

CHOCOLATE SPOTTED

Once known in Britain as "Egyptian Maus", the name was changed to avoid confusion with a different breed known by that name in the United States.
• FEATURES The spotting is the result of rich shades of chocolate-brown, with lighter tones being preferred. The spotted markings should stand out clearly against the bronze agouti ground colour. The spots must be rounded and evenly spaced.
• REMARK While kittens may have a solid spinal line, in adult cats this is seen as a serious fault.

FUR TYPE: short, fine, and glossy

ears emphasize wedge-shaped head

spinal line broken into spots

long neck

chocolate rings on tail

Longhair option Chocolate Spotted Oriental Longhair	Temperament Lively

Country of origin Great Britain	Ancestry Siamese crosses	Origins 1950s

LILAC CLASSIC TABBY

Clear definition of markings is an important feature of these cats; the darker coloration should be dense, contrasting with the ground colour.
• FEATURES The lilac tabby markings are set against a cool, beige ground colour and must be clearly defined. The underside of the body is lighter overall with lilac spotting. The markings on each shoulder are butterfly shaped while those on the flanks are oyster shaped, with rings encircling them.
• REMARK The Lilac is sometimes known as the "Lavender" in the United States.

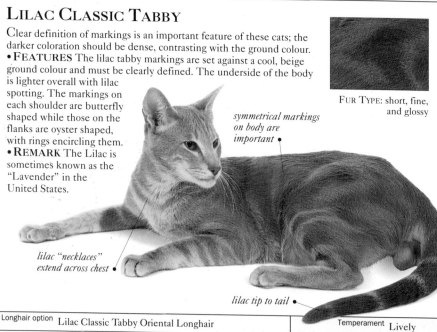

FUR TYPE: short, fine, and glossy

symmetrical markings on body are important

lilac "necklaces" extend across chest

lilac tip to tail

Longhair option Lilac Classic Tabby Oriental Longhair	Temperament Lively

Country of origin Great Britain	Ancestry Siamese crosses	Origins 1950s

BLACK SMOKE

These cats result from matings between Siamese and Chinchilla Longhairs with the use of Blacks and Havanas to establish type. A Red Point Siamese bred to a Silver Shaded Longhair produced the first Oriental Smoke during the 1970s.

• **FEATURES** The black appearance is belied by the white undercoat, which should be approximately one third of the total hair length. An even Smoke effect is desirable, without prominent silver brindling.

• **REMARK** Ghost tabby markings are often apparent on Oriental Smokes, giving a watered silk effect to the cat's appearance.

white undercoat evident as cat moves

green eyes

slim legs

the Smoke effect on body should correspond to that on head

shadowy tabby markings apparent

colour of pads matches basic colour

FUR TYPE: short, fine, and glossy

long, tapering tail

Longhair option Black Smoke Oriental Longhair	Temperament Lively

Country of origin Great Britain	Ancestry Siamese crosses	Origins 1950s

BLACK SMOKE AND WHITE

Any colour is accepted in the Oriental Smoke category, a group that has developed rapidly in recent years. This is one of the first bi-colours to be bred.

• **FEATURES** The undercoat is pure white and the top-coat is heavily tipped with black, giving the impression of a black and white bi-colour. The distribution of black and white patches varies according to the individual.

• **REMARK** The bi-coloured Oriental has arisen from the Seychellois breeding programme, which is aiming for mainly white bi-colours.

large, wide ears continue line of head

FUR TYPE: short, fine, and glossy

clear definition between white and black Smoke areas of fur

restricted white markings

small, oval paws

Longhair option Black Smoke and White Oriental Longhair	Temperament Lively

Country of origin Great Britain	Ancestry Siamese crosses	Origins 1950s

RED TICKED TABBY

The ticked tabbies can be distinguished by the lack of patterning in their coats, compared with the other three tabby variants established in Orientals.
• **FEATURES** There should be two and ideally three bands of darker red coloration on the individual hairs. Contrast here is based on the warm, rich red banding on a lighter, bright apricot ground colour.
• **REMARK** There should be no solid spinal line down the back, but tabby stripes should be apparent on the face, legs, and tail.

• *wide base to ears*

FUR TYPE: short, fine, and glossy

• *a complete or broken "necklace" must be visible*

straight line of head •

• *tabby stripes visible on legs*

• *red tip to tail*

Longhair option Red Ticked Tabby Oriental Longhair	Temperament Lively

Country of origin Great Britain	Ancestry Siamese crosses	Origins 1950s

LILAC TICKED TABBY

Contrast is a key feature of the ticked tabbies, but any sign of traditional tabby patterning on the body is penalized. Darker shading may, however, be apparent on the back.
• **FEATURES** In this case, the darker lilac ticking is displayed against a cool beige colour. The nose, pads, and eye rims are of a faded lilac shade, though some pinkish coloration may be seen on the nose and pads. The eyes should be green, with no flecks of any other colour.
• **REMARK** There may well be evidence of tabby markings on the underside of the body.

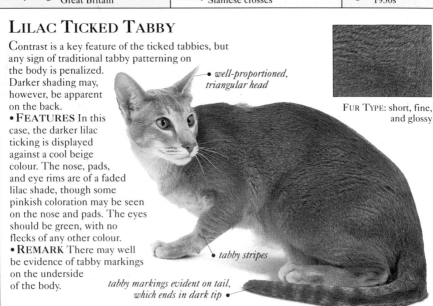

• *well-proportioned, triangular head*

FUR TYPE: short, fine, and glossy

• *tabby stripes*

tabby markings evident on tail, which ends in dark tip •

Longhair option Lilac Ticked Tabby Oriental Longhair	Temperament Lively

Country of origin Great Britain	Ancestry Siamese crosses	Origins 1950s

CARAMEL TICKED TABBY

The sparkling effect of the coat results from the ticking on individual hairs, which should have two or three bands of colour along their length.
• **FEATURES** The cool, bluish fawn markings contrast with a beige agouti ground colour. There should be no blotches, stripes, or spots, but traces of tabby markings are permitted on the undersides. The darker caramel colour must extend up the hind legs and should be present at the tip of the tail.
• **REMARK** Although the fur is darker along the back, any trace of a solid line here is a flaw.

FUR TYPE: short, fine, and glossy

• *darker ticking apparent over back*

tabby markings on tail •

recognizable tabby stripes present on legs •

Longhair option Caramel Ticked Tabby Oriental Longhair	Temperament Lively

Country of origin Great Britain	Ancestry Siamese crosses	Origins 1950s

CHOCOLATE CLASSIC TABBY

Oriental tabbies may show whitish areas on their lips and lower jaw, but this should generally not extend over a wider area.
• **FEATURES** Classic tabby patterning is out-lined in chocolate-brown, offset against the bronze agouti ground coloration. The eyes are green.
• **REMARK** The eye rims are chocolate-brown, offset by the green eye colour.

solid oyster marking •

• *darker "necklaces" present on neck and upper chest*

• *sleek body*

• *"bracelets" of darker fur extend down legs*

chocolate tip to tail •

FUR TYPE: short, fine, and glossy

Longhair option Chocolate Classic Tabby Oriental Longhair	Temperament Lively

Country of origin Great Britain	Ancestry Siamese crosses	Origins 1950s

CHOCOLATE TICKED TABBY

The origin of today's Oriental tabbies can be traced back to the breeding of tabby-pointed Siamese, at a time when Siamese were mated with non-pedigree tabbies. Later refinement of the breed occurred with the pairing of Havanas and tabby-pointed Siamese.
• FEATURES The chocolate ticking contrasts with the bronze agouti ground colour on the body, creating a sparkling effect. The tipping at the end of the hairs is darkest. In this example, typical tabby markings are confined to the head, legs, and tail.
• REMARK This, and other Chocolate Oriental varieties, are often better known in the United States as "Chestnut". Eye coloration in this group of cats, as in the majority of Oriental tabbies, should be pure green, with no flecks of other colours apparent.

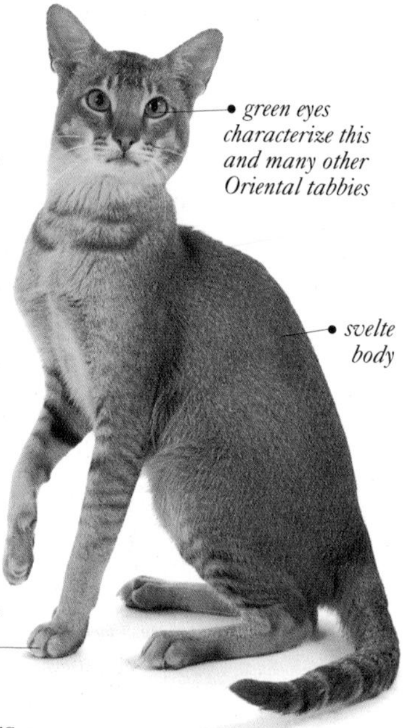

• green eyes characterize this and many other Oriental tabbies

• svelte body

long tail •

• clear signs of tabby markings must be apparent on head

small paws •

darker shading on back •

long, wedge-shaped head with straight nose •

• at least one "necklace" around neck

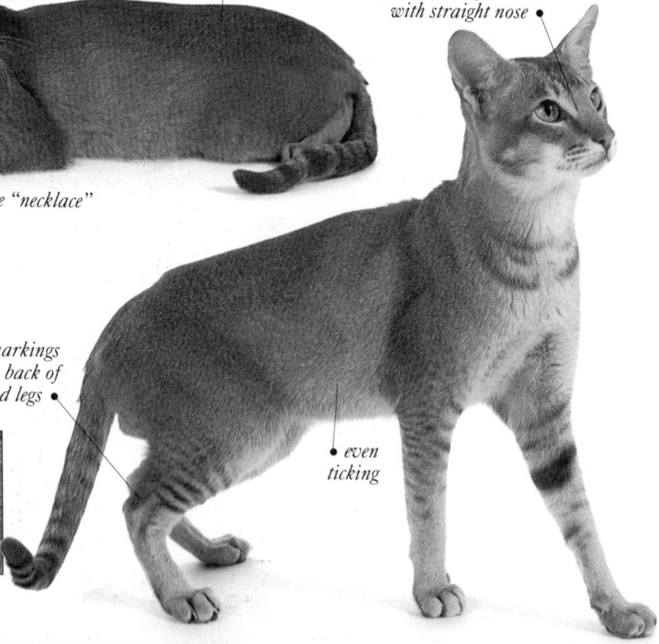

chocolate markings extend up back of both hind legs •

• even ticking

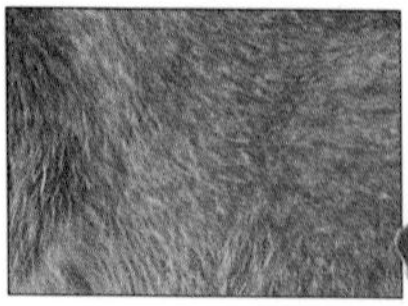

FUR TYPE: short, fine, and glossy

Longhair option Chocolate Ticked Tabby Oriental Longhair	Temperament Lively

Country of origin	Great Britain	Ancestry	Siamese crosses	Origins	1950s

BLACK SILVER SPOTTED

This is one of the most striking of the Oriental Spotted group, with a vivid contrast between coat and markings.
• **FEATURES** While the head markings resemble those of the Classic Tabby, the body markings consist of a series of spots of varying size that should be well distributed over the coat, and not overlapping or forming blotches.
• **REMARK** Two rows of spots should be apparent on the underside, with spotted patterning in place of a solid line along the back.

typical "M"-shaped tabby marking on head

long, svelte body shape

FUR TYPE: short, fine, and glossy

spots or bars permitted on legs

Longhair option	Black Silver Spotted Oriental Longhair	Temperament	Lively

Country of origin	Great Britain	Ancestry	Siamese crosses	Origins	1950s

CHOCOLATE SILVER CLASSIC TABBY

The contrast between the ground colour and the markings is most apparent in the darker forms, such as the Chocolate.
• **FEATURES** In this colour form, the chocolate markings are offset against a paler silvery chocolate ground colour. The wedge-shaped, triangular face of Oriental cats is distinctive.
• **REMARK** The intelligent and playful nature of these cats, plus the wide range of colours and patterns in which they are now being bred, have ensured their popularity.

Oriental-shaped eyes, slanting towards nose

long, slender neck

silvery white coloration may extend to throat in silver tabbies

good contrast between markings and ground colour

slim legs with small, oval paws

long, tapering tail showing tabby markings

sleek appearance, with healthy gloss on coat

FUR TYPE: short, fine, and glossy

Longhair option	Chocolate Silver Tabby Oriental Longhair	Temperament	Lively

EGYPTIAN MAU

THIS GROUP of spotted cats has been developed in the United States from European stock. They show a striking similarity to the cats of ancient Egypt, featured on tomb paintings and papyrus scrolls dating back thousands of years. The Egyptian Mau is a relatively scarce breed, even today, but attempts have been made in Europe to create cats that look similar. This bloodline was originally based on tabbies produced during the breeding of the Tabby Point Siamese. Such cats are now described as Oriental Spotted Tabbies, rather than as Egyptian Maus, in order to prevent any confusion.

Country of origin Egypt	Ancestry Non-pedigree Shorthairs	Origins 1950s

SILVER

The development of this breed in North America had its roots in the Mediterranean area. Having fallen in love with cats showing these markings, the Princess Troubetskoy obtained a specimen from Cairo and mated her with an Italian cat, producing two kittens. In 1956, the Princess took her Egyptian Maus to the United States, where the breed was registered and exhibited for the first time the following year.

• **FEATURES** These cats are intermediate between the cobby outline of the American Shorthair and the svelte profile of Oriental breeds. The wedge-shaped head is gently rounded; the muzzle should not be pointed. The angle changes from the cat's forehead down to the nose.

• **REMARK** Females tend to be slightly smaller than males.

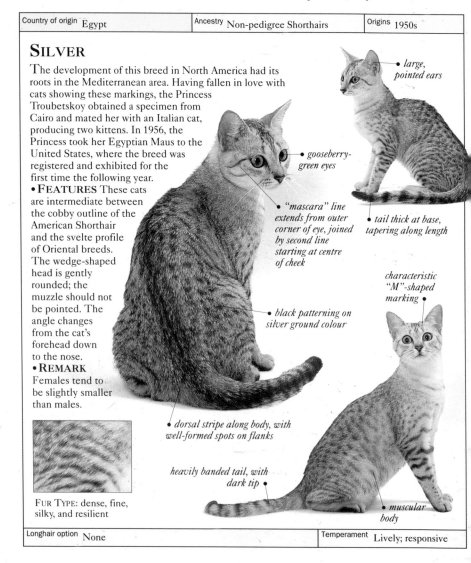

large, pointed ears

gooseberry-green eyes

"mascara" line extends from outer corner of eye, joined by second line starting at centre of cheek

tail thick at base, tapering along length

characteristic "M"-shaped marking

black patterning on silver ground colour

dorsal stripe along body, with well-formed spots on flanks

heavily banded tail, with dark tip

muscular body

FUR TYPE: dense, fine, silky, and resilient

Longhair option None	Temperament Lively; responsive

| Country of origin Egypt | Ancestry Non-pedigree Shorthairs | Origins 1950s |

BRONZE

There are only three colour forms of the traditional Egyptian Mau, all of which have the usual spotted patterning associated with tabbies. The spots themselves must be clearly defined. The ground colour is made up of banded hairs with black tips. At least two bands, if not more, should be apparent on each hair.

• **FEATURES** The spots should be round and evenly distributed over the body. There are also so-called "vest buttons" of spots on the underside. In newly born kittens the spots tend to be less clearly defined.

• **REMARK** During the moult the spotting becomes less distinct.

arched neck

medium-length hair with distinctive ticking

black barring on bronze ground colour

dainty, oval paws

FUR TYPE: dense, fine, silky, and resilient

| Longhair option None | Temperament Lively; responsive |

| Country of origin Egypt | Ancestry Non-pedigree Shorthairs | Origins 1950s |

BLACK SMOKE

The contrast in the coloration of these cats takes up to two years to develop fully. There is no ticking apparent; the hairs have whitish roots and black tips, creating a contrast as the cat moves.

• **FEATURES** The eyes are very large, oval in shape, and slanting. The distinctive green coloration can be relatively slow to develop and, in later life, the eyes tend to become paler green.

• **REMARK** Egyptian Maus are quiet cats, compared to Oriental breeds. The black coloration may become bleached a lighter brown if the cat is exposed to bright sunshine.

characteristic green eyes

broad forehead gives width between ears

jet-black spots on dark grey ground colour

muscular neck

very long toes on hind feet

tail equal to body length

FUR TYPE: dense, fine, silky, and resilient

| Longhair option None | Temperament Lively; responsive |

ABYSSINIAN

SIMILAR IN APPEARANCE to the cats of ancient Egypt, the Abyssinian is believed, by some, to be one of the oldest breeds of domestic cat. The first cats of this type were brought to Britain by soldiers returning home from the Abyssinian War in 1868. Attempts to develop the breed in Great Britain, by crossings involving British Shorthairs, modified the appearance and coloration of the Abyssinian. Although slow to breed, not being particularly prolific, the Abyssinian was finally recognized as a breed in its own right in 1882.

Country of origin Great Britain	Ancestry Non-pedigree Ticked Shorthairs	Origins 1860s

LILAC

There has been a considerable development of Abyssinian colours in recent years and the Lilac is now quite common. It displays an intelligent and slightly aloof temperament.

• **FEATURES** Abyssinians are of foreign type with a lithe, muscular body. The head is wedge shaped, with a slight indentation on the nose, and the eyes are large and almond shaped. In the case of the Lilac Abyssinian, the body should be a warm shade of pinkish dove-grey, with darker ticking of this colour. The underparts and insides of the legs are paler.

• **REMARK** At present, the Lilac, along with a number of other new Abyssinian colours, has limited worldwide recognition from cat organizations.

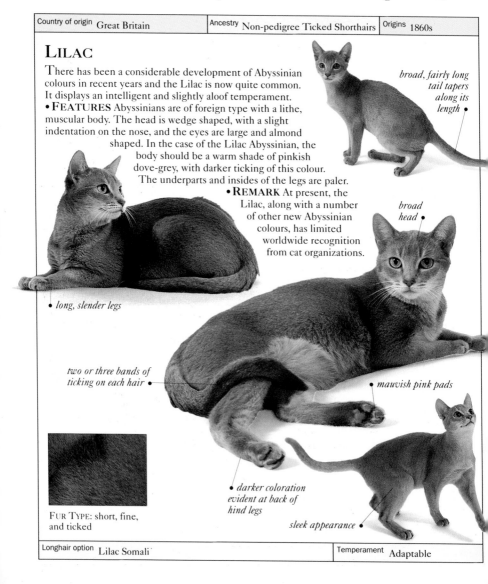

broad, fairly long tail tapers along its length

broad head

long, slender legs

two or three bands of ticking on each hair

mauvish pink pads

darker coloration evident at back of hind legs

sleek appearance

FUR TYPE: short, fine, and ticked

Longhair option Lilac Somali	Temperament Adaptable

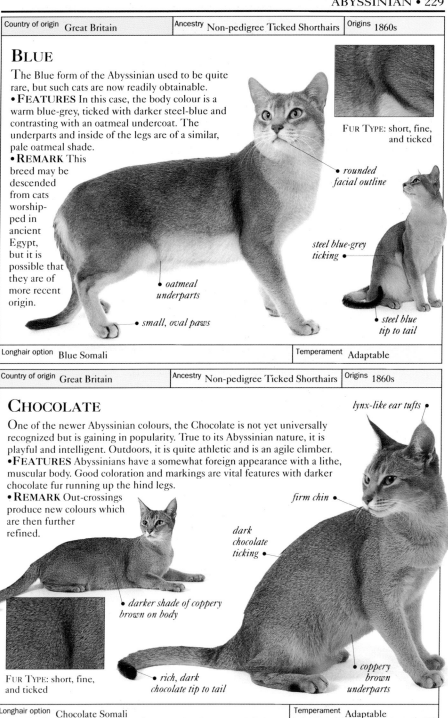

Country of origin Great Britain	Ancestry Non-pedigree Ticked Shorthairs	Origins 1860s

BLUE

The Blue form of the Abyssinian used to be quite rare, but such cats are now readily obtainable.

• **FEATURES** In this case, the body colour is a warm blue-grey, ticked with darker steel-blue and contrasting with an oatmeal undercoat. The underparts and inside of the legs are of a similar, pale oatmeal shade.

• **REMARK** This breed may be descended from cats worshipped in ancient Egypt, but it is possible that they are of more recent origin.

FUR TYPE: short, fine, and ticked

• *rounded facial outline*

• *steel blue-grey ticking*

• *oatmeal underparts*

• *small, oval paws*

• *steel blue tip to tail*

Longhair option Blue Somali	Temperament Adaptable

Country of origin Great Britain	Ancestry Non-pedigree Ticked Shorthairs	Origins 1860s

CHOCOLATE

lynx-like ear tufts •

One of the newer Abyssinian colours, the Chocolate is not yet universally recognized but is gaining in popularity. True to its Abyssinian nature, it is playful and intelligent. Outdoors, it is quite athletic and is an agile climber.

• **FEATURES** Abyssinians have a somewhat foreign appearance with a lithe, muscular body. Good coloration and markings are vital features with darker chocolate fur running up the hind legs.

• **REMARK** Out-crossings produce new colours which are then further refined.

firm chin •

dark chocolate ticking •

• *darker shade of coppery brown on body*

FUR TYPE: short, fine, and ticked

• *rich, dark chocolate tip to tail*

• *coppery brown underparts*

Longhair option Chocolate Somali	Temperament Adaptable

| Country of origin | Great Britain | Ancestry | Non-pedigree Ticked Shorthairs | Origins | 1860s |

BLACK SILVER

Several forms of the Silver
Abyssinian are recognized,
including Black (shown
here), Sorrel, and Blue,
but in each case the
undercoat must be white.
• **FEATURES** Here, the
shading over the spine is
black, as are the tip of the
tail and the solid coloration
on the hind legs. Traces of
yellow in the coat are
considered undesirable.
• **REMARK** The Silver
form has been
developed to a high
standard in both
Britain and New
Zealand during
recent years.

*dark outline
to eyes*

*clear silver with
black ticking*

*darker
coloration
evident
along
spine*

*white
under-
parts*

black pads

FUR TYPE: short, fine,
and ticked

| Longhair option | Silver Somali | Temperament | Adaptable |

| Country of origin | Great Britain | Ancestry | Non-pedigree Ticked Shorthairs | Origins | 1860s |

FAWN

Abyssinian kittens have a dark skull cap and
noticeably darker ticking than adults,
although ticking does not appear until
they are about three weeks old.
• **FEATURES** The Fawn is a dilute
form of the Sorrel. The basic fur colour
here is a pinkish dove-grey, with bands of
darker fawn ticking. Barring on the
chest, legs, or tail is considered a
fault. The nose is pink.
• **REMARK** This colour
is perhaps best
established in the
United States at
the present time.

*elegant
neck*

*large,
bright
eyes*

*slim, fine-boned
legs, and neat,
compact paws*

*only traces of
white allowed
around lips
and lower jaw*

*solid fawn
tip to tail*

*mauvish
pink pads*

FUR TYPE: short, fine,
and ticked

| Longhair option | Fawn Somali | Temperament | Adaptable |

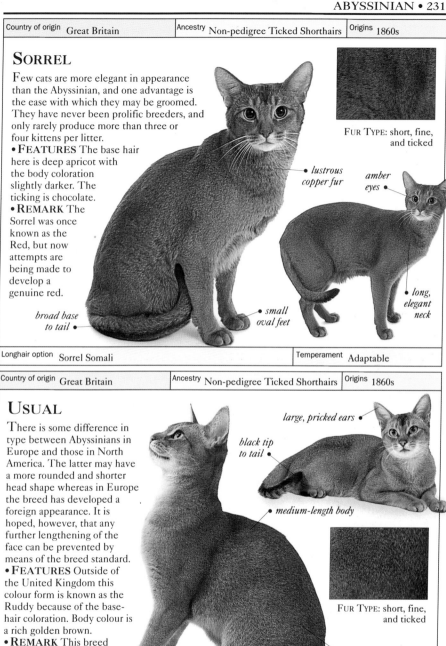

| Country of origin | Great Britain | Ancestry | Non-pedigree Ticked Shorthairs | Origins | 1860s |

SORREL

Few cats are more elegant in appearance than the Abyssinian, and one advantage is the ease with which they may be groomed. They have never been prolific breeders, and only rarely produce more than three or four kittens per litter.

• **FEATURES** The base hair here is deep apricot with the body coloration slightly darker. The ticking is chocolate.

• **REMARK** The Sorrel was once known as the Red, but now attempts are being made to develop a genuine red.

broad base to tail •

FUR TYPE: short, fine, and ticked

• *lustrous copper fur*

amber eyes •

• *small oval feet*

• *long, elegant neck*

| Longhair option | Sorrel Somali | Temperament | Adaptable |

| Country of origin | Great Britain | Ancestry | Non-pedigree Ticked Shorthairs | Origins | 1860s |

USUAL

There is some difference in type between Abyssinians in Europe and those in North America. The latter may have a more rounded and shorter head shape whereas in Europe the breed has developed a foreign appearance. It is hoped, however, that any further lengthening of the face can be prevented by means of the breed standard.

• **FEATURES** Outside of the United Kingdom this colour form is known as the Ruddy because of the base-hair coloration. Body colour is a rich golden brown.

• **REMARK** This breed was recognized in Great Britain in 1882.

long, slender legs •

large, pricked ears •

black tip to tail •

• *medium-length body*

FUR TYPE: short, fine, and ticked

• *ticking clearly visible*

| Longhair option | Ruddy Somali | Temperament | Adaptable |

Country of origin Great Britain	Ancestry Non-pedigree Ticked Shorthairs	Origins 1860s

SORREL SILVER

The Abyssinian patterning is equivalent to the ticked tabby, but selective breeding has led to the disappearance of markings on the legs and tail, as well as of the "necklaces" of darker fur encircling the neck in this case. Any of these traits are now considered serious flaws in the contemporary Abyssinian. Another problem that has proved harder to eradicate is the presence of white fur: any white areas, apart from those around the lips and lower jaw, are regarded as faults.

• **FEATURES** These cats are distinguished by a white undercoat. Their body coloration is silvery peach, with chocolate ticking. Both the pads and the nose should be pink, and there must be a line of dark pigment encircling the eyes. Eye coloration of amber, green, or hazel is acceptable.

• **REMARK** The only clearly distinctive tabby markings are present on the heads of these cats.

large, widely spaced ears; broad at base •

• lithe, muscular body with no tendency to cobby shape

tufted ears preferred •

slanting eyes •

• spinal shading may be present

tapering tail •

• two or three bands of ticking on each individual hair

tip of tail matches ticking •

• fine-boned, slim legs terminating in small, oval feet

"M"-shaped tabby marking clearly apparent, with darker pencil lines also evident •

• broad, tapering, wedge-shaped head with slight nose break

• medium-length body

• compact paws

• darker hair extends up back of hind legs

FUR TYPE: short, fine, and ticked

Longhair option Sorrel Silver Somali	Temperament Adaptable

WILD ABYSSINIAN

DURING RECENT YEARS, cat fanciers have given a great deal of attention to cats with Abyssinian-type coat patterning. Already the Singapura is quite well known, and enthusiasts of the Wild Abyssinian hope that their cats will follow suit. It is thought to be similar in its markings to the early Abyssinians seen in Victorian Britain, but is not a hybrid developed from crossing wild and domestic cats as its name might suggest. A third member of this group, the Ceylonese, is somewhat similar to the Wild Abyssinian and was developed as a result of the endeavours of the Cat Club of Ceylon (now Sri Lanka). The Wild Abyssinian is now being bred in Italy and elsewhere.

Country of origin Singapore	Ancestry Non-pedigree Shorthairs	Origins 1980s

USUAL

The ancestors of these cats, which had been living wild in Singapore, were taken to the United States where Tord Svenson and other breeders are now developing the breed. In order to maintain their original "wild" appearance, and to minimize the detrimental effects of in-breeding, it has been decided that within the pedigree of each cat there should be at least one imported individual shown within five generations.

FUR TYPE: short, fine, dense, and close-lying

• **FEATURES** Larger than the Abyssinian itself, these cats at present exist only in the Usual (or Ruddy) form; their coloration is a rich shade of golden brown, with a ruddy-orange undercoat. Black ticking is visible on the coat and, in contrast to the Abyssinian, barring is visible on the legs; the tail has a series of distinctive black rings.

• **REMARK** Selective breeding of the Abyssinian, which is actually a ticked tabby, has eliminated the normal tabby barring, so that the coat is simply ticked. This is seen as a distinctive characteristic of the Wild Abyssinian.

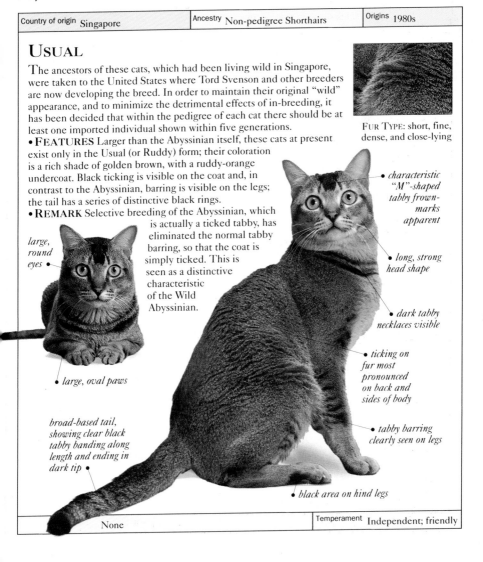

characteristic "M"-shaped tabby frown-marks apparent

long, strong head shape

large, round eyes

dark tabby necklaces visible

ticking on fur most pronounced on back and sides of body

large, oval paws

broad-based tail, showing clear black tabby banding along length and ending in dark tip

tabby barring clearly seen on legs

black area on hind legs

None	Temperament Independent; friendly

OCICAT

T HIS RELATIVELY RECENT addition to the cat world appeared in 1964 after a chance mating between a male Chocolate Point Siamese and a female Abyssinian x Seal Point Siamese. The owner of these cats, Virginia Daly, who was living in Michigan State, USA, was attracted to the wild-cat appearance of the resulting kitten, which she called *Dalai Talua*. She repeated the mating and another breeder, Tom Brown, later helped to develop the bloodline.

Country of origin USA	Ancestry Siamese x Siamese / Abyssinian	Origins 1964

CHOCOLATE

In the United States, American Shorthairs were used to increase the size and range of colours in these cats. Development in Europe from separate stock began quite recently, the first kitten being born in 1984.

• FEATURES These are large cats, with a well-designed pattern of spots. There is no link between coat and eye colour; blue eyes are not permitted. An impression of power and strength is an important feature of this breed. Newborn kittens have a cub-like appearance.

FUR TYPE: short, soft, and lustrous

• REMARK The name combines two previous names: "Ocelette" for the similarity to the ocelot, and "Accicat" as the breed arose from an accidental mating.

• *rise from bridge of nose to brow apparent*

• *longish tail*

• *clear contrast between markings and ground colour*

• *clearly defined spots*

• *powerful, muscular legs with sturdy, oval paws*

Longhair option None	Temperament Friendly and alert

Country of origin USA	Ancestry Siamese x Siamese / Abyssinian	Origins 1964

USUAL

The Ocicat is of intermediate type, neither cobby nor Oriental overall. The entire coat, apart from the tip of the tail, consists of banded hairs, and spotting is evident over the cat's body.

• **FEATURES** Lighter coloration is present around the eyes, chin, lower jaw as well as underneath the body. The markings on the head, legs, and tail areas are typically darker in colour than those on the body.

• **REMARK** During the moulting period, the clarity of the spotted markings is often reduced.

"M"-shaped tabby marking extends over top of head •

FUR TYPE: short, soft, and lustrous

patterned tail, terminating in black tip •

long legs •

Longhair option None		Temperament Friendly and alert

Country of origin USA	Ancestry Siamese x Siamese / Abyssinian	Origins 1964

SILVER

A distinctive feature of the Ocicat is that the dark lines around the neck and on the legs should be broken up into spots. The lines that extend along the spine will be replaced by spots as the cat matures.

• **FEATURES** The contrast is provided by a pattern of black spots on a silvery white ground colour. The pads should be black; the brick-red nose is edged with black.

• **REMARK** American Shorthairs were used in breeding to introduce the silver gene.

• "mascara" lines extend from eyes to cheeks

large, almond-shaped eyes slant towards ears •

• large ears, preferably tufted

tail tapers slightly along length •

• spots on flanks about size and shape of thumb-print

FUR TYPE: short, soft, and lustrous

• strong, neat paws

Longhair option None		Temperament Friendly and alert

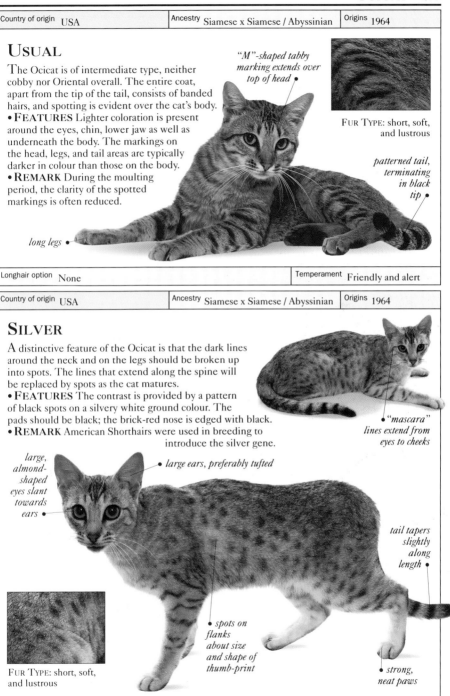

CALIFORNIA SPANGLED

T HE CALIFORNIA SPANGLED was launched in a blaze of publicity through the 1986 Christmas mail-order catalogue of a well-known American store. The breed was the creation of a Californian scriptwriter, Paul Casey, who assembled a variety of cat breeds from around the world, including a Spotted Manx, Silver Spotted Tabby Longhair, Seal Point Siamese, and British and American Shorthairs. He also used street cats from Cairo and other non-pedigree cats from Asia, to produce a spotted cat with the look of its wild relatives.

Country of origin USA	Ancestry Pedigree and Non-pedigree cats	Origins 1971

GOLD

The spotted patterning of this breed took five generations to develop, while establishing the precise type of these cats took six generations from the start of the breeding programme. The appearance of the California Spangled today is suggestive of a much bigger cat, rather like the leopard that gave Paul Casey the idea of creating this breed, following a visit to Africa.

• **FEATURES** Although golden coloration is apparent in the coat, the pattern of markings is much more significant. Stripes extend from between the ears, down the neck to the shoulders, with spots on the back and sides.

• **REMARK** Names from native Californian Indian tribes were chosen for the earliest cats.

well-defined oval, round, square, or triangular spots

medium-length tail

almond-shaped eyes

prominent whisker pads

FUR TYPE: short, soft, and sleek

long, lean, muscular body reminiscent of many wild cats

fur on tail quite long

stripes extending from neck down over shoulders

clear dark bar evident at top of each foreleg

Longhair option None	Temperament Affectionate; lively

| Country of origin USA | Ancestry Pedigree and Non-pedigree cats | Origins 1971 |

SILVER

The "natural" appearance of these cats was achieved without any recourse to wild cats and did not entail any in-breeding; it was based on eight separate bloodlines. Such was the interest in the California Spangled that there is still invariably a waiting-list for kittens from the relatively few breeders with stock.

• **FEATURES** The black markings are set against a silvery ground colour; this contrast is considered an important aspect of the cat's patterning.

• **REMARK** This is one of Paul Casey's own kittens, at the age of ten months.

more than two dark rings should be present at end of tail •

• rounded ears

• muscular thighs

• prominent cheekbones

• longer fur on underparts

markings clearly apparent •

FUR TYPE: short, soft, and sleek

• large paws

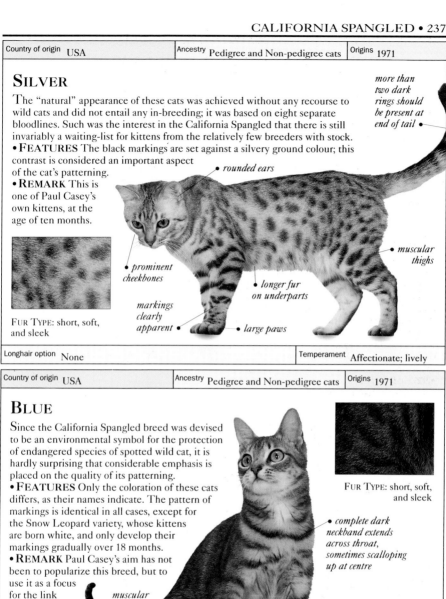

| Longhair option None | | Temperament Affectionate; lively |

| Country of origin USA | Ancestry Pedigree and Non-pedigree cats | Origins 1971 |

BLUE

Since the California Spangled breed was devised to be an environmental symbol for the protection of endangered species of spotted wild cat, it is hardly surprising that considerable emphasis is placed on the quality of its patterning.

• **FEATURES** Only the coloration of these cats differs, as their names indicate. The pattern of markings is identical in all cases, except for the Snow Leopard variety, whose kittens are born white, and only develop their markings gradually over 18 months.

• **REMARK** Paul Casey's aim has not been to popularize this breed, but to use it as a focus for the link between domestic cats and the plight of many of their wild relatives.

FUR TYPE: short, soft, and sleek

• complete dark neckband extends across throat, sometimes scalloping up at centre

muscular body •

• ears set well back on head, away from face

kittens are lively and playful •

• agile paws

| Longhair option None | | Temperament Affectionate; lively |

| Country of origin USA | Ancestry Pedigree and Non-pedigree cats | Origins 1971 |

CHARCOAL

It is not just the appearance of these cats that is important: they must also be intelligent and fit; they benefit from climbing frames and other toys to keep them occupied. Sociable by nature, they get on well with other cats and even dogs, and become devoted to their owners.
• **FEATURES** Good contrast is a feature of the Charcoal.
• **REMARK** The expressive face highlights the breed's individual nature.

• widely spaced, slanting eyes

• unbroken line should run from shoulder to armpit

strong legs •

• powerful feet

FUR TYPE: short, soft, and sleek

• athletic, muscular body

• dark tip to tail

| Longhair option None | Temperament Affectionate; lively |

| Country of origin USA | Ancestry Pedigree and Non-pedigree cats | Origins 1971 |

BROWN

The head of the California Spangled is medium both in length and width, with the shape of the cheekbones giving the eyes a sculpted setting. Both the jaw and chin are well developed.
• **FEATURES** A notable characteristic of these cats is the way the body remains close to the ground when they walk, in spite of their relatively long legs. This is a result of their angled joints – the forelegs, for example, almost make a right angle to the elbow and, as a result, they are effectively slung backwards beneath the body when the cat is walking.
• **REMARK** Their hind legs are similarly developed, and extend well back beyond the body when the cat is stalking.

prominent cheekbones •

• spots on back and sides

• small, white bib marking allowed on throat

FUR TYPE: short, soft, and sleek

• patterning continues on tail

| Longhair option None | Temperament Affectionate; lively |

BENGAL

C ROSSINGS BETWEEN small wild cats and domestic cats have been documented for more than a century, and some of the resulting hybrids were exhibited at cat shows in Victorian times. At least ten species have been used, and such matings became popular again during the 1960s. The Bengal evolved from an American breeding programme, begun in 1963, in which a geneticist named Jean Sugden crossed a male domestic cat with a female Asian leopard cat, attempting to transfer the wild cat's markings to a domestic breed.

Country of origin USA	Ancestry Asian leopard cat crosses	Origins 1963

LEOPARD

One kitten, christened *Kinkin*, was produced and fostered alongside a litter of domestic cats. In due course she was mated back to her father and produced both self and spotted kittens. In 1981, Jean Mill (*née* Sugden) and Dr Willard Centerwall, another geneticist, both began work in earnest on the development of the Bengal.

• **FEATURES** The Bengal's spotted patterning is highly distinctive and quite unlike that of a spotted tabby. The large spots are arranged horizontally, ideally showing signs of developing into rosettes. Sound temperament is a vital feature of the breed, due to its wild origins.

• **REMARK** Sorrel (orange with brown spotting) and Mink (black marks on rich mahogany) varieties are among other colours that have now been created. So-called Snow Bengals are the result of Siamese crosses.

long, muscular body

markings present on tail

strong, rounded head

large, open ears

wide nose

coat may not achieve its full reddish colour until kitten is one year old

clearly defined spotted pattern - a striped variety of this breed also now exists

kitten's coat relatively coarse

dark tip to tail

FUR TYPE: dense, soft, and silky

Longhair option None	Temperament Friendly and gentle

NON-PEDIGREE

T HESE ARE PROBABLY the most common cats in the world, and are often known simply as "moggies". They can be found in the full range of colours and patterns, although the bi-colours tend to predominate and the "foreign" colours, such as chocolate, are quite scarce. These colours can be produced, however, by unplanned matings with a pedigree partner. Although non-pedigree cats, by definition, are not of recognizable type, they can evolve into a distinctive form through repeated matings of similar cats. These shorthairs tend to be of cobby shape with rather rounded faces.

Country of origin Egypt	Ancestry African wild cat	Origins 1500BC

BLUE AND WHITE

It is from cats such as these that Victorian breeders began to develop the British Shorthair breed. It was necessary to eliminate the white markings, however, in order to produce the solid-coloured cats, such as the Blue, associated with this breed today. The lack of selection in pairings of non-pedigree shorthairs means that white markings are still conspicuous in most of these cases.
• **FEATURES** In non-pedigree cats, white and blue hairs may intermingle. There may also be some signs of darker tabby barring.
• **REMARK** Selective breeding of pedigree cats has concentrated on developing certain specific features present in the non-pedigree population.

FUR TYPE: short, dense, and crisp

medium-sized ears, with round tips and furnishings •

• *rounded face shape, with short, straight nose*

greenish eyes •

• *quite broad, muscular body*

straight whiskers •

• *distribution of blue and white areas remains consistent throughout cat's life*

short, thick tail, often showing darker tabby rings •

large paws •

Longhair option Blue and White Non-pedigree Longhair	Temperament Friendly

Country of origin Egypt	Ancestry African wild cat	Origins 1500BC

BLACK AND WHITE

These cats were popular as pets during the 19th century, but they suffered a decline as more exotic breeds became fashionable. Such cats are still an excellent choice, however, being adaptable and easy to care for.
• **FEATURES** The appearance of non-pedigree bi-colours is much more variable than in the case of pedigree cats. In this example, white hairs are clearly visible among areas of predominantly black fur.
• **REMARK** Eye colour can differ according to the individual.

white facial blaze •

• stocky body shape

• white hairs intermingled with black

FUR TYPE: short, dense, and crisp

variable patterning •

Longhair option Black and White Non-pedigree Longhair	Temperament Friendly

Country of origin Egypt	Ancestry African wild cat	Origins 1500BC

WHITE AND TORTIE

The red gene, responsible for tortoiseshell coloration in cats, probably appeared first in Turkey and North Africa, and is also common in the Orient.
• **FEATURES** The typical tortoiseshell markings, comprising black with shades of red coloration, are offset in this case by white fur.
• **REMARK** Cats with tortoiseshell markings are usually good-natured, as well as being long-lived.

• intermingled colours

• rounded head shape

FUR TYPE: short, dense, and crisp

• white underparts

• traces of pale pink, black, and richer red coloration

• thick tail

• mottled paw pads

Longhair option White and Tortie Non-pedigree Longhair	Temperament Friendly

Country of origin Egypt	Ancestry African wild cat	Origins 1500BC

BLUE-CREAM

Blue-creams typically result from the mating of a cream and a blue cat. They are the dilute form of the Tortoiseshell.
• FEATURES In Britain, (standards differ in the United States) a pedigree Blue-cream should have well mixed blue and cream hairs. In a non-pedigree, however, distinct patches of blue and cream colour are more likely to be seen.
• REMARK Male blue and cream cats can only be produced if they have a rare extra chromosome in their genetic make-up.

rounded tips to ears

powerful jaws

contrasting areas of cream and blue fur in coat

legs usually quite short

FUR TYPE: short, dense, and crisp

Longhair option Blue-cream Non-pedigree Longhair	Temperament Friendly

Country of origin Egypt	Ancestry African wild cat	Origins 1500BC

TORTIE AND WHITE

Even if the mother is attractively marked, it is impossible to predict the likely markings of tortoiseshell kittens; they are always variable.
• FEATURES In this case the characteristic tortoiseshell colours, rather than the areas of white fur, predominate in the cat's coat.
• REMARK Tortoiseshell patterning occurs as the result of a gradual shut-down of one of the female's paired sex chromosomes during an early stage of embryonic growth, when coloration corresponds to genes on one chromosone or the other. The red gene chromosome switches off in some cells; in others it is the black.

FUR TYPE: short, dense, and crisp

round eyes

facial blaze apparent

patches of colour not clearly defined in non-pedigrees

extent of coloured patches variable

Longhair option Tortie and White Non-pedigree Longhair	Temperament Friendly

Country of origin	Ancestry	Origins
Egypt	African wild cat	1500BC

RED CLASSIC TABBY AND WHITE

Non-pedigree cats of this colour are sometimes known as "ginger and white" because of the rather orange tinge to their red fur. The tabby markings are a darker shade of red.

• **FEATURES** The white fur is distributed entirely randomly, and some overlap between white and coloured areas is not unusual. In type, these cats show a similarity to the British Shorthair, but they are usually smaller in size.

• **REMARK** The tabby markings are not as well-ordered in this case as they are in a pedigree tabby.

darker frown lines apparent on head

FUR TYPE: short, dense, and crisp

• *variable markings*

white paws •

broad tail with rounded tip •

Longhair option	Temperament
Red Classic Tabby and White Non-pedigree Longhair	Friendly

Country of origin	Ancestry	Origins
Egypt	African wild cat	1500BC

BLUE MACKEREL TABBY AND WHITE

Tabby markings in cats have been known for centuries; this mackerel form originated in Britain, possibly during the 17th century.

• **FEATURES** Not only do the markings vary from cat to cat, but the depth of blue coloration is not entirely consistent. In some cases, the contrast between the ground coloration and the tabby markings is less pronounced than in others.

• **REMARK** The relative size and distribution of the white patches will not alter from the kitten stage.

FUR TYPE: short, dense, and crisp

• *pure white areas contrast with blue*

• *rounded head with relatively small ears*

tabby markings clearly discernible •

Longhair option	Temperament
Blue Mackerel Tabby & White Non-pedigree Longhair	Friendly

| Country of origin Egypt | Ancestry African wild cat | Origins 1500BC |

BROWN CLASSIC TABBY AND WHITE

• *ringed tail* •

The disruptive coat markings that result from the darker tabby patterning help these cats to conceal themselves quite effectively when hunting.

• **FEATURES** The dark tabby markings are clearly contrasted here with the lighter brown body coloration. White areas in this case are very restricted.

• *round head set on short, muscular neck*

straight tail •

• **REMARK** This placid tabby is probably the most common cat in Britain.

• *patching clearly apparent on side of body*

• *barring present on legs*

FUR TYPE: short, dense, and crisp

• *short, powerful legs*

| Longhair option Brown Classic Tabby and White Non-pedigree Longhair | Temperament Friendly |

| Country of origin Egypt | Ancestry African wild cat | Origins 1500BC |

BROWN SPOTTED

"M"-shaped tabby marking •

One of the reasons that tabby markings are so common amongst ordinary household cats is that such patterning is genetically dominant. Since many non-pedigree cats are the result of random matings, tabby genes have become widely distributed and are often evident in the country's cat population.

thick, unbroken "bracelet" around neck •

• **FEATURES** This tabby has a mackerel-type coat pattern although some of the vertical lines are broken.

• **REMARK** Selective breeding has enabled this patterning to be developed into the symmetrical, balanced markings associated with pedigree mackerel tabbies today.

• *striped patterning running vertically down sides of body*

• *black stripes*

FUR TYPE: short, dense, and crisp

bars on legs •

• *heavy black line*

| Longhair option Brown Spotted Non-pedigree Longhair | Temperament Friendly |

| Country of origin Egypt | Ancestry African wild cat | Origins 1500BC |

WHITE AND BROWN TABBY

Tabby markings do not
extend over areas of
white fur, as is clearly
shown in this cat.
• **FEATURES** This
amount of white would
not be acceptable in the
equivalent pedigree
shorthair. Although the
tabby markings are
restricted, it is clear that
this is a blotched rather
than a mackerel tabby.
• **REMARK** A study of non-
pedigree cat populations in
countries such as Australia has
shown that tabbies are more
common in the newer cities,
resulting from the cats taken
overseas by immigrants.

pure white fur

white facial blaze between eyes

odd white hairs may be present in tabby areas

FUR TYPE: short, dense, and crisp

no tabby markings on white legs

thick tail

| Longhair option White and Brown Tabby Non-pedigree Longhair | Temperament Friendly |

| Country of origin Egypt | Ancestry African wild cat | Origins 1500BC |

BROWN MACKEREL TABBY

furnishing of hair within ears

Although the chin area is usually whitish
in these tabbies, in the example shown the
white areas are more widespread, and
extend to the nose and above the jaws.
• **FEATURES** The markings are not
especially even, so that black areas are
more prominent in some parts of
the coat than in others. The
bands on the cat's tail are
also irregular.
• **REMARK** Tabby
patterning is a
dominant trait, so
a number of
tabby kittens
will always be
produced in a
tabbie litter.

large black blotch on hind foot

FUR TYPE: short, dense, and crisp

pinkish red nose with darker border

irregular tabby patterning extends along length of tail

| Longhair option Brown Tabby Non-pedigree Longhair | Temperament Friendly |

CAT CREDITS

We are indebted and immensely grateful to the many owners and breeders who brought their cats from far and wide to be photographed for this book; without their help and enthusiastic cooperation, it could not have been produced. The cats, along with the names of their owners and breeders, are listed in page order, with references to indicate the exact position of each cat on the page.

KEY TO ABBREVIATIONS

Page numbers, in bold type, are followed by position references:
b bottom
c centre
l left
r right
t top

The cats' names are prefixed by an abbreviated reference to their current championship status:
GrPr Grand Premier
Pr Premier
GrCh Grand Champion
Ch Champion
EurCh European Champion
IntCh International Champion
GrEurCh Grand European Champion
SupGrCh Supreme Grand Champion
SupGrPr Supreme Grand Premier

• **1 c** *Midamist Shynal* J Bright (C Bone)
• **2 tl (grandmother)** *Ch Fleic Mimosa Magic* P & J Choppen (P & J Choppen); **tc (great grandfather)** *GrCh Fleic Chocolate Imperial* P & J Choppen (P & J Choppen); **tr (mother)** *Ch Jasrobinka Angelique* P & J Choppen (P & J Choppen); **bl (kitten)** *Jasrobinka Annamonique* P & J Choppen (P & J Choppen)
• **3 c** *Pandapaws Mr Biggs* S Ward-Smith (J Varley & J Dicks)
• **5 b** *Skogens Volla* A S Watt (A Moss & J Higgins); **cl** *Bealltainn Bezique* T Stracstone (T Stracstone); **tr** *UK GrCh Nobilero Loric Vilesilensa* AE & RE Hobson (M Reed)
• **8 br** *Marble Masquerade* F Wagner (B Street & G Pascoe); **cl** *Kajenka Juniper* K Jenkins (J North)
• **9 bc & tr** *IntGrCh Gardenia du Vaumichon* G Bock (J Simmonet); **bl (kitten)** *IntCh Giroflée du Bois de Meudon* G Bock (G Bock)
• **11 br** *Friskie* (Bethlehem Cat Sanctuary)
• **12-13 c** *GrCh Aerostar Spectre* J E D Mackie (S Callen & I Hotten)
• **13 cl (white)** *Ch Miletree Memories* R Towse (P Kratz); **rc (ruff)** *Sitah Orllando* M Harvey (M Harvey)
• **16 bc (kitten)** *Sheephouse Diamond Lil* J Bradley (J Bradley); **bl (adult)**

Ch Lancendel Santa Claw P Ross (G Ellins & B Hollandt); **br (kitten)** *Sheephouse Precious Pearl* J Bradley (J Bradley); **cl** *Satinmist Charlie Brown* I Worsley-Waring (I Worsley-Waring); **cr (kitten)** L Berry *Kavida Amethyst* (L Berry); **cr (kitten)** L Berry *Kavida Cadberry* L Berry (L Berry); **cr (kitten)** *Kavida Primetime* L Berry (L Berry); **lc (adult)** *Adixish Talisman* M Acton (M Acton); **t (kitten)** *Lipema Monty Moon* P Brown (P Brown); **t (kitten)** *Lipema Melisa* P Brown (P Brown); **t (kitten)** *Lipema Muriel* P Brown (P Brown); **tl (adult)** *Adkrish Mary Contarie* C Andrews (P Brown)
• **17 bl kitten** *Rejuta Irrissitable* T & R Quick (T & R Quick); **bl kitten** *Rejuta Prize Guy* T & R Quick (T & R Quick); **bl kitten** *Rejuta Sacramentosam* T & R Quick (T & R Quick); **br Adult** *Sarouks Sweet William* W & J Benson (T & R Quick); **cl (kitten)** *Sargenta Blue Gismo* U Graves (U Graves); **cl (left kitten)** *Leolee Larnyen Poppy* (S Lee Soper); **cl (right kitten)** *Leolee Leetee* (S Lee Soper); **cr** *GrCh Wellmar Flamenco* J Martin (M Frew); **tc** *GrCh Miletree Masquerade* R K Towse (P Allen); **tl (kitten)** *Westways Jane Seemoor* A West (E Button); **tr** *Ch Leolee Sweet Song* (S Lee Soper); **tr (below)** *Indalo Knights Templar* B Pridham (B Pridham)
• **18 br** *GrPr Honeycharm Pandarella* B Patch (A Tonks); **tr** *Pr Shermese Elysium* C Simpson (F & D Powell)
• **19 bc** *Cobby Chops Kitten* M Tolliday (M Tolliday); **bc** *Cobby Chops Kitten* M Tolliday (M Tolliday); **bl** *Cobby Chops Kitten* M Tolliday (M Tolliday); **c** *Cobby Chops Clarida* M Tolliday (M Tolliday); **t** *Cobby Chops Confetti* M Tolliday (M Tolliday)
• **20 br** *Ch Watlove Windser* H Watson (H Watson)
• **21 tr (great grandfather)** *GrCh Fleic Chocolate Imperial* P & J Choppen (P & J Choppen); **step-by-step kitten** *Jasrobinka Annamonique* P & J Choppen (P & J Choppen); **step-by-step kitten** *Jasrobinka Dominique* P & J Choppen (P & J Choppen); **step-by-step kitten** *Jasrobinka Jade Princess* P & J Choppen (P & J Choppen); **step-by-step kitten** *Jasrobinka Jean Pierre* P & J Choppen (P & J Choppen)
• **22 all steps** *Picwick Puff Dragon* P Rogers (P Rogers); **br** *GrCh Miletree Masquerade* R K Towse (P Allen)
• **23 cr, bl, bc, & br** *GrCh Pannaduloa Yentantethra* Bred by J Hansson (J Hansson)
• **23 tc & tr** *GrCh Aerostar Spectre* J E D Mackie (S Callen & I Hotten)
• **26 bl** *Honeymist Blue Seastar* M Howes (M Howes); **br** *Kaleetay*

Dextoniatoo J Marshall (T Cornwall); **cr** *Lipema Shimazaki* P Brown (G Dean); **cr** *Jardinage Penny Royale* D Jardine (G Dean)
• **27 b** *Shaird Bare Essentials* A Rushbrook & J Plumb (A Rushbrook & J Plumb); **cr** *GrCh Maruja Samson* M Moorhead (M Moorhead); **tr** *Pr Bobire Justin Tyme* I E Longhurst (A Charlton)
• **30 bl** *Susian Just Judy* S Kempster (M Way); **tl** *GrCh Chermicican Santa Fe* G & S Sanders (G & S Sanders); **tr** *Ch Bartania Pomme Frits* B Beck (B Beck)
• **31 cl** *Parthia Angelica* (M A Skelton); **cr** *Ch Sargenta Silver Dan* U Graves (U Graves); **tl** *Ch Leolee Sweet Song* S Lee Soper (S Lee Soper); **tr** *Ch Ballantyne Sadrazam* L Miles (L Miles)
• **32 b** *Shaird Bare Essentials* A Rushbrook & J Plumb (A Rushbrook & J Plumb); **c** *GrCh Aerostar Spectre* J E D Mackie (S Callen & I Hotten) **t** *Zultan Paquita Ballet* J Powell (B & B Raine)
• **35 cl (Somali)** *Sitah Orllando* M Harvey (M Harvey)
• **36 bc** *IntGrCh Gardenia du Vaumichon* G Bock (J Simmonet)

LONG-HAIRED CATS
• **40 all** *GrCh Adievo Ladydido* P Woodman (P Woodman)
• **41 bl &cr** *Annelida Shalom* A Ashford (M Butler Aust); **tl** *Ch Gleeway Iceberg* G Lee (G Lee); **tr** *Ch Lafrabella Queynote* I Bangs (G & S Sanders)
• **42 bl & br** *Picwick Puff Dragon* P Rogers (P Rogers); **tl & tr** *Ch Chrysellus Cream Emperor* R Smith (G Miller)
• **43 bl** *Honeymist Blue Seastar* M Howes (M Howes); **br** *Ch Lollipop Blue Rascall* M Edwicker (G Miller); **t** *Bowmans Lilac Rhapsody* E Frankland (D Thompson)
• **44 bl & br** *Ch Honeymist Black Domino* M Howes (M Howes); **tl & tr** *Ch Bowmans Rose Dream* A L Frankland (A L Frankland)
• **45 bl** *GrCh Chermicican Santa Fe* G & S Sanders (G & S Sanders); **br** *Ch Honeycharm Amanda* B Patch (B Patch); **tl & tr** *Ch & GrPr Cherub Hendel* A Cromton (A Bowman)
• **46 bl** *Chermicican Teaseme* G & S Sanders (G & S Sanders); **tl & tr** *Crystaldee Bi Design* C & K Smith (E Baldwin)
• **47 bl** *Chermicican Who Dundat* G & S Sanders (G & S Sanders); **br** *Myway Beau Sabreur* I Witney (A Tonks); **tl & tr** *Adirtsa Choc Ice* D Tynan (C & K Smith)
• **48 bl & br** *SupGrCh Honeycharm Jasmine* B Patch (B Patch); **tc & tr**

Honeymist Roxana M Howes
(M Howes)
• **49 tc** *Humdinga Heartsease* B Haigh
(C Evans); **tr** *Angieal Naughty Butnice*
A Mitchell (A Mitchell)
• **50 b** *Honeycharm Channell* B Patch
(B Patch); **cl** *Annelida Madonna*
A Ashford (A Ashford); **tr** *GrPr
Honeycharm Pandarella* B Patch
(A Tonks)
• **51 b** *Crystaldee Hope* C & K Smith
(C & K Smith); **tl & tr** *Casalina Dolly
Mixture* E Baldwin (E Baldwin)
• **52 bl & br** *Primabella Blueberry pie*
(C Gook); **t** *Watlove Hamish* H Watson
(H Watson)
• **53 bl & br** *Adraylo Silva Gabriella*
N Holt (M Harvey); **tl & c**
Ch Pieris Thomasina A & M Baker
(A & M Baker)
• **54 b** *Honeymist Taboo* M Howes
(M Howes); **cr** *Sarasamsan Honkytonk
Angel* S Corris (C Gook); **t (kitten)**
Rejuta Irrisistible T & R Quick (T & R
Quick); **t kitten** *Rejuta Prize Guy*
T & R Quick (T & R Quick);
t (kitten *Rejuta Sacramentosam* T & R
Quick (T & R); **tr (Adult)**
Sarouks Sweet William W & J Benson
(T & R Quick)
• **55 bl** *Celebrity Silver Bonbon* D Slater
(D Slater); **br** *GrCh Bellablanca
Thumbelina* S Greaves (S Greaves);
tl & tc *Mowbray Tanamera* D Cleford
(D Cleford)
• **56 bl & br** *Mandarin Halcyon*
D Thomson (D Thomson); **tc & tr**
Ch Diwenna Mandarin D Went
(D Thomson)
• **57 b** *Zultan Paquita Ballet* J Powell
(B & B Raine); **tc & tr** *Penumbra
Samsons Secret* J Palfreyman
(J Palfreyman)
• **58 bl & br** *Ch & GrPr Bessjet Silver
Dollar* J Smith (C Wall); **t** *Pickwick
Exquisite Pixie* P Rogers (P Rogers)
• **59 b** *Taloola Oopsadaisy* J Saunders
(J Saunders); **cl & tr (adult)** *Cashel
Golden Yuppie* A Curley (A Curley);
cr (kitten) *Cashel Golden Alice*
A Curley (A Curley)
• **60 b** *GrPr Bellrai Faberge* B & B
Raine (B & B Raine); **tl & tr**
Bellrai Creme Chanel B & B Raine
(B & B Raine)
• **61 cl** *Ch Ambergem Orlandos* A Burke
(A Burke); **cr & b** *Adhuilo
Meadowlands Alias* P Hurrell
(S Josling); **tr** *Klaxon Matterhorn* Mary
Harrington (M Harrington)
• **62 all** *Anneby Sunset* A Bailey
(A Bailey)
• **63 b** *Impeza Chokolotti* C Rowark
(E Baldwin); **t** *Ch Watlove Mollie
Mophead* H Watson (H Watson)
• **64 b** *Amocasa Beau Brummel* I Elliott
(I Elliott); **tr & c** *GrCh Anneby
Trendsetter* A Bailey (A Bailey)
• **65 bl & br** *Ch Dermask Dolly
Daydream* J Bettany (M Allum);
tl & tr *GrCh Anneby Charisma*
A Bailey (A Bailey)
• **66 b** *Ch Watlove Windser* H Watson

(H Watson); **tl & tr** *Ch Jonalynn
Munchkin* J & L Wallett
(J & L Wallett)
• **67 bl & br** *Casaline Malteaser* E
Baldwin (E Baldwin); **t** *Ch
Crystaldee Frilly Knickers* C & K Smith
(C & K Smith)
• **68 all** *Saybrianna Tomorrows Cream*
A Carritt (A Carritt)
• **69 bl & br** *Schwenthe Kisca*
F E Brigliadori (F E Brigliadori &
K Robson); **tl & tr** *Panjandrum
Bestman* A Madden (E Leach)
• **70 bc & br** *Ch & GrPr Panjandrum
April Suprice* A Madden (A Madden);
t *GrCh Adivelo Anchantress* D Wedmore
(C Flynn)
• **71 all** *Shwechinthe Katha*
F Brigliadori (F Robinson)
• **72 bl & br** *Boemm Shantung Silk*
K Bairstairs (G Rankin); **t** *Aesthetikat
Toty Temptress* Mrs G Sharpe
(H Hewitt)
• **73 bc & br** *Panjandrum Pan Yan*
A Madden (A Madden); **c (kitten)**
Shandatal Yelena S Talboys
(S Talboys); **cl & tr** *Panjandrum
Swansong* Anne Madden (S Talboys)
• **74 b** *Shanna's Snowy Fleur* M Harms
(M Harms); **br** *Shanna's Demiz Sayah*
M Harms (I Halewyck); **cr (Adult)**
Ch Yemin de Saint Glinglin H Den
Ouden (M Harms)
• **75 cr & b** *Shanna's Essen Demir*
M Harms (D Hondijk Zuuring);
t *Shanna's Tombis Hanta Yo* M Harms-
Moeskops (G Rebel van Kemenade)
• **76 b & cr** *Shanna's Boncuk Bertje*
M Harms (Ad Senders); **t** *Shanna's
Yasmine Sevince* M Harms (H Dieman)
• **77 b & cr** *Shanna's Yacinta-Sajida*
M Harms (M Harms); **tc & tr**
Kazibelli Kedi's Tamar M Bosch
(G Rebel van Kemenade)
• **78 all** *Ch Lady Lubna Leanne
Chatkantarra* T Boumeister
(J van der Werff)
• **79 all** *Ch Ballantyne Sadrazam*
L Miles (L Miles)
• **80 all** *Chantonel Snowball Express*
R Elliot (R Elliot)
• **81 b & cr** *Jardinage Penny Royale*
D Jardine (G Dean); **tc (adult)** *Ohope
White Mischief* C Andrews (P Brown);
tr & c (kitten) *Lipema Major
Balmerino* P Brown (P Brown)
• **82 b** *Lipema Shimazaki* P Brown
(G Dean); **t (kitten)** *Lipema Monty
Moon* P Brown (P Brown); **t (kitten)**
Lipema Melisa P Brown (P Brown);
t (kitten) *Lipema Muriel* P Brown
(P Brown); **tr (adult)** *Adkrish Mary
Contarie* C Andrews (P Brown)
• **83 all** *Quinkent Honey's
Mi-Lei-Fo* I A van der Reckweg
(I A van der Reckweg)
• **84 all** *Koonluv White Fury* A Rowsell
(T Cornwall)
• **85 cr & br** *Charlemma Blue Balco*
D Froud (D Gourd); **tl & tc** *USA GrCh
Honeycoon Voodoo Boy* K Muller
(T Cornwall)
• **86 bl & br** *Namrib Silvasand*

H Horton (J Lindsey); **c (kitten)**
Caprix Dinah T Cornwall (Mr and Mrs
Harley); **cl (adult)** *Caprix Marvellous
Marvin* T Cornwall (T Cornwall);
tr *Caprix Dynamite* T Cornwall
(T Cornwall)
• **87 bl & br** *Kaleetay Dextoniatoo*
J Marshall (T Cornwall); **tc & tr**
Purpuss Mainchance T & S A Morgan
(T Morgan)
• **88 b** *Caprix Silver Mist* T Cornwall
(T Cornwall); **c** *Charlemma Fire Dancer*
D Froud (Col. & E Stapleton);
tr *Koonluv Chevrolet* A Rowsell
(T Cornwall)
• **89 bc & br** *Bealltainn Cadillac*
Sheeman (T Cornwall); **cl & tr**
Adixillo Coon Laura C Evans
(H Horton)
• **90 all** *Skogens Modi* A S Watt
(G Elston & K Harvey)
• **91 br** *Skogens Volla* A S Watt (A Moss
& J Higgins); **cl & tc** *Skogens Magni*
A S Watt (K Garrett)
• **92 bc & cr** *Skogens Odin* M & M
Laine (A S Watt); **tc & tr** *Skogens SF
Eddan Romeo* A S Watt (S Garrett)
• **93 all** *Olocha* A Danveef
(H von Groneburg)
• **94 all** *Ladibyrd Ragadam* S Ward-
Smith (C M Carter & M Sumpter)
• **95 all** *Pandapaws Blue Flash* S Ward-
Smith (C M Carter & M Sumpter);
bc *Pandapaws Mr Biggs* S Ward-Smith
(J Varley & Jon Dicks)
• **96 all** *Adhuish Alefeles Topaz*
R J Allen (P G & M Frayne)
• **97 br** *Sitah Kissamayo* M Harvey
(M Harvey); **tl & tc** *Sir Duncan Van
Manja* M Van Zweden (L Warwick)
• **98 bc & cr** *Vestisler Risingstar*
L Warwick (L Warwick); **tl & tr** *Bonzer
Fandango* J Ponsford (L Warwick)
• **99 bl & bc** *Melody Von
Haimhaurschloss* N Reiger (J Holderer-
Hortensius); **cr** *Bealltainn Bezique*
T Stracstone (T Stracstone);
tr *Kelmscott Falcon* T Stracstone
(T Stracstone)
• **100 all** *Frafadi's Silver Aurora*
D Hondijk Zuuring (D Hondijk
Zuuring)
• **101 bc** *Uptomalian Forgetmenot*
F Upton (F Upton); **c & tr** *Uptomalian
Jessica Rabbit* F Upton (L Warwick)
• **102 all** *Pakvjia Pennyfromheaven*
J Buroughs (T Tidey)
• **103 b** *Pr Pandai Feargal* E Corps
(B V Rickwood); **tc & tr** *Blancsanglier
Rosensoleil* A Bird (A Bird)
• **104 bc & cr** *Pr Blancsanglier Beau
Brummel* A Bird (A Bird); **t** *Ronsline
Whistfull Spirit* R Farthing
(R Farthing)
• **105 bc & cr** *Jeuphi Golden Girl*
J Phillips (L Cory); **tr & tc** *Dasilva
Tasha* J St. John (C Russel &
P Scrivener)
• **106 b** *Ch Apricat Silvercascade*
R Smyth (E & J Robinson); **tr & c**
GrCh Soleil Imperial Rufus L Howard
(L Howard)
• **107 b** *Mossgems Sheik Shimizu*

M Mosscrop (H Grenney); tc & tr
GrPr Nighteyes Cinderfella J Pell (J Pell)
• 108 all Favagello Hamlet J Bryson
(R I Bryson)
• 109 b & cr Kennbury Dulcienea
C Lovell (K Harmon); c & tr Favagello
Brown Whispa J Bryson (J Bryson)
• 110 all Polar Star L Price
(L Williams)
• 111 all Shilley Wilderbras
C M Balemans (Family Wouters)
• 114 all Maggie (Bethlehem Cat
Sanctuary)
• 115 bl & bc Dumpling (Bethlehem
Cat Sanctuary); tc Dan-I-Lion
(V Warriner)
• 116 cl & tr Dan (D & C Ellis)
• 117 cr & br Mr Beau (V Warriner);
tc & tr Stardust (V Warriner)

SHORT-HAIRED CATS
• 118 all Ch & SupGrPr Welquest
Snowman A Welsh (A Welsh)
• 119 b Ch Lancendel Girl Friday
P Ross (J Bradley); tl & tr GrCh
Miletree Twinkle R Towse (R Towse)
• 120 bc (adult) Adixish Talisman
M Acton (M Acton)
c (kitten) Kavida Primetime L Berry
(L Berry); cr (kitten) Kavida Amethyst
L Berry (L Berry); tc & tr GrCh
Westways Purfect Amee A West
(G B Ellins)
• 121 tc & tr GrCh Maruja Samson
M Moorhead (M Moorhead);
bl (kitten) Kavida Cadberry L Berry
(L Berry); br Satinmist Charlie Brown
I Worsley-Waring (I Worsley-Waring)
• 122 bc & br GrCh Blakewood Tuteine
G B Ellins (G B Ellins); l Miletree Black
Rod R Towse (R Towse); tr Susian
Cara Mia S Kempster (S Kempster)
• 123 bc & cr Ch Bartania Pomme
Frits B Beck (B Beck); tl (kitten)
Sheephouse Tallullah J Bradley
(J Skinners); tr Bradlesmere Nerine
J Shaw (B Hollandt)
• 124 b Ch Sargenta Silver Dan
U Graves (U Graves); cr (kitten)
Sargenta Blue Gismo U Graves
(U Graves); tc GrCh Wellmar Flamenco
J Martin (M Frew)
• 125 bc & br Tammeko Tamoshanter
M Simon (R Taylor); tr Ch Wellmar
Boson J Martin (J Martin)
• 126 bc GrCh Tammeko Marmaduke
M Simon (M Simon); tl & tc Ch
Tammeko Cappuccino M Simon
(M Simon)
• 127 cl & br Susian Just Judy
S Kempster (M Way); tl & tr
GrCh Miletree Masquerade R K Towse
(P Allen)
• 128 b Miletree Magpie R Towse
(M Le Monnier); cr (adult) Ch
Lancendel Santa Claw P Ross (G Ellins
& B Hollandt); tc (kitten) Sheephouse
Precious Pearl J Bradley (J Bradley);
tr (kitten) Sheephouse Diamond Lil
J Bradley (J Bradley)
• 129 bl & cr Wellmar Keziah J Martin
(A M Gothard); tr GrCh Starfrost
Dominic E Conlin (C Greenall)

• 130 bc & br Ch Adreesh Lotte
J Bradley (K McKenna)
• 130 c & tr Ch Semra Smokeancoke
M Sutton (J M Allison)
• 131 bc & cr GrCh (CA) Ch (GCCF)
Westways Dusty Miller A West (A West)
• 131 cl & tr Ch Phykell Milliways
M Sparshot (Mrs R K Towse)
• 132 all Kavida Hamilton L Berry
(V Clerkin)
• 133 bc Boadicat Bertie P Griffiths
(J Jones); cr Cordelia Cassandra
J Codling (C Excell); l & tr Boadicat
Bizzie Lizzie P Griffiths (L Berry)
• 134 bl & br Kavida Sweet Georgia
Brown L Berry (L Berry); cr Beeblebox
Plum Crazy J Crafer (C Boyd);
tr Adhuish Cattino C Excell (C Excell)
• 135 bl & cr Boadicat Camilla
P Griffiths (L Berry); tc Adhuish
Carnival Queen C Excell (C Excell);
tr Kavida Misty Daydream L Berry
(L Berry)
• 136 cl & cr Blondene Choochy chops
G Butler (M Smith); tl Tzarksak Aint
Misbehavin J Rogers (M Smith)
• 137 c & b Adqwesh Avra Mrs Farmer
(S W McEwen); tr Pennydown Penny
Black S W McEwen (S W McEwen)
• 138 bl & bc IntCh Silvery Glow
Dwarrelhof A P Groeneugen
(A P Groeneugen); c French Can Can
M Schuriderski (E Christian Tilli)
• 139 bc & cr EurCh None Such of the
Golden Rainbow A P Groeneugen
(A P Groeneugen); tc Pennydown
Touch of Class S W McEwen
(S W McEwen)
• 140 all Myrneen Cloudy Man Sell
L Price (L Williams)
• 141 bc & cr Myrneen Timmiswara
L Williams (L Williams); tr Minty
L Williams (H Walker & K Bullin)
• 142 br Adrish Alenka L Price
(L Williams); tc & cr Tattleberry Signed
J Hellman (L Williams)
• 143 all Ngkomo Ota A Scruggs
(L Marcel)
• 144 all Delicious Panda Vanzechique
M Wijers (M Wijers)
• 145 all Lucky Boy Wildebras
C M Balemans (C M Balemans)
• 146 b Esmaralda Wildebras
C M Balemans (C M Balemans);
cl & tc Ambre de Brentwood Drive
M Lisart (M Wijers)
• 147 bl & tr (kitten) Linkret Evie
M Trompetto (J Swinyard); br & cl
Linkret Barclay Mews M Trompetto
(M Trompetto)
• 160 all IntCh & Pr Rimsky de
Santanoe L Kenter (L Kenter)
• 161 bl & br Eldoria's Crazy Girl
O van Beck and Aat Quast (O van
Beck and Aat Quast); t Eldoria's
Graziana O van Beck and Aat Quast
(O van Beck and Aat Quast)
• 162 bl & cr Eldoria's Goldfinger
O van Beck and Aat Quast (O van
Beck and Aat Quast); t Eldoria's
Yossarian O van Beck and Aat Quast
(O van Beck and Aat Quast)
• 163 all IntCh Orions Guru Lomaers

(Mulder-Hopma)
• 164 all Aurora de Santanoe L Kenter
(L Kenter)
• 165 bc & tr IntGrCh Gardenia du
Vaumichon G Bock (J Simmonet);
bl (kitten) IntCh Giroflée du
Bois de Meudon G Bock
(G Bock)
• 166 all Pr Adkrish Samson
P K Weissman (P K Weissman)
• 167 b Ch Adhuish Anak Barong
P K Weisman (P K Weissman); tc & tr
Rastacat Yzella J Cross (J Cross)
• 168 bc & cr Amaska Fantasia
S Luxford-Watts (S Luxford-Watts);
tl & tr Leshocha Little Gem
E Himmerston (E Himmerston)
• 169 bc & cr Amaska Tia Maria
S Luxford-Watts (S Luxford-Watts);
cl & tr Amaska Silver Cinnerama
S Luxford-Watts (S Luxford-Watts)
• 170 br Leshocha Azure My Friend
E Himmerston (E Himmerston);
tc & tr Myowal Rudolph J Cornish
(T Compton)
• 171 br Lohteyn Whispered Word
L Heath (J Green); tc & tr Ch Myowal
Moppers Blues G Cornish (G Cornish)
• 172 all Capillatus White Simba
J Cook (J Cook)
• 173 bl & cr Adhuish Grainne
N Jarrett (J Burton); tc & tr Adhuish
Happy Joker M & H Benson (J Burton)
• 174 b GrCh Ikari Donna S Davey
(J Plumb); tc & tr Sailorman Horay
Henery K Hardwick (K Hardwick)
• 175 bl & cr Washtog Oil Slick
C Plumbly (C Plumbly); tr Washtog
Intoeverything C Plumbly (C Plumbly)
• 176 b GrPr Berilleon Dandi Lyon
B Lyon (M Chitty); cl & tr Myowal
Susie Sioux G Cornish (J and B Archer)
• 177 br Pr Bobire Justin Tyme
I E Longhurst (A Charlton); tl & tc
UK GrCh Nobilero Loric Vilesilensa
AE & RE Hobson (M Reed)
• 178 all Riahon Auda Bebare Shana
Scanlin (A Rushbrook & J Plumb)
• 179 all Shaird Bare Essentials
A Rushbrook & J Plumb
(A Rushbrook & J Plumb)
• 180 all Shearling Faerie Neem Mary
Harrington (M Harrington)
• 181 bc (adult) Shearling Annie Smith
Peck Mary Harrington (M Harrington);
bl (kitten) Shearling Swiss Bliss Mary
Harrington (M Harrington)
• 182 all Astahazy Zeffirelli (M von
Kirchberg)
• 183 all GrCh Aerostar Spectre
J E D Mackie (S Callen & I Hotten)
• 184 all GrCh Pannaduloa Yentantethra
J Hansson (J Hansson)
• 185 bl & br Ch Willowbreeze Goinsolo
Mr & Mrs Robinson (T K Hull-
Williams); tr Dawnus Caruso
A Douglas (A Douglas)
• 186 bl Leolee Sweet Song S Lee Soper
(S Lee Soper); cr Leolee Larnyen Poppy
S Lee Soper (S Lee Soper); tc & tr
Ch Pannaduloa Phaedra J Hansson
(J Hansson)
• 187 b & cr GrCh Dawnus

Primadonna A Douglas (A Douglas);
tl & tr *Pr Parthia Black Watch*
M Skelton (O Watson)
• **188** b *Midamist Shynal* J Bright
(C Bone); **tc & tr** *Rocamadour
Heightofashion* K Holder (K Holder)
• **189** b *Midamist Taffetalace* J Bright
(J Bright); **tc & tr** *Ch Darling Copper
Kingdom* I George (S Mauchline)
• **190** bc & cr *Ch Sisar Brie*
L Pummell (L Pummell); **tc & tr** *GrPr
Bluecroft Sunsationallad* P Mapes
(M Brazier)
• **191** bc & cr *Indalo Knights Templar*
B Pridham (B Pridham); **t** *Parthia
Giselle* M Skelton (S Johnson &
P Norman);
• **192** b *Peryorsia Casandra* L E Martin
(L E Martin); **tc & tr** *Jophas Mysticetti*
J Reed (M Saunders)
• **193** b *Ch Bosan Carmen* S Bell
(L E Martin); **t** *Ch Rondell Christmas
Cracker* F Jackson (F Jackson)
• **194** all *Braeside Moonflower*
H Hewitt (H Hewitt)
• **195** bc & cr *Ch Hobberdy Hokey
Cokey* A Virtue (A Virtue); **tl & tr**
Braeside Red Sensation H Hewitt
(H Hewitt)
• **196** bc & cr *GrCh Bambino Alice
Bugown* B Boizard-Neil (B Boizard-
Neil); **t** *Ch Bambino Seawitch*
B Boizard-Neil (B Boizard-Neil)
• **197** b & cr *Kamehahd Pecious Purrdy*
D Tomlinson (D Tomlinson); **tc & tr**
Ch Mootam Flyaway Peter S Fearon
(S Hillman)
• **198** all *Ch Bambino Dreamy*
B Boizard-Neil (B Boizard-Neil)
• **199** bl & br *Impromptu Crystal*
M Garrod (M Garrod); **tc & tr**
Oakenshield Blue Willow C Kemp
(C Kemp)
• **200** br *Adhuish Atlas* T J H Bishop
(M S Hodgekinson); **cl & tr** *Adonis*
D Bishop (D Bartlett)
• **201** bl *Yanazen Birmanie* D Bartlett
(M Harvey); **br** *Tajens Rula Girl*
T Jenkinson (D Bartlett); **cr (kitten)**
Tajens Irridescent Opal T Jenkinson
(T Jenkinson); **tc** *Pearls Princess*
M Martin (T Jenkinson)
• **202** bc *Tajens Isabella* T Jenkinson
(T Jenkinson); **bl (kitten)** *Tajens
Oliver* T Jenkinson (T Jenkinson);
cr *Yanazen Bonnechance* D Bartlett
(M Harvey); **tc** *Yankie Doodle Dandy*
J Elkington (S Klein)
• **203** bc & cr *Adhuish Plumtree*
N J & C Young (M S Hodgekinson);
t *Amber* H Foreshaw (A Crowther)
• **204** all *Lasiesta Miss Puddleduck*
G W Dyson (G W Dyson)
• **205** br & cr *Ballego Betty Boo*
J Gillies (J Gillies); **tl & tr** *Lasiesta
Nutcracker* J P Dyson (D Boad)
• **206** bc & cr *Kartush Benifer* C & T
Clark (C & T Clark); **tc & tr** *Kartush
Cyberleh* C & T Clark (C & T Clark)
• **207** all *Favagello Tabitha* J Bryson
(J Bryson)
• **208** b *Astahazy Zoltan* (M von
Kirchberg); **cl (kitten)** *Braeside*

Sunsukinyasohn
H Hewitt
(H Hewitt);
tc *Yolanda Maple
Zuzi* Late Y
Symes
(H Hewitt)
• **209** b & cr
*Lasiesta
Blackberry Girl*
G W Dyson
(G W Dyson); **cl & tc** *Vatan Mimi*
D Beech & J Chalmers (J Moore)
• **210** all *Boronga Black Savahra*
P Impson (R Stanbrook)
• **211** (kittens) *Silvaner Pollyanna* &
Un-named kitten C Thompson
(C Thompson); **c (adult)** *Silvaner
Kuan* C Thompson (C Thompson)
• **212** all *GrCh Sukinfer Samari*
J O'Boyle (J O'Boyle)
• **213** bl & bc *Ch Pr Adixish Minos
Mercury* A Concanon (A Concanon);
t *Patrican Palomino* S Humphris
(G Ford)
• **214** all *Adhuish Champignon Sattin*
N Williams (N Williams); **cr** *Adhuish
Tuwhit Tuwhoo* N Williams
(N Williams); **t** *Marilane Bryony*
G Ford (G Ford)
• **215** b & cr *Sunjade Brandy Snap*
E Wildon (E Tomlinson); **t** *Scilouette
Angzhi* C & T Clark (C & T Clark)
• **216** b & cr *GrPr Jasrobinka Jeronimo*
P & J Choppen (B & T Plumb);
cl & tr *Shelemay Logan* B Castle
(L Flint)
• **217** bl & cr *Simonski Sylvester
Sneakly* S Cosgrove (S Cosgrove);
tl & tr *Tenaj Blue Max* J Tonkinson
(K Iremonger)
• **218** bl & br *Sayonora Cinnamon
Specs* G Worthy (C Harrison); **t** *Salste
Mr Mistoffelees* S Franklin (S Franklin)
• **219** b *Bosskats Jenny Anydots*
G Hemmings (G Hemmings); **tc & tr**
Ercit Diadem Chelone K & L Spencer-
Mills (K & L Spencer-Mills)
• **220** b *Joysewel Ernisteminway*
J Stevens (L Muffett); **tl & tr** *Ch
Jasrobinka Angelique* (P & J Choppen)
• **221** b *Felides Vivres Purr-sé*
Y C Kleyn (A P Groeneuegen); **tc & tr**
Myomah Madelaine K Toft (S Elliot)
• **222** b *Siaforebur Black Marketeer*
L Muffett (L Muffett); **tl (adult)**
Salste Kaneelbusterboy S Franklin
(K McGrath); **tc (kitten)** *Salste
Kaneelbobby* S Franklin (S Franklin);
tr (kitten) *Salste Kaneelbusterboy*
S Franklin (S Franklin)
• **223** bc & cr *Parthia Angelica*
M A Skelton (M A Skelton); **cl & tc**
Lynfield New Moon E Morse
(L Muffett)
• **224** all *Salste Edwin* S Franklin
(D & A Popham)
• **225** bc & br *Scintilla Silver Whirligig*
P Turner (D Walker); **tc & tr**
Greysbrook Polly Doodle M Hornet
(P R Wilkinson)
• **228** br (kitten) *Karthwine Elven
Moonstalk* R Clayton (M Crane);

cl & cr (adult) *Kingcup
Lilac Wine* M Cook
(P Gillison); **tr (kitten)** *Karthwine
Elven Moonstalk* R Clayton
(M Crane)
• **229** cl & br *Giselle Chocolate Ceres*
C Bachellier (V Spragg); **tc & cr**
GrCh Emarelle Milos M R Lyall
(R Hopkins)
• **230** bl *Charriet Cupid* H &
C Patey (H & C Patey); **cr (kitten)**
Satusai Fawn Amy I Reid (I Reid);
tc *Giselle Silver Spirit* C Bachelier
(E & S Hoyle); **tr (kitten)**
Braeside Marimba H Hewitt
(H Hewitt)
• **231** bc & cr *Ch Anera Ula*
C Macaulay (C Symonds); **tc & tr**
Lionelle Rupert Bear C Bailey
(C Tencor)
• **232** all *Adqwesh Chi Chi Chablis*
A Cooper (A Cooper)
• **234** all *Gogees Jungle Jim* G Johnson
(M Hornett)
• **235** b & cr *Thickthorn Carroway*
G Johnson (S Sweeny); **t** *Gogees
Firespot* G Johnson (M Hornett)
• **236** all *Carragato Lassik* T Edwards
(V Maria Tatti)
• **238** bc & cr *Carragato Kotaki*
T Edwards (V Maria Tatti);
• **239** bl *Jungle Spirit* F Wagner
(G Pascoe & B Street); **cl** *Jezabel
Jamberee* F Wagner (G Pascoe &
B Street); **cr & tr (adult)** *Gogees
Warhawk* G Johnson (G Pascoe &
B Street)
• **240** bl (kitten) *Misty* (P Pickering);
cl & br *Sinbad Sailor Blue* (V Lew)
• **241** bl & br *Crumpet* (Bethlehem
Cat Sanctuary); **tl** *Esther* (D & C Ellis);
tr *Peanut* (P Pickering)
• **242** b *Vikivashti* (D Fagg); **tc & tr**
Dreamy Woman (Bethlehem Cat
Sanctuary); **tl & tr** *Thomson*
(D & C Ellis)
• **243** bl & br *Truffles* (V Warriner)
• **244** bc & cr *Tiger* (D & C Ellis);
t *Friskie* (Bethlehem Cat Sanctuary)
• **245** bl & br *Rosie* (V Warriner);
tc & tr *Nigel* (D & C Ellis)
• **249** cr *Grimswald de Shiva Devale*
M & S Gubbel-Noens (M & S
Gubbel-Noens)
• **252** b *Eldoria's Crazy Girl* O van
Beck and Aat Quast (O van Beck &
A Quast)
• **254** tl & tr *Braeside Pikilo* H Hewitt
(H Hewitt)
• **256** b *GrCh Starfrost Dominic*
E Conlin (C Greenall)

GLOSSARY

- **AGOUTI**
Combination of light and dark banding along length of individual hairs, notably in tabbies.
- **ALBINO**
Cat with no colour pigment whatsoever, appearing pure white with pinkish eyes.
- **ASIAN**
Cat of Burmese **type**, but not showing Burmese coloration, patterning, or coat length.
- **AWN HAIRS**
Coarser form of secondary hair, with thickened tips.
- **BARRING**
Striped patterning, associated with tabbies but considered to be a fault in self-coloured cats.
- **BI-COLOUR**
Coat showing areas of one solid colour and patches of white.
- **BLAZE**
Marking, usually white, between eyes extending from forehead down to nose.
- **BLOODLINE**
Group of cats related to each other through several generations or by their **pedigrees**.
- **BLUE**
Blue-grey coloration.
- **BREAK**
Alteration to nose profile; also known as a stop.
- **BREED**
Cats having similar, defined appearance and related ancestry.
- **BREED STANDARD**
Criteria against which cats of particular breed are judged.
- **BRINDLING**
Scattered hairs of wrong colour apparent in coat.
- **BRUSH**
Describes profuse covering of hair on tail, typical of long-haired cats.
- **CALICO**
American description for Tortoiseshell and White.
- **CALLING**
Distinctive vocalization of female cat when in **oestrus**.
- **CAMEO**
Hair with cream or red **tipping**, referring to Chinchilla, Shaded, or Smoke cats.
- **CARNIVORE**
Animal feeding mainly on food of animal origin.

- **CARPAL PAD**
Pads present at level of carpus on both front feet.
- **CAT FANCY**
Organized, selective breeding and exhibiting of cats.
- **CATTERY**
Where cats are kept and bred, with cattery's name included as part of **pedigree** name.
- **CHAMPAGNE**
American description for Lilac form of Tonkinese and Chocolate Burmese.
- **CHAMPION**
Title accorded to cat after a number of wins at shows.
- **CHINCHILLA**
Tip of fur coloured, with remainder pale or white.
- **CHOCOLATE**
Medium to pale brown. Lighter than Seal in **pointed** cats.
- **CHROMOSOME**
Thread-like paired structure present in cell nucleii, carrying genetic material encoded in genes.
- **COBBY**
Short, compact body shape, as exemplified by British Shorthair.
- **CONGENITAL**
Non-hereditary health problem arising before birth.
- **CROSS-BREEDING**
The mating together of two different breeds.
- **DILUTE**
Paler version of colour, such as Cream (dilute form of Red).
- **DOMINANT**
Genetic term, describing characteristic inherited from one parent and appearing in offspring.
- **DOUBLE COAT**
Thick, longer **top-coat** over short, soft **undercoat**.
- **DOWN HAIR**
Soft, short, secondary hairs.
- **EAR FURNISHINGS**
Hair growing within ears.
- **ENTIRE**
Not **neutered**.
- **FAMILY**
In taxonomy, grouping between order and individual genera.
- **FELINE**
Member of cat family.
- **FERAL**
Domestic cat that has reverted to living wild.

- **FOREIGN**
Cat with lithe, fine-boned appearance, such as Siamese.
- **FRILL**
Neck **ruff** of longer fur.
- **GENES**
Contain encoded information for all features of cat (or other organism).
- **G.C.C.F.**
Governing Council of the Cat Fancy (U.K.)
- **GHOST MARKINGS**
Traces of faint tabby markings often seen in kittens.
- **GLOVES**
White areas of fur on back of feet of Birmans.
- **GUARD HAIRS**
Longer hairs forming **top-coat**.
- **HARLEQUIN**
Description used in America for **Van patterning**.
- **HEAT**
Female's period of **oestrus**.
- **HIMALAYAN PATTERNING**
Darker coloration at extremities of body, which can be affected by body temperature.
- **HYBRIDIZATION**
Production of offspring by mating different species or breeds.
- **IN-BREEDING**
Mating together of very closely related cats, such as the pairing of brother and sister.
- **JOWLS**
Cheek folds, prominent in mature, unneutered, male cats.
- **KINK**
Malformation, typically of tail, most commonly associated with Siamese and other breeds of Oriental origin.
- **LACES**
White fur extending from paws up hind legs in Birmans.
- **LEVEL BITE**
Jaws correctly aligned, and not with one overlapping other.
- **LILAC**
Pale pinkish grey coloration.
- **LITTER**
Kittens born to female at same time. (Also lining for dirt tray.)
- **LYNX POINT**
American term used to describe tabby **points**.
- **MACKEREL MARKINGS**
Distinctive pattern of striping on body of tabbies, said to resemble fish's skeleton.

- **MANTLE**
Area of back, closest to head.
- **MASCARA LINES**
Dark lines connecting to eyes.
- **MASK**
Contrasting darker coloration present on face of **pointed** breeds such as Siamese.
- **MELANIN**
Black pigmentation.
- **MITTENS**
White fur on front feet, as seen in Ragdolls.
- **MOGGY**
Describes domestic cat of non-pedigree origins.
- **MOULT**
Shedding of coat, usually in response to seasonal changes.
- **MUTATION**
Change in genes, giving rise to unexpected alteration in appearance of kittens, compared with that of parents.
- **MUZZLE**
Comprises nose and jaws.
- **NATURAL MINK**
Colour description for darkest form of Tonkinese, equivalent to Seal Point Siamese.
- **NECKLACE**
Darker markings encircling neck; not always complete.
- **NEUTER**
Cat that has been castrated (males) or spayed (females).
- **NICTITATING MEMBRANE**
Thin, transparent membrane that may become apparent at corner of eyes if cat is sick or malnourished. Otherwise known as the "haw" or the third eyelid.
- **NOSE LEATHER**
Area of coloured skin on nose, not covered by fur.
- **ODD-EYED**
Eyes of different colours, typically blue and orange.
- **OESTRUS**
Breeding period in females.
- **ORIENTAL**
Term used to describe cat of fine-boned, lithe, **foreign** appearance, such as the Siamese.
- **OUT-CROSS**
Pairing with unrelated individual, possibly of different breed.
- **OUTER COAT**
Comprises longer **guard hairs**.
- **PADS**
Leathery areas without hair on feet.
- **PARTI-COLOURED**
Coat consisting of two or more colours, such as Tortie and White.

- **PATCHED TABBY**
Tortoiseshell Tabby.
- **PEDIGREE**
Line of descent of pure-bred cat, showing the ancestry over a number of generations.
- **PENCILLING**
Thin, darker lines, resembling pencils, seen in tabbies.
- **PERSIAN**
Equivalent to Longhair in Britain.
- **PEWTER**
Describing Silver Shaded cat, with orange or coppery eyes.
- **POINTS**
Darker coloured areas of body, on head, ears, legs, paws, and tail, associated with Siamese and similar pointed breeds.
- **POLYDACTYL**
Having extra digits on feet.
- **PREMIER**
Neutered champion.
- **PRICKED**
Describes ears held erect.
- **PRIMARY HAIRS**
Longer **guard hairs** of **top-coat**.
- **PURE-BRED**
The result of controlled pairings over a number of generations.
- **QUEEN**
Unneutered female to be used for breeding purposes.
- **RECESSIVE**
Genetic feature passed from one generation to the next, but not always being evident.
- **RECOGNITION**
Acceptance of **standard** for new breed by cat association.
- **REGISTRATION**
Recording of kitten's birth and ancestry with cat association.
- **RUFF**
Longer hair around neck.
- **RUMPY**
Manx with no trace of tail.
- **RUMPY RISER**
Manx showing trace of tail.
- **RUSTINESS**
Trace of reddish brown fur apparent in coat of black cat.
- **SABLE**
American description of brown Burmese (the darkest form).
- **SCARAB MARKING**
"M"-shaped darker marking on the head of tabbies.
- **SEAL**
Dark brown coloration, typically describing **points** of Siamese.
- **SEX CHROMOSOMES**
Pair of chromosomes responsible for determining gender.

- **SEX LINEAGE**
Genetic trait associated with **sex chromosomes**.
- **SHADING**
Widespread darker area toning with basic coloration of coat.
- **SPAYING**
Neutering of female cat.
- **SPINA BIFIDA**
Congenital malformation of backbone.
- **SPRAYING**
Territorial habit, especially of intact males, using urine to mark territory.
- **SQUINT**
Deformity causing eyes to stare at nose, giving cross-eyed impression.
- **STANDARD OF POINTS**
Description and scoring system used by show judges.
- **STIFLE**
Cat's knee joint on hind leg.
- **STUD**
Male cat kept for breeding.
- **STUD TAIL**
Accumulation of greasy secretion around tail area, especially in **unneutered** males.
- **STUMPY**
Manx with residual tail.
- **TABBY**
Coat markings that can be striped, blotched, spotted, or ticked **agouti**.
- **TICKING**
Bands of colour seen on hairs.
- **TIPPED**
Coloured ends to hairs.
- **TOM**
Intact or **unneutered** male cat.
- **TOP-COAT**
Comprises **guard hairs**.
- **TORBIE**
Tortoiseshell Tabby.
- **TORTOISESHELL**
Cat, usually female, showing black, and light and dark red areas in coat.
- **TRI-COLOURED**
Coat with three distinct colours apparent in coat.
- **TYPE**
Overall size and shape of cat.
- **UNDERCOAT**
Soft hairs beneath **guard hairs**, providing insulation.
- **VAN PATTERN**
Coat mainly white, with tail and head being coloured.
- **WEDGE-SHAPED**
Describes head shape of Siamese and similar breeds.
- **WHIP TAIL**
Long, thin, tapering tail.
- **WILD TYPE**
Feral or wild cat appearance.

INDEX

USEFUL ADDRESSES

The Governing Council of the Cat Fancy (GCCF), 4–6 Penel Orlieu, Bridgwater, Somerset TA6 3PG

The Cat's Protection League, 17 Kings Road, Horsham, West Sussex RH13 5PP

Cat Association of Britain (CA), Mill House, Letcombe Regis, Oxon OX12 9JD

Feline Association of South Australia, 7 Athelney Avenue, Brighton SA 5048 Australia

Fédération Internationale Féline, (FIFe), Boerhaavelaan 23, NO-5644 BB Eindhoven The Netherlands

New Zealand Cat Fancies Inc. 20 Warren Kelly Street, Richmond Nelson, New Zealand

Feline Advisory Bureau, 235 Upper Richmond Road, Putney, London SW15 6SN

Cat World, 10 Western Road, Shoreham-by-Sea, West Sussex BN43 5WD

— 🐈 —

ACKNOWLEDGMENTS

THE AUTHOR would like to thank the many kind cat fanciers who allowed their cats to be photographed for the book. Particular thanks are due to Fiona Henrie and Phyllis Choppen for co-ordinating this process, and to Marga Harms and Marijke Wijers who helped to organize cats for photography in the Netherlands. He would also like to thank: Marc Henrie, with whom it is always a pleasure to work; Colin Walton and Irene Lyford for their care and expertise in respectively designing and editing the book; and Jane Laing, Mary-Clare Jerram, and Gill Della Casa at Dorling Kindersley for their valuable input at various stages of the project. He would like to thank Rita Hemsley for her typing skills and, last but not least, he would like to thank Therese Clarke, Daphne Negus, and Baroness Miranda von Kirchberg for their invaluable advice and contributions.

DORLING KINDERSLEY would like to thank: Paul Casey for help on California Spangleds; Phyllis and John Choppen for their hospitality when photographing the Orientals; Andrea Fair for help with Grooming and Choosing a Kitten photography; Jan Osborne of *Purrsonal Touch* for hospitality, equipment, and the co-operation of *Rapunzel Cherokee Chief*; Ruta and Peter Towse for their help with photography of Shorthairs and Foreigns.

We would also like to thank Dr A.W. Gentry of the Natural History Museum, and Dr Andrew S. Nash of Glasgow University Veterinary School for their invaluable co-operation and advice.

We are indebted to: Michael Allaby for proofreading and compiling the Index; Mike Darton for proof-reading; Angeles Gavira, Carol McGlynn, and Bella Pringle for editorial assistance; Steve Tilling for help with the Identification Key; Alastair Wardle for invaluable technical assistance.

PICTURE CREDITS
All specially commissioned photographs by Marc Henrie, except those on *pp.14-15* by Jane Burton.

The publishers would like to thank the following photographers and organizations for their permission to reproduce the photographs indicated below: Bridgeman Art Library 7 bl; Stephe Bruin 9 all; 36 bc; 165 all; Chanan Photography 7 t; 31 bl; 36 tcl; 149 b; 149 tl; 149 tr; 151 t; 152 b; 152 tl; 152 tr; 153 t; 157 b; 157 t; 237 c; 237 bl; 237 br; 237 t; 238 t; Michael Holford 6 tl; Johnson Photography 25 tr; Dr Andrew S. Nash, University of Glasgow Veterinary School 26 t; Science Photo Library 8 tr; Through the Cat's Eye 153 b; Tony Stone Worldwide 8 c; Tetsu Yamazaki 27 cl; 31 br; 49 b; 112 b; 112 t; 113 bl; 113 br; 113 t; 148 l; 148 r; 150 bl; 150 tl; 150 br; 150 tr; 154 bl; 154 br; 154 tl; 154 tr; 155 bl; 155 br; 155 tl; 155 tr; 156 l; 156 r; 158 ; 159 bl; 159 tl; 159 br; 159tr; 181 t; 226 br; 226 c; 226 tr; 227 bl; 227 br; 227 tl; 227 tr; 233 r; 233 l; Dave King 7 br; 116 bc; 116 cr; 151 bl; 151 cr;
The black and white photographs on *p.6* and *p.18* were taken from *The Book of the Cat,* by Frances Simpson (Cassell and Co. Ltd; 1903).

Endpapers by Caroline Church
All other artwork by Janos Marffy
Picture research: Julia Pashley

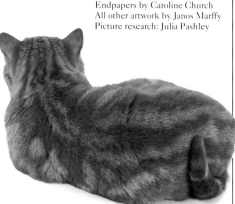